MORE PRAISE FOR *FINDING ULTRA*

"If you liked *Born to Run*, you'll love *Finding Ultra* . . . **one of the best books about health and fitness that I've ever read.**"

> —NEAL D. BARNARD, M.D., President of the Physicians Committee for Responsible Medicine

"*Finding Ultra* **is the ultimate story of hope, perseverance, and endurance against life's biggest challenges.**"

> —WILLIAM COPE MOYERS, *New York Times* bestselling author of *Broken: My Story of Addiction and Redemption*

"**I loved this. A rare book, unusual for its honesty and willingness to bare all, that really does deserve such superlatives as 'riveting' and 'compelling.'** I was moved by watching Roll conquer his demons, and felt privileged to share in his eventual enlightenment. By laying it on the line, Roll absolutely wins us over."

> —RIP ESSELSTYN, *New York Times* bestselling author of *The Engine 2 Diet*

"An incredibly inspirational book about achieving greatness at any age through self-belief and a positive attitude. Rich Roll is a true champion of life and sport."

—LEVI LEIPHEIMER, two-time stage winner of the Tour de France and Olympic time-trial bronze medalist

"*Finding Ultra* is an inspired first-person account of fast living and even faster swimming, biking, and running that will leave you convinced of the power of your own will."

—BRENDAN BRAZIER, bestselling author of *Thrive*

"An inspiring story of a man whose life took a tragic turn but then rebounded spectacularly. Down but not out, Rich Roll rose like a phoenix, taking the commitment to his own health to a new level and achieving a remarkable transformation. I believe everyone will be able to relate to this plant-powered athlete's riveting story and perhaps garner some inspiration for their own journey. A top read!"

—LUKE McKENZIE, five-time Ironman champion

FINDING ULTRA

*REJECTING MIDDLE AGE,
BECOMING ONE OF THE WORLD'S FITTEST
MEN, AND DISCOVERING MYSELF*

RICH ROLL

CROWN ARCHETYPE
NEW YORK

CROWN ARCHETYPE with colophon is a trademark of
Random House, Inc.

Library of Congress Cataloging-in-Publication Data

Roll, Rich.
Finding Ultra : rejecting middle age, becoming one of the world's
fittest men, and discovering myself / by Rich Roll.—1st ed.
1. Roll, Rich.   2. Triathletes—United States—Biography.
3. Older athletes—United States—Biography.   4. Ironman
triathlons.   5. Ultraman World Championships.   I. Title.
GV1060.72.R65A3 2011
796.42'57092—dc53
[B]   2012003094

ISBN 978-0-307-95219-6
eISBN 978-0-307-95221-9

PRINTED IN THE UNITED STATES OF AMERICA

Book design by Gretchen Achilles
Jacket design by Nupoor Gordon
Jacket photograph © John Segesta

10 9 8 7 6 5 4 3 2 1

FIRST EDITION

TO JULIE

CONTENTS

PREFACE

The crash comes out of nowhere. One second I'm feeling good, cycling as fast as I can at a good clip, even through the pouring rain. Then I feel a slight bump and my left hand slips off the damp handlebar. I'm hurled off the bike seat and through the air. I experience a momentary loss of gravity, then *bam!* My head slams hard to the ground as my body skids twenty feet across wet pavement, bits of gravel biting into my left knee and burning my shoulder raw as my bike tumbles along on top of me, my right foot still clamped in the pedal.

A second later I'm lying faceup with the rain beating down and the taste of blood on my lips. I struggle to release my right foot and pull myself up using the shoulder that doesn't seem to be bleeding. Somehow, I find a sitting position. I make a fist with my left hand and pain shoots up to the shoulder—the skin has been sheared clean off, and blood mixes with rainwater in little rivers. My left knee has a similar look. I try to bend it—bad idea. My eyes close, and behind them there's a pulsating purple-and-red color, a pounding in my ears. I take a deep breath, let it out. I think of the thousand-plus hours of training I've done to get this far. I have to do this, I have to get up. It's a race. *I have to get back in it.* Then I see it. My left pedal shattered, carbon pieces strewn about the pavement. One hundred and thirty-five miles still to go today—hard enough with two working pedals. But with only one? Impossible.

It's barely daybreak on the Big Island of Hawaii, and I'm on a pristine stretch of terrain known as the Red Road, which owes its name to its red cinder surface, bits of which are now deeply lodged in my skin. Just moments before, I was the overall race leader at about 35 miles into the 170-mile, Day Two stage of the 2009 Ultraman World Championships, a three-day, 320-mile, double-ironman distance triathlon. Circumnavigating the entire Big Island, Ultraman is an invitation-only endurance-fest, limited to thirty-five competitors fit enough and crazy enough to attempt it. Day One entails a 6.2-mile ocean swim, followed by a 90-mile bike ride. Day Two is 170 miles on the bike. And the event's culmination on Day Three is a 52.4-mile run on the searing hot lava fields of the Kona Coast.

This is my second try at Ultraman—the first occurred just one year before—and I have high hopes. Last year, I stunned the endurance sports community by coming out of nowhere at the ripe age of forty-two to place a respectable eleventh overall after only six months of serious training, and that was after decades of reckless drug and alcohol abuse that nearly killed me and others, plus no physical exertion more strenuous than lugging groceries into the house and maybe repotting a plant. Before that first race, people said that, for a guy like me, attempting something like Ultraman was harebrained, even stupid. After all, they knew me as a sedentary, middle-aged lawyer, a guy with a wife, children, and a career to think about, now off chasing a fool's errand. Not to mention the fact that I was training—and intended to compete—on an entirely plant-based diet. *Impossible,* they told me. *Vegans are spindly weaklings, incapable of anything more athletic than kicking a Hacky Sack. No proteins in plants, you'll never make it.* I heard it all. But deep down, I knew I could do it.

And I did—proving them wrong and defying not just "middle age," but the seemingly immutable stereotypes about the physical capabilities of a person who eats nothing but plants. And now here I was again, back at it a second time.

Just one day before, I'd begun the race in great form. I completed the Day One 6.2-mile swim at Keauhou Bay in first place, a full ten minutes ahead of the next competitor. Clocking the sixth-fastest swim split in Ultraman's twenty-five-year history, I was off to an amazing start. In the late 1980s, I'd competed as a swimmer at Stanford, so this wasn't a huge surprise. But cycling? Different story altogether. Three years ago I didn't even *own* a bike, let alone know how to *race* one. And on that first day of the race, after I'd blasted out two and a half hours in strong ocean currents, deep fatigue had set in. With salt water–singed lungs and my throat raw from vomiting up my breakfast half a dozen times in Kailua Bay, I faced ninety miles in blistering humidity and gale-force headwinds en route to Volcanoes National Park. I did the math. It was only a matter of time before the cycling specialists would quickly make up lost time and I'd get passed on the final twenty miles of the day, a backbreaking four-thousand-foot climb up to the volcano. I kept looking back, fully expecting to see the Brazilian three-time Ultraman champ, Alexandre Ribiero, fast on my heels, tracking me like prey. But he was nowhere to be seen. In fact, I never saw a single other competitor all day. I could hardly believe it as I rounded the final turn through the finish-line chute, my wife Julie and stepson Tyler screaming from our crew van as I *won* the Day One stage! Leaping from the van, Julie and Tyler ran into my arms; I buried myself in their embrace, tears pouring down my face. And even more shocking was just how long I waited for the next competitor to arrive—a full ten minutes! *I was winning Ultraman by ten minutes!* It wasn't just a dream come true; I'd made an indelible mark on the endurance sports landscape, one for the record books. And for a guy like me—a plant-eating, middle-aged dad—well, with everything I'd faced and overcome, it was nothing short of remarkable.

So the morning of Day Two, all eyes were on me as I waited

with the other athletes at the start line in Volcanoes National Park, tensed and spring-coiled in the early-morning dark, cold rain falling. When the gun sounded, all the top guys leapt like jaguars, trying to establish a quick lead and form an organized front peloton. It's an understatement to say that I wasn't prepared to begin the 170-mile ride with a flat-out, gut-busting sprint; I hadn't warmed up before and was caught completely off guard by just how fast the pace would be. Accelerating downhill at a speed close to fifty miles per hour, I dug deep to hold pace and maintain a position within the lead group, but my legs quickly bloated with lactate and I drifted off the back of the pack.

For this initial twenty-mile rapid descent down the volcano, the situation is what's called "draft legal," meaning you can ride behind other riders and safely ensconce yourself in a "wind pocket." Once enveloped in the group, you're able to ride pace at a fraction of the energy output. The last thing you want to do is get "dropped," leaving you to fend for yourself, a lone wolf struggling against the wind on nothing but your own energy. But that's exactly what I'd become. I was behind the lead pack, yet far ahead of the next "chase" group. Only I felt less like a wolf than a skinny rat. A wet, cold skinny rat, irritated and mad at myself for my bad start, already winded and staring at eight hard hours of riding ahead. The rain made everything worse, plus the fact that I'd forgotten covers for my shoes, so my feet were soaked and frozen numb. Not a lot bothers me, including pain, but wet, cold feet make me crazy. I considered slowing down to let the chase group catch up, but they were too far back. My only option was to soldier on, solo.

When I reached the bottom of the descent, I made the turn down to the southeastern tip of the island just as the sun was rising. I was finally beginning to feel warmed up by the time I made the turn onto the Red Road. This section is the one part of the entire race that's off-limits to crew support—no support cars allowed.

For fifteen miles, you're on your own. I saw no other riders as I flew through this rolling and lush but diabolical terrain, the pavement marked by potholes and sharp, difficult turns, gravel flying up constantly. Utterly alone, I concentrated on the whir and push of my bike, the silence of tropical dawn broken only by my own thoughts of how wet I was. I was also irritated that my wife Julie and the rest of my crew had blown the hydration hand-off before the "no car" zone, leaving me bone-dry for this lonely stretch. And just like that, I hit that bump. A Red Road face-plant.

I unsnap my helmet. It's broken, a long crack threading through the center. I touch the top of my head, and under my matted, sweaty hair the skin feels tender. I squeeze my eyes shut, open them, and wiggle my fingers in front of my face. They're all there, all five. I cover one eye, then the other. I can see just fine. Wincing, I straighten out my knee and look around. Aside from a bird that I should probably be able to identify—it's long-necked with a sweeping black tail and a yellow chest—pecking at the ground by the bike, there's not a soul around. I listen hard, straining to hear the rising approach of the next group of riders. But there's nothing but the peaceful caw of a bird, a rustling in a tree close by, the slam of a screen door echoing through the trees, and over and over, the small crash of nearby ocean waves on sand.

Nausea moves through me. I hold my hand over my stomach and concentrate for a minute on the rise and fall of the skin beneath my hand, the in and out of my breath. I count to ten, then twenty. Anything to distract me from the pain now entering my shoulder like an army at full gallop—anything to keep me from focusing on the pulpy skin on my knee. The nausea subsides.

My shoulder is freezing up and I try to move it. It's no good. I feel like the Tin Man, calling out for the oilcan. I flap my feet back and forth, my damn wet feet. I stand up gingerly and put weight on the bad knee. Grunting, I lift the bike up and straddle it, flipping at the one remaining pedal with my foot. No matter what, I have to somehow make it another mile to the end of the Red Road, where the crews are waiting, where Julie will take care of me and clean me up. We'll put the bike in the van and shuttle back to the hotel.

My head throbs as I make a wobbly push-off and begin riding with one leg, the other dangling free, blood dripping from the knee. Beside me the sky is clearing into full morning over the ocean, a gray-white slate above muting the tropical sea to a dark-hued green, spotted with rain. I think of the thousands and thousands of hours I've trained for this, how far I've come from the overweight, cheeseburger-addicted, out-of-shape guy I was just two years ago. I think of how I completely overhauled not just my diet, and my body—but my entire *lifestyle*—inside and out. Another look at my broken pedal, and then I think about the 135 miles still ahead in the race: *impossible.* That's it, I think, equal parts shame and relief flooding through me. For me, this race is over.

Somehow I press through that last mile or so of the Red Road, and soon I can make out the crews waiting ahead, vehicles parked, supplies and gear spread out in anticipation of tending to the approaching competitors. My heart begins to beat faster and I force myself to keep going toward them. I'll have to face my wife and stepson Tyler, tell them what happened, tell them how I've failed not just me, but them—my family that has sacrificed so much in support of this dream. *You don't have to,* a voice inside me whispers. *Why don't you just turn around—or, better yet, slink into the foliage before anyone sees you coming?*

I see Julie pushing past the other people to greet me. It takes a moment before she realizes what has happened. Then it hits her, and I see shock and worry cross her face. I feel the tears well up in my eyes and tell myself to keep it together.

In the spirit of *ohana,* the Hawaiian word for "family" that is the soul of this race, I'm suddenly surrounded by half a dozen crew members—from *other* competitors' crews—all rushing to my aid. Before Julie can even speak, Vito Biala, crewing today as part of a three-person relay team known as the "Night Train," materializes with a first-aid kit and begins taking care of my wounds. "Let's get you back on the road," he states calmly. Vito is somewhat of an Ultraman legend and elder statesman, so I try to muster up the strength to return his wry smile. But the truth is, I can't.

"Not gonna happen," I tell him sheepishly. "Broken pedal. It's over for me." I gesture at the place on the bike where the left pedal used to be.

And I feel, somehow, a bit better. Just saying those words— actually telling Vito that I've decided to quit—lifts something dark off my shoulders. I'm relieved at what I've blundered into: an easy, graceful exit out of this mess, and very soon a warm hotel bed. I can already feel the soft sheets, imagine my head on the pillow. And tomorrow, instead of running a double marathon, I'll take the family to the beach.

Next to Vito is competitor Kathy Winkler's crew captain, Peter McIntosh. He looks at me and squints. "What kind of pedal?" he asks.

"A Look Kēo," I stammer, wondering why he wants to know.

Peter vanishes as a pit crew of mechanics seize my bike and swing into action. As if trying to get an Indy 500 car back on the speedway, they begin running diagnostics—checking the frame for cracks, testing the brakes and derailleurs, eyeing the true of my wheels, Allen wrenches flying in all directions. I frown. *What are they doing? Can't they see I'm done!*

Seconds later, Peter reappears—*holding a brand-new pedal, identical to mine.*

"But I—" My mind works furiously to understand how this situation has changed so dramatically from what I'd planned. They're fixing me up, it's dawning on me. They expect me to stay in the race! I wince as someone swabs my shoulder. This isn't how it was going to be! I'd made up my mind: I'm hurt, the bike is broken; it's over, isn't it?

Julie, kneeling and bandaging my knee, glances up. She smiles. "I think it's going to be okay," she says.

Peter McIntosh rises from where he's been adjusting the pedal into place. Staring directly into my eyes and sounding like a five-star general, he says, "This is not over. Now, get back on your bike and get it done."

I am speechless. I swallow hard and look at the ground. Around me I can sense that the crews are all looking at me now, awaiting my response. They expect me to listen to Peter, to jump back on the bike, get going. *Get back in it.*

There are another 135 miles ahead of me. It is still raining. I've relinquished my lead and lost a huge amount of time to my competitors. Besides being completely checked out mentally, I'm hurt, wet, and physically drained. I take a deep breath, let it out. I close my eyes. The chatter and noise around me seem to fade, recede, and then altogether disappear. Silence. Just my heartbeat and the long, long road in front of me.

I do what I have to do. I turn off that voice in my head urging me to quit. And I get back on the bike. My race, it seems, is only just beginning.

CHAPTER ONE

A LINE IN THE SAND

It was the night before I turned forty. That cool, late-October evening in 2006, Julie and our three kids were sound asleep as I tried to enjoy some peaceful moments in our otherwise rowdy household. My nightly routine involved losing myself in the comfort of my giant flat-screen cranked to maximum volume. While basking in the haze of *Law & Order* reruns, I'd put away a plate of cheeseburgers and followed that welcome head-rush with a mouthful of nicotine gum. This was just my way of relaxing, I'd convinced myself. After a hard day, I felt I deserved it, and that it was harmless.

After all, I knew about harm. Eight years earlier, I'd awoken from a multiday, blackout binge to find myself in a drug and alcohol treatment center in rural Oregon. Since then I'd miraculously gotten sober, and one day at a time was staying that way. I no longer drank. I didn't do drugs. I figured I had the right to pig out on a little junk food.

But something happened on this birthday eve. At almost 2 A.M., I was well into my third hour of doltish television and approaching sodium toxicity with a calorie count in the thousands. With my belly full and nicotine buzz fading, I decided to call it a night. I performed a quick check on my stepsons, Tyler and Trapper, in their room off the kitchen. I loved watching them sleep. Aged eleven and ten, respectively, they'd soon be teenagers, grasping for independence. But for now, they were still pajama-clad boys in their bunk beds, dreaming of skateboarding and Harry Potter.

With the lights already out, I had begun hauling my 208-pound frame upstairs when midway I had to pause—my legs were heavy, my breathing labored. My face felt hot and I had to bend over just to catch my breath, my belly folding over jeans that no longer fit. Nauseous, I looked down at the steps I'd climbed. There were eight. About that many remained to be mounted. *Eight steps.* I was thirty-nine years-old and I was winded by eight steps. *Man,* I thought, *is this what I've become?*

Slowly, I made it to the top and entered our bedroom, careful not to wake Julie or our two-year-old daughter, Mathis, snuggled up against her mom in our bed—my two angels, illuminated by the moonlight coming through the window. Holding still, I paused to watch them sleep, waiting for my pulse to slow. Tears began to trickle down my face as I was overcome by a confusing mix of emotions—love, certainly, but also guilt, shame, and a sudden and acute fear. In my mind, a crystal-clear image flashed of Mathis on her wedding day, smiling, flanked by her proud groomsmen brothers and beaming mother. But in this waking dream, I knew something was profoundly amiss. I wasn't there. I was dead.

A tingling sensation surfaced at the base of my neck and quickly spread down my spine as a sense of panic set in. A drop of sweat fell to the dark wood floor, and I became transfixed by the droplet, as if it were the only thing keeping me from collapsing. The tiny crystal ball foretold my grim future—that I wouldn't live to see my daughter's wedding day.

Snap out of it. A shake of the head, a deep inhale. I labored to the bathroom sink and splashed my face with cold water. As I lifted my head, I caught my reflection in the mirror. And froze. Gone was that long-held image of myself as the handsome young swimming champion I'd once been. And in that moment, denial was shattered; reality set in for the first time. I was a fat, out-of-shape, and very *unhealthy* man hurtling into middle age—a depressed, self-destructive person utterly disconnected from who I was and what I wanted to be.

To the outside observer, everything appeared to be perfect. It had been more than eight years since my last drink, and during that time I'd repaired what was a broken and desperate life, reshaping it into the very model of modern American success. After snagging degrees from Stanford and Cornell and spending years as a corporate lawyer—an alcohol-fueled decade of mind-numbing eighty-hour workweeks, dictatorial bosses, and late-night partying—I'd finally escaped into sobriety and even launched my own successful boutique entertainment law firm. I had a beautiful, loving, and supportive wife and three healthy children who adored me. And together, we'd built the house of our dreams.

So what was wrong with me? Why did I feel this way? I'd done everything I was supposed to do and then some. I wasn't just confused. I was in free fall.

Yet in that precise moment, I was overcome with the profound knowledge not just that I needed to change, but that I was *willing* to change. From my adventures in the subculture of addiction recovery, I'd learned that the trajectory of one's life often boils down to a few identifiable moments—decisions that change everything. I knew all too well that moments like these were not to be squandered. Rather, they were to be respected and seized at all costs, for they just didn't come around that often, if ever. Even if you experienced only one powerful moment like this one, you were lucky. Blink or look away for even an instant and the door didn't just close, it literally vanished. In my case, this was the second time I'd been blessed with such an opportunity, the first being that precious moment of clarity that precipitated my sobriety in rehab. Looking into the mirror that night, I could feel that portal opening again. I needed to act.

But how?

Here's the thing: I'm a man of extremes. I can't just have one drink. I'm either bone dry or I binge until I wake up naked in a hotel room in Vegas without any idea how I got there. I'm crawling out of bed at 4:45 A.M. to swim laps in a pool—as I did throughout my teens—or I'm pounding Big Macs on the couch. I can't just have one cup of coffee. It has to be a Venti, laced with two to five extra shots of espresso, just for fun. To this day "balance" remains my final frontier, a fickle lover I continue to pursue despite her lack of interest. Knowing this about myself, and harnessing the tools I'd developed in recovery, I understood that any true or lasting lifestyle change would require rigor, specificity, and accountability. Vague notions of "eating better" or maybe "going to the gym more often" just weren't going to work. I needed an urgent and stringent plan. *I needed to draw a firm line in the sand.*

The next morning, the first thing I did was turn to my wife Julie for help.

As long as I've known her, Julie has been deeply into yoga and alternative healing methods, with some (to put it mildly) "progressive" notions about nutrition and wellness. Always an early riser, Julie greeted each day with meditation and a series of Sun Salutations, followed by a breakfast of odoriferous herbs and teas. Seeking personal growth and counsel, Julie has sat at the feet of many a guru—from Eckhart Tolle, to Annette, a blue-eyed clairvoyant, to Chief Golden Eagle of the South Dakota Lakota tribe, to Paramhansa Nithyananda, a youthful and handsome Indian sage. Just last year, in fact, Julie traveled by herself to southern India to visit Arunachala, a sacred holy mountain revered in yogic culture as a "spiritual incubator." I'd always admired her for her willingness to explore; it sure seemed to work for her. But this kind of "alternative thinking" was strictly *her* territory, never mine.

Particularly when it came to food. To open our refrigerator was to see an invisible but obvious line running down the middle. On one side were the typical American heart attack–inducing items: hot dogs, mayonnaise, blocks of cheese, processed snack foods, soda, and ice cream. On the other side—Julie's—were mysterious Baggies filled with herbal preparations and an unmarked Mason jar or two filled with putrid-smelling medicinal pastes of unknown origins. There was something she patiently told me was called "ghee," and also chyawanprash, a pungent, brown-colored sticky jam made from an Indian gooseberry known as the "elixir of life" in Ayurveda, a form of ancient Indian alternative medicine. I never tired of poking fun at Julie's ritualistic preparations of these strange foods. Though I'd grown accustomed to her attempting to get me to eat things like sprouted mung beans or seitan burgers, to say it "never took" is an understatement. "Cardboard," I'd announce, shaking my head and reaching instead for my juicy beef burger.

That kind of food was fine for Julie, and certainly fine for our kids, but I needed *my* food. My *real* food. To her immense credit, Julie had never nagged me to change my ways. Frankly, I assumed she'd simply given up on me. But in truth she understood a crucial spiritual principle I'd yet to grasp. You can stand in the light. And you can set a positive example. But you simply cannot *make* someone change.

But today was different. The previous night had given me a gift: a profound sense not just that I needed to change, but that I wanted to change—*really* change. As I poured a massive cup of very strong coffee, I nervously raised the issue across the breakfast table.

"So, uh," I began, "you know that detox, juice-cleanse thing you did last year?"

From a bite of hemp bread spread with chyawanprash jam, Julie peered up at me, a small smile of curiosity playing at her lips. "Yes. The cleanse."

"Well, I think I might, well, uh, maybe I should, you know, give it a shot?" I couldn't believe the words were coming out of my mouth. Even though Julie was one of the healthiest people I knew, and I'd seen how her diet and use of alternative medicine had helped her through so much—even miraculously, at one point—just twenty-four hours before, I would have argued till I was blue in the face that a "cleanse" was useless, even harmful. I'd never found any evidence to support the idea that a cleanse was healthy or that it somehow removed "toxins" from the body. Ask any traditional Western medicine doctor and he'll agree: "These cleanses are not just innocuous, they're downright unhealthy." And by the way, what are these mysterious toxins, anyway, and how would a cleanse possibly remove them? It was all nonsense, I'd thought, pure fabrication, the babbling of snake oil salesmen.

But today, I was desperate. I could still feel the previous night's panic, still feel my temples pounding. The drop of sweat and its dark portent, flashing before my eyes, were all too real. Clearly, my way was not working.

"Sure," Julie said softly. She didn't ask what had prompted this curious request, and I didn't offer an explanation. As clichéd as it sounds, Julie was my soul mate and best friend—the one person who knew me better than anyone. Yet for reasons I still don't fully understand, I couldn't bring myself to tell her about what I'd experienced the night before. Maybe it was embarrassment. Or more likely, the fear I'd felt was simply too acute for words. Julie is too intuitive not to have noticed that something was clearly up, but she didn't ask a single question; she just let it unfold, without expectation.

In fact, Julie's expectations were so low that I had to ask her three more times before she actually returned from the alternative pharmacist with the goods needed to begin the cleanse—a journey that would soon change everything.

Together we embarked on a seven-day progressive regime that involved a variety of herbs, teas, and fruit and vegetable juices (for more information on my recommended cleansing program, see Appendix III, Resources, Jai Renew Detox and Cleansing Program). It's important to understand that this was not a "starvation" protocol. Each and every day I made certain to fortify my body with essential nutrients in liquid form. I cast aside my doubts and threw myself into the process with everything I had. We cleared the fridge of my Reddi-Wip, Go-Gurts, and salami, filling the empty shelves with large vats of tea boiled from a potpourri of what looked like leaves raked from our lawn. I juiced with vigor, downing liquid concoctions of spinach and carrots laced with garlic, followed by herbal remedies in capsule form chased by gagging on a tea with a distinct manure aftertaste.

A day later I was curled up in a ball on the couch, sweating. Try quitting caffeine, nicotine, *and food* all at once. I looked horrible. And felt worse. I couldn't move. But I couldn't sleep either. Everything was upside down. Julie remarked that I looked like I was detoxing heroin. Indeed, I felt like I was back in rehab.

But Julie urged me to hang tough; she said that the hardest part was soon to pass. I trusted her, and true to her word, each day proved easier than the day before. The gagging subsided, replaced by gratitude just to put something—anything—down my throat. By day three, the fog began to clear. My taste buds adapted and I actually began enjoying the regime. And despite so few calories, I began feeling a surge of energy, followed by a profound sense of renewal. I was sold. Day four was better, and by day five, I felt like an entirely new person. I was able to sleep well, and I only needed a few hours of sleep. My mind was clear and my body felt light, infused with a sense of vibrancy and exhilaration that I hadn't known was possible. Suddenly I was jogging up the staircase with Mathis on my back, my heart rate barely elevated. I even went out for a short "run" and felt great, despite the fact that I hadn't laced up a pair of running shoes in years and was on my fifth day without any real food! It was astounding. Like a person with poor eyesight donning a pair of glasses for the first time, I was amazed to discover that a person could feel this good. Until then a hopeless and life-long coffee addict, I entered into a momentous collaboration with Julie on day two of the cleanse when we unplugged our beloved coffeepot and together walked it out to the garbage bin—an act neither of us would have thought possible in a million years.

At the conclusion of the seven-day protocol, it was time to return to eating real food. Julie prepared a nutritious breakfast for me—granola with berries, some toast with butter, and my favorite, poached eggs. After going seven days with no solid food, I might have been excused for inhaling the meal in seconds flat. But instead, I just stared at it. I turned to Julie. "I think I'm just going to keep going."

"What are you talking about?"

"I feel so good. Why go back? To food, I mean. Let's just keep going." I smiled broadly.

To understand me is to understand that I am an alcoholic, through and through. If something is good, then more is better, right? Balance is for ordinary people. Why not strive for extra-ordinary? This had always been my rule—and my ruin.

Julie had tilted her head and frowned, clearly about to say something, when Mathis accidentally dumped her orange juice all over the table, a daily occurrence. Julie and I both jumped to the rescue before the juice spilled onto the floor. "Whoops," Mathis giggled, and Julie and I both smiled. I swabbed at the sticky mess, and just like that, I was jolted out of my crazy idea. Suddenly the thought of juicing and cleansing forever seemed as stupid as it actually is. "Never mind," I said sheepishly. I looked down at my plate and speared a blueberry. It was the best blueberry I'd ever eaten in my whole life.

"Good?" Julie asked.

I nodded and ate another, then another. Beside me Mathis gurgled and smiled.

So I'd achieved my first goal by seizing that precious moment— walking through the open door and taking a stand. But now I needed a plan to build on what I'd started. I was going to have to find some kind of balance. Terrified of simply returning to past practices, I needed a solid strategy to move forward. Not a "diet" per se, but a regimen I could stick to long-term. In truth, I needed an entirely new *lifestyle*.

Without any real study, thought, or responsible inquiry, I decided the first step would be to try a vegetarian diet, with a commitment to working out three days a week. Cut out the meat, the fish, and the eggs. It seemed challenging yet still reasonable, and more important, *doable*. Remembering the lessons I'd learned in becoming sober, I decided not to dwell on the idea of "never having a cheeseburger [or drink] ever again" and just focus on taking it day by day. To show her support, Julie even bought me a bike for my birthday and encouraged me to exercise. And I held up my end of the bargain, opting for burritos without the carnitas, veggie burgers instead of beef, and casual Saturday morning bike rides with friends in place of cheese omelet brunches.

But it was not long before my spirits began to plummet. Despite jumping back into the pool and the occasional jog or bike ride, the extra weight simply wasn't coming off, and I was steady at 205 pounds—a far cry from my 160-pound college swimming weight. But even more disconcerting was the fact that my energy levels soon declined to my pre-cleanse state of lethargy. I was happy that I'd returned to exercising again and had reminded myself of my long-lost love of the water and outdoors. But the truth was that after six months on this vegetarian diet, I didn't feel much better than I had that night on the staircase. Still forty pounds overweight, I was despondent and ready to abandon the vegetarian plan altogether.

What I failed to realize at the time was just how *poorly* one can eat on a vegetarian diet. I'd convinced myself that I was healthy, but when I paused to reflect on what exactly I was eating, I realized that my diet was dominated by a high-cholesterol, artery-clogging lineup of processed foods, high-fructose corn syrup, and fatty dairy products—stuff like cheese pizza, nachos, soda, fries, potato chips, grilled cheese sandwiches, and a wide array of salty snack foods. Technically, I was "vegetarian." But healthy? Not even close. Without any true understanding of nutrition, even I knew this wasn't a good plan. Time to reevaluate once again. On my own this time, I made the radical decision to entirely remove not just meat but all animal products from my diet—dairy included.

I opted to go entirely vegan.

Despite Julie's vigilant commitment to healthy living, even *she* wasn't vegan. So at least within the Roll household I was entering uncharted waters. I just remember feeling the need to up the ante, or throw in the towel altogether. In fact, I specifically recollect thinking that I'd give this vegan thing a whirl, fully believing that it *wouldn't work,* thereby paving a return to eating my beloved cheeseburgers. If such came to pass, I'd be comforted by the thought that I'd tried everything.

Full disclosure: The word "vegan," because it is so heavily associated with a political point of view and persona utterly at odds with how I perceived myself, was one that I couldn't at first get comfortable with. I've always been left-leaning politically. But I'm also the furthest thing from a hippie or earthy-crunchy type—the sort of person that the word "vegan" had always conjured in my mind. Even today, I struggle a little with the term "vegan" as it applies to me. Yet despite everything, there I was, giving it a shot. What followed was a miracle, altering my life's trajectory forever.

When I began my post-cleanse vegetarian phase, I found the elimination of meat from my diet not that difficult. I barely noticed the difference. But the removal of dairy? Different story altogether. I considered giving myself occasional permission to enjoy my beloved cheese and milk. What on earth is wrong with a nice cold glass of milk, anyway? Could there be anything healthier? Not so fast. As I began to study food more intently, I was amazed by what I discovered. Dairy, it turns out, is linked to heart disease, Type 1 diabetes, the formation of hormone-related cancers, congestive problems, rheumatoid arthritis, iron deficiency, certain food allergies, and—as counterintuitive as it sounds—osteoporosis. Simply put, dairy had to go. But the task became even more daunting when further study unearthed just how much of what I ate (and what most people eat, for that matter) contained some form of a dairy product or derivative. For example, did you know that most breads contain amino acid extracts derived from whey protein, a by-product of cheese production? And that whey protein or its dairy cousin, casein, can be found in most boxed cereals, crackers, nutrition bars, veggie "meat" products, and condiments? I certainly didn't. And what about my beloved muffins? Forget it.

As my eyes began to widen, I was once again back in rehab—at least, it felt that way.

The first few days were brutal, the cravings severe. I found myself just staring at that wedge of cheddar still in the fridge, transfixed. Burning with envy, I glared at my daughter as she sucked on her bottle of milk. Driving past a pizza parlor, I could feel my mouth water, the saliva literally pooling in my mouth.

But if I knew anything, it was how to weather a detox. This was familiar territory. And in a perverse sort of way, I welcomed the painful challenge.

Fortunately, after only a week, the cravings for cheese and even that glass of milk dissipated. And at ten days in, I was surprised to recapture the full extent of the vibrancy I'd experienced during the cleanse. In this interim period, my sleep patterns were uneven, yet I was buffeted by skyrocketing energy levels. Overcome by a sense of wellness, I quite literally started bouncing off the walls. Previously too lethargic to engage Mathis in an evening game of hide-and-seek, I was now feverishly chasing her around the house until she collapsed in exhaustion—no small feat! And out in the yard, I found myself for the first time practicing soccer drills with Trapper. Clearly, my desire to prove this vegan thing pointless had failed. Instead, I was sold.

For the first time in nearly two decades I began working out almost daily—running, biking, and swimming. I had no thought of returning to competitive sports; I was just getting in shape. After all, I was closing in on forty-one. Any desire I had to compete in something physical had dried up in my early twenties. I simply needed a healthy channel to burn off my energy reserves. Nothing more.

Then came what I like to call *the Run.*

About a month into my vegan experiment, I headed out early one spring morning for what was intended to be an easy trail run on nearby "Dirt Mulholland"—a tranquil but hilly nine-mile stretch of fire road that cuts along the pristine ridgeline atop the hills of Topanga State Park near Los Angeles. Connecting Calabasas to Bel Air and Brentwood beyond, it's an oasis of untouched nature smack in the middle of L.A.'s sprawl, a wide sandy home to scurrying rabbits, coyotes, and the occasional rattlesnake, which offers stunning views of the San Fernando Valley, the Pacific Ocean, and downtown. I parked my truck and stretched a bit, then started my run. I didn't plan on running more than an hour at the most. But it was a beautiful day, and feeling energized by the clean air, I let myself go.

And go.

I didn't just feel good; I didn't just feel amazing. I felt *free*. As I ascended shirtless, the welcome sensation of the warm sun baking my shoulders, time folded in on itself as I seemingly lost all conscious thought, the only sound that of my easy breath and my legs pumping effortlessly beneath me. I recall later thinking, *This must be what it means to meditate.* I mean really meditate. For the first time in my life, I felt that sense of "oneness" I'd only previously read about in spiritual texts. Indeed, I was having an out-of-body experience.

So instead of turning back after thirty minutes as I'd planned, I kept running, with a mind switched off but a spirit fully engaged. At two hours in, I was painlessly cruising over rolling grasslands above Brentwood and the famed Getty Museum, without a soul in sight. And as if being aroused from a sleepwalk, I slowly began to come out of my trance-like state to find myself transfixed by the dip and rise of a hawk flying overhead. A moment later the realization hit—I was still running *away* from my truck! *What is going on? What am I doing so far away from home? Am I nuts? It's only a matter of minutes before my calf seizes up in a cramp and I'm lying facedown in a meadow in the middle of nowhere without a phone or any way home! What if I get bitten by a rattlesnake?* But I didn't care. I didn't want this feeling to end. Ever.

I crested a small hill to see a fellow runner coming my way—the first person I'd seen all morning. As he passed, he gave me a quick nod and a gentle thumbs-up. There was just something about this tiny gesture that was profound. It was barely noticeable. Yet it was everything, some kind of message—from above, perhaps— touching my soul. It let me know not just that I'd be okay, but that

I was on the right track—that, in fact, this wasn't just a run. It was the beginning of a new life.

I did turn around, eventually, even though I really didn't want to. It certainly wasn't out of fatigue, dehydration, or fear, but because I realized I'd scheduled an important conference call that I couldn't responsibly skip. As I ascended a particularly steep hill on my journey back, reason told me I should at least slow down a bit. Or better yet, why not stop and take a break? Instead, I accelerated, chasing a rabbit that scurried out of the brush and harnessing a power in my legs and lungs that I'd had no idea I possessed. I was on top of the world—both energetically and literally—peering down on the Valley far below as I painlessly hurled myself up a sandstone ridge, fluidly cresting yet another steep, craggy ascent, bearing the full brunt of what was now the midday desert sun without notice or care. And not only did I make it back to my truck in one piece, I felt superb right to the very end, even quickening my pace over the last five miles to a flat-out, downhill sprint, my dust-covered running shoes kicking up bits of gravel in my wake. *I was flying.*

When I arrived where I'd begun almost four hours earlier, I was overcome by an absolute certainty that I could have kept going all day. Without ingesting any water or food as I went, I'd run what I later discovered (after reviewing trail maps) was in excess of twenty-four miles—the farthest I'd ever run in my life by a long shot. For a guy who hadn't run more than a few easy miles in countless years, it was remarkable.

It wasn't until much later that I'd fully appreciate the extent and impact of the morning. But as I showered the grit and grime from my worn legs that afternoon, my body hummed with excitement and possibility. And without conscious thought, a huge grin spread across my face. In this moment I knew one thing for certain: I'd soon be seeking a challenge—and it would be a big one.

This middle-aged guy—who'd just run a huge distance, who'd just awoken something inside himself, something that was fierce and tough and wanted to win—this guy would soon be making a return to athletics. And not just for fun. To actually *be competitive. To contend.*

CHAPTER TWO

CHLORINE DREAMS

Long before I'd ever met Julie or heard the word "vegan" or thought about running up a hill—before, even, I'd run one step, not to mention walked—*I swam.* I had yet to reach my first birthday when my mom hoisted my scrawny, diapered body off the cement deck of the neighborhood swimming pool and launched me into deep water, leaving me to thrash and struggle. Not until I was about to drown did she come to the rescue, scooping me up as I gasped for air. But I didn't cry. Instead, she tells me, I just smiled and cast a glance that, in her interpretation, could mean only one thing—*When can I do that again?*

I can't say I remember the moment, but I wish I did. What she did may seem harsh, but her motivation was pure: She simply wanted to give me a love of the water. It was the same love that defined her father and my namesake—a man who died long before I was born yet, I'd later come to understand, embodied so much of who I'd soon become.

Thus began my own lifelong love affair with water—a passion that would carry me far, yet prove no match for the grip of addiction. It was a devotion I'd rediscover in sober middle age, once again floating my life with meaning and purpose.

Long before that day, Nancy Spindle was a cheerleader with a deep tan, twinkling brown eyes, and short-cropped dark hair, swirling pom-poms for her high school sweetheart Dave Roll, who played center for the Grosse Pointe High football team. The year was 1957, when life could seem at times like a series of scenes out of *American Graffiti*. Affectionately known as "Muffin," my father was a hardworking senior with big dreams, a popular school leader and textbook match for the cute girl with the kind smile known as "Spinner," a few years his junior.

Despite the years and miles that divided them when my father enrolled in Amherst College in 1958, they successfully kept their courtship going and were reunited when my father returned to go to law school at the University of Michigan, where my mother was still an undergraduate and a member of the Kappa Kappa Gamma sorority.

Diligently studying through the summer months, Dad completed his law school courses early, married Spinner, and settled into law-firm life back home in Grosse Pointe, with a modest house in the suburbs and a white Dodge Dart in the driveway. It wasn't long after that I entered the world, on October 20, 1966. With my birth came no indication that I'd have a future in athletics. In fact, all evidence was to the contrary. I was a frail baby: rawboned and often ill, prone to earaches and allergy attacks; a cross-eyed weakling and a regular at the local pediatrician's office.

My earliest memory surrounds the birth of my younger sister Mary Elizabeth, two years my junior. Fearing that I'd feel "left out," my parents bought me a toy garage set. Frankly, I don't remember feeling any inkling of abandonment. Instead, I relished the alone time with my toys, the chance to become deeply immersed in something. It was an attitude that foretold the loner I'd later become. As it turned out, Molly, unlike me, was a robust baby, strong and full of vigor. Affectionately known at the time as "Butter Ball" (a nickname my now beautiful sister would rather forget), she, and not I, was the safer bet to one day be the Roll child who covered herself in athletic glory.

In 1972, when I was six, my father was offered a position with the Antitrust Division of the Federal Trade Commission, and we settled into the middle-class suburban enclave known as Greenwich Forest in Bethesda, Maryland, just outside D.C. It was a safe neighborhood that teemed with young families, and I distinctly remember the cherry blossom trees that canopied the streets in white and pink during spring. I began first grade at the local public school, Bethesda Elementary. And the three years that followed marked my descent down the public school system's academic chute and into the rabbit hole of prepubescent social exile. New to town and feeling overwhelmed by the forty-plus kids crammed into each classroom, I was surpassingly shy. It was easy for me to withdraw into a dreamworld—and so I did.

Worsening my situation was an outward appearance that made it even harder to fit in. In an effort to strengthen the weak left eye that had left me cross-eyed since birth, I wore beneath my thick horn-rimmed glasses an eye patch over my stronger right eye. And if that wasn't enough, I had to wear orthodontic headgear—a 1970s torture contraption in which heavy metal wire emanated from my mouth and ran across my cheeks, where it was pulled tight by an elastic head strap. Then there was the *playground*— that awful coliseum of pain. Even with corrective eyewear, I've always lacked any semblance of hand-eye coordination. To this day, I can't throw or catch a ball to save my life. Needless to say, I was always the kid picked last for any game—whether it was softball, touch football, or basketball. Tennis? Forget it. Golf? You must be kidding. I was—and still am—terrible at all of them. So I usually found the kickball bouncing off the glasses that shielded my patched eye. In an effort to correct this terrible wrong, I joined the local soccer team. And my football-loving father even volunteered to coach. Not only was I hopeless, I was completely uninterested. Typically, I could be found staring off at some bird flying overhead or sitting down in the middle of the game picking daisies. Soccer was not for me. In fact, it looked as though I had no future in sports whatsoever.

In retrospect, I can't say I blame the other kids for making fun of me. I made it too easy for everyone. I stuck out like a sore thumb: a weakness that had to be rooted out, put on display, and exploited as part of the natural order of things. Kids will be kids. But the inevitability of it all didn't salve my intense pain. At the school bus stop just up the street from my house, Tommy Birnbach, Mark Johnson, and a band of older kids would shove me, fully aware that I wouldn't strike back. And whether it was on the bus or in the school cafeteria, I generally sat alone. During winter months, the kids would make a hilarious daily game out of stealing the wool beanie that I wore. On countless occasions I'd slink home from the bus after school, defeated and hatless, my head hung low, and cry in the warm embrace of my mother's arms.

And as I continued to withdraw, my grades followed suit. I didn't care about what was happening in the classroom. The academic train was pulling out of the station. It was only third grade, but I was already quickly getting left behind.

Solace came during the summer months, when my family would vacation in quaint cottages on Lake Michigan with my beloved cousins, or at Deep Creek Lake in rural Maryland. And during Washington downtime, I could generally be found at Edgemoor, our local neighborhood swim and tennis club. Times were different back then: Mom would simply drop off my sister and me at Edgemoor in the morning and leave us there all day under the guidance of the lifeguards, only to pick us up when it got dark. I officially joined my first swim team at the age of six, dog-paddling my way across the pool to modest results in summer-league meets. But the results didn't matter. From the moment Mom submerged my infant self, I loved everything about the water. From the smell of chlorine to the whistles of the lifeguards, I relished it all. Most of all, I loved the silence of submersion—that womblike feeling of protection that enveloped me when underwater. What can I say— there was a feeling of completeness, *of being home.* And so, left to my own devices, I learned to swim.

And then I learned to swim fast.

By the time I was eight, I was winning local summer-league swim team races with regularity. I'd stumbled into something I was actually good at. I enjoyed being part of a team, but more important, I loved the self-determination of it all. The idea that hard work and discipline left me solely responsible for the result—win or lose—was a revelation.

Summer-league swim team meets were the highlight of my youth. I felt part of something meaningful, but more important, I was having fun. The Edgemoor team was composed of kids of all ages, from six to eighteen. I looked up to the older kids, even idolized a few, especially Tom Verdin, a Harvard-bound Adonis who seemed to own every pool record and win every race he entered. He was a great swimmer, and smart. *Someday I'm going to be a great swimmer, just like Tom,* I thought. And so I followed him around like a lost puppy, relentlessly pestering him until he took me under his wing. *How did you get so fast? How long can you hold your breath? I'm gonna go to Harvard, too!* And on and on. But to his great credit, Tom patiently mentored me. He made me feel special—that I could be someone like him. Before leaving for Harvard, he even gave me his swimsuit—a suit he'd worn in many a victory. It was a passing of the torch, and meant the world to me. I'll never forget that. *Screw those kids at the bus stop,* I thought. In this world, I could be myself. I could look people in the eye and smile. I could even excel.

At the age of ten, I set my first true athletic goal—to win the local summer-league title in the ten-and-under age bracket of the

25-meter butterfly. I even sacrificed my beloved summer vacation on Lake Michigan, staying home with my dad to attend practices in preparation as my sister and mom headed north for July. Unfortunately, I didn't win the race, ending up second by a fingernail to my nemesis Harry Cain. But my time of 16.9 seconds was a team record—a record set in 1977 that would stand for the better part of the next thirty years. And the narrow loss gave me a sense of unfinished business, of work to be done. From that moment forward, I was in with 100 percent of everything I had. *I was a swimmer.*

In an effort to address my rapidly disintegrating academic and social life, my parents made the wise decision to pull me out of public school. And so I entered the fifth grade at St. Patrick's Episcopal Day School, a parochial school on the outskirts of Georgetown—a move that literally saved me. The staff at St. Patrick's created a nurturing and supportive environment with small class sizes that catered to the individual. For the first time, I felt like I fit in. My grades quickly picked up and I made friends. My fifth-grade teacher, Eric Sivertsen, even showed up at my swim meets during the summer to cheer me on. It was a long way from staring at my feet at the bus stop.

Meanwhile, my swimming improved. I even began practicing year-round on a team made up of friendly kids at the local YMCA.

But things would soon take a turn for the worse. After completing elementary school at St. Patrick's, I once again had to try to fit in at a new school. The year was 1980, and I'd just entered my first year at the Landon School for Boys—a prep school Shangri-la that boasted perfectly manicured playing fields, stonemasonry, and country lanes lined with large rocks painted blinding white. Widely considered one of Washington's most prestigious all-boys prep schools, Landon was—and in many ways still is—a machismo paradise. It's a preppy haven known as much for its football and lacrosse prowess as its Ivy League matriculation rate.

Unfortunately, I didn't play lacrosse—or football. And despite my developing mastery of the chlorine currents, I was still the awkward nerd with the thick glasses, quietly toting a dog-eared copy of *Catcher in the Rye* while my tweed-jacketed, madras tie–donning classmates practiced lacrosse skills on open fields. I was proud, though, that I had been accepted into this unparalleled academic institution, and so were my parents. By this time my father had moved into private practice with the Steptoe & Johnson law firm. And my mother, fresh off receiving her master's degree in special education at American University after years of night school, taught children with learning disabilities at Washington's Lab School. But even with the increase in income, my parents had to dig deep into their savings to pay Landon's steep tuition. The education that students received there was a golden ticket to a bright future, and I'll never forget my parents' willingness to sacrifice to ensure a great outcome for me. The only problem? I didn't fit in. I was water in a sea of oil.

It's not that I didn't try. It was during the winter months of the seventh grade—what Landon still calls "Form I"—that I decided to try out for the middle school basketball team. If you could have seen me back then in all my inelegant and maladroit glory, you'd have considered this a bold move. By some bizarre stroke of fate I managed to survive the cuts and become the last person named to the team. The problem was, I had no place among this crew, many of whom had been playing together since their first days at Landon, all the way back to the third grade. I was proud that I'd made the squad, but confused, knowing I was in way over my head. And I was resented for bouncing a longtime peer from the lineup. On the court, I was simply awful. I couldn't run the plays. I froze up. Tense and anxiety-ridden, I'd habitually pass the ball to the opposing team. Throwing up air balls was routine. And despite practicing at home with my dad, who'd erected a hoop in our driveway in support, I was hopeless. And I paid for it with relentless ridicule. Soon I was the butt of every joke. And beatings would quickly follow.

One day in the locker room after practice, I suddenly found myself surrounded and wearing only a towel. A group of my teammates circled close. Todd Rollap, twice my strength, stepped forward and got right in my face.

"You don't belong here. Time to quit the team and just go back where you came from."

"Just leave me alone, Todd," I replied, cowering.

Todd laughed. My teammates circled tighter, poking me in the chest, taunting me to try something. And I obliged, finally shoving Todd, who was standing right in my face. *Game on.* My teammates shoved back, pushing me around like this was a game of hot potato.

"Get off me! Go away! Leave me alone!" I cried. Sensing weakness, the throng cheered for blood and moved in for the kill. In a last-ditch effort to escape, I took a swing at Todd but missed his face entirely. Predictable. Like my jump shot, nothing but air.

Then *BOOM!* Todd landed one right on my jaw. The next thing I remember I was lying on my back, staring up at my teammates, who were laughing hysterically at my embarrassing crumple. They were chanting what would become a mantra of ridicule. *"Rich Roll—man under control! Rich Roll—man under control!"*

Half-naked, horrified, and utterly humiliated, I grabbed my clothes and ran crying from the locker room, bringing the curtain down on one of my countless vintage Landon moments.

The next day Coach Williams pulled me aside into an empty classroom. "I heard about what happened. Are you okay?"

"I'm fine," I replied, doing my best to hold back the emotions that were boiling inside.

"Do you know why I wanted you on the team?" he asked, his

balding forehead glistening as he peered at me through his John Lennon–esque wire-rimmed glasses. I stared back at his mustache blankly. Given what had occurred, I couldn't think of a single reason. I didn't want anything to do with Landon anymore, let alone basketball. "It's not because of your ability to play the game," he continued. *You think?!* "It's because you're a leader. You have a rare enthusiasm and a contagious optimism. The team needs that."

Maybe so. But I didn't need the team. That much I knew. And I couldn't understand why he saw me as a leader. By my account, I lacked any evidence of such skills.

"But I understand if you want to quit. It's up to you."

I badly wanted to quit. But I also knew that if I did, my fate would be sealed. I'd never hear the end of it. And so I agreed to stick it out. It was far from pleasant. The ridicule continued—escalated even. But I did my best to stand my ground. I couldn't let them win.

But what I *did* do was do what I did best. Withdraw. From that day forward through high school graduation, I opted out of everything social that Landon had to offer. I kept my head down, studied hard, and found myself entirely alone. I'd reap what I could academically from Landon, but that was it.

By fifteen, I'd outgrown what the YMCA had to offer my development as a swimmer. If I wanted to play with the big boys, it was time to step it up. And even if Landon had a swimming program—which they didn't—I needed the guidance of an expert hand to take whatever talent I had to the next level.

And so I announced to my parents that I wanted to join the Curl Swim Club, an outfit newly formed by Coach Rick Curl, who'd begun his career launching athletes to the national level with crosstown rival Solotar Swim Club and had now struck out on his own with a new team. At the Y, I'd been a big fish in a small pond.

At Curl, I'd be the smallest fish in the biggest pond available to me. Not only would every swimmer my age eclipse my talent and ability, I'd be required to attend ten swim workouts a week—four seventy-five-minute sessions before school, five two-hour weekday sessions after school, and a three-hour workout every Saturday. Daunting, for certain. And my parents were responsibly concerned, unsure about whether such a huge commitment was in my best interest. For them, education was king, and they understandably didn't want this megadose of swimming to undermine my grades, which were finally beginning to head in the right direction. But I convinced them I could make it work. And I knew that if I gave it my all, the sky was the limit. Rick could take me there. But most of all, I was desperate to be away from anything and everything Landon.

There was only one hitch in the plan. Landon was very proud of its mandatory after-school sports program. Every student was *required* to play a school sport when the classroom bell rang at 3 P.M. No exceptions. I needed to find an end run around this rule if I wanted to swim, really swim. And so with the help of my parents, I petitioned Headmaster Malcolm Coates and Athletic Director Lowell Davis for an exemption. No big deal, I thought. With its emphasis on athletic excellence, I figured the school would want to support a student who hungered to take his sport to the highest level, something Landon simply couldn't offer me.

I couldn't have been more wrong. A.D. Davis was adamantly against the idea from the outset. In the history of Landon, a school that was founded in 1929, no student had ever been granted an exemption from the pride and joy that is Landon's athletic program, and they weren't about to start now. Could this really be an issue? It wasn't as if I were *needed* on the gridiron. Shouldn't sports be about *building* confidence? At Landon, mine couldn't have been lower. And it wasn't like I was asking to pick daisies, either. All I wanted was the simple right to train like a *real* athlete, with a vigor, intensity, and time commitment more than triple Landon's requirement. But the door was closed. Not backing down, I put my petition in writing, pleading my case like the appellate attorney I'd later become. What ensued were several intimidating meetings with the powers that be. There was concern about the precedent it would set. And lip service given to how I might properly develop as a young man. *What if you need to play tennis or golf for business? What will you do then?* Well, that wasn't going to happen anyway.

During this time, my head hit the pillow every night with just one thought. *Why won't they let me just swim!?*

To his credit, Headmaster Coates responded to my persistence, lending a kind ear to my case. Swayed by the indefatigable effort I'd put into my petition, he ultimately persuaded Davis to grant my request. To my knowledge, I remain the only student to whom Landon has granted such an exemption. And I wasn't about to put it to waste.

Life changed immediately. From the next day forward, my alarm bell rang every morning at 4:44. In a remarkable show of support, my dad would rise right along with me (until I could obtain my driver's license a year later), and together we'd make the dark twenty-minute drive in his beloved MG Midget—a car that to this day he continues to drive—to the dingy basement natatorium at Georgetown Preparatory School, where Curl rented pool time. While I swam, Dad would sit in the car, marking up legal briefs. Never once did he complain. The locker rooms were cockroach-infested and covered in mud. The pool was dark, gloomy, and cold. Green mold grew everywhere, and a black, tar-like substance dripped from the aging mildewed ceiling through the damp lingering fog into the over-chlorinated water. But from the moment I set eyes on the place, I loved it for the promise it brought into my life.

From the outset, I was thrown in with the sharks. The lanes teemed with kids responsible for dozens of national age-group records. Among my teammates were several Olympic Trials quali- fiers and even a few national champions. If you lived in the D.C. area and wanted to swim with the best, there was only one place to be, and this was it. I had a lot of catching up to do, but I wasted no time in getting to work.

Determined to rise to the level of my swimming peers as rap- idly as possible, I rarely missed a workout. And improvement came rapidly. But I quickly became aware that I lacked a certain level of God-given talent. If I wanted to catch up and make the leap to the national level, I couldn't rely on innate gifts. I was going to have to go the extra mile. I decided to focus almost entirely on the 200-yard butterfly; widely considered one of the most difficult and draining events, most people had no interest in swimming it. This gave me an immediate advantage. Less interest and fewer competi- tors meant better chances for success.

I was willing to bridge my talent-deficit gap by doubling down with yardage and intensity. Rick took notice and created spe- cial workouts specifically designed to see just how far I could be pushed. But I never backed down. I welcomed the suffering that came with unheard-of routines like twenty 200-yard butterfly re- peats on a descending interval that started with thirty seconds' rest after the first repeat and slowly dropped to just five seconds by the end. Or ten consecutive 400-yard butterfly efforts, each successive repeat harder and faster than the previous.

I loved the pain, and the pain loved me back; in fact, I couldn't get enough—something that would serve me well in ultra-endurance training later in life. On a conscious level, I was doing everything in my power to excel. But in retrospect, I know that underneath it all, my daily torture sessions were an unconscious and masochistic attempt to exorcise the pain of my Landon experience. Striving for excellence made me feel alive, in contrast to the disconnection and emotional numbness that defined my time at Landon.

Life in those days revolved entirely around swimming. Other than go to school, I did nothing but eat, live, and breathe the sport. No matter how exhausted I was, I never overslept and was typically the first person to arrive for each practice session, often springing from the car to run into the pool. Even during snowstorms when school was called off, I'd venture out onto the icy thoroughfares in the family Volvo, skidding and sliding my way across town in order to make practice. And because I was more reliable than even the coach, I was given a key to the pool, to use in the event Rick was late or, worse yet, didn't show up at all, which happened from time to time.

My goal times could be found written in giant block letters on my school notebooks, inside my school locker, and pasted on my bathroom mirror. And every inch of the corkboard that blanketed an entire wall of my bedroom was covered with glossy pictures and posters of my heroes torn from the pages of *Swimming World* magazine—world record holders and Olympic champions such as Rowdy Gaines, John Moffet, Jeff Kostoff, and Pablo Morales. Of all the photographs my favorite was the one of speed skater extraordinaire Eric Heiden in his golden bodysuit—a shot that appeared on the cover of *Sports Illustrated* during the 1980 Winter Olympic Games in Lake Placid. With leg muscles the size of tree trunks, Heiden had completely rewritten the record books in almost every speed skating event, from sprint to distance, garnering five gold medals in the process. Sure, he wasn't a swimmer, but in my mind he was the very essence of athletic virtue and excellence.

I couldn't have been older than fifteen when I read in the *Washington Post* that a professional bike race would be held on the "Ellipse"—a large oval stretch of road picturesquely facing the White House on Washington's Mall, the expanse of green that was part of French architect Pierre-Charles L'Enfant's famous design for our nation's capital. At that point, Eric Heiden had made a rare transition from speed skating to pro cycling, and he'd be competing with his 7-Eleven Team, America's first top professional outfit. I dragged my dad to the race and watched intensely. I think Dad was bored, but I'd never seen such athletic pageantry. Whipping around the looped course at impossible speeds, the tightly packed group of riders known as the "peloton" captivated me, their spinning wheels a beehive-purr soundtrack to the rainbow blur of the brightly colored jerseys careening past. After the race, I snuck through security to get close to the 7-Eleven Team van, catching glimpses of Heiden casually chatting with reporters. Never before, and never since, have I been so starstruck. And in that moment, I fell in love with the sport of cycling. I wanted to race bikes. But I didn't know any other kids who raced. And the timing was all wrong. I didn't possess nearly enough bandwidth for this aspiration if I wanted to excel as a swimmer. And so for the next twenty-five years it would remain nothing more than a dream deferred.

I was forced to manage my rigorous schedule with extreme precision. While my classmates stayed out late, experimenting with drugs and alcohol and enjoying parties that I wasn't invited to, with the girls from Landon's sister school, Holton Arms, I maintained a strict regimen of studying, sleeping, training, and racing. Even if I *had* been invited to the parties, I would have declined, if for no other reason than that I was just too damn tired. And so, by default, I became the model son and student. During the week I had no free time—just swim, school, eat, swim, study, sleep. And even on the weekends my goals didn't allow me to get into any trouble. Most weekends were spent traipsing up and down the East Coast to compete in meets, from Tuscaloosa to Pittsburgh to Hackensack.

For competitions within driving range, my parents would dutifully load up the wagon and haul me—and often my sister, who'd now joined me in the pool and would become an outstanding swimmer in her own right—to endless meets that, for a spectator, were about as exciting as watching grass grow.

But the work quickly began to pay off. By the time I was sixteen—a little more than a year since I'd joined Rick Curl—I'd achieved my goal of obtaining a national ranking, landing eighth in the country for my age in the 200-meter butterfly. I was qualifying for national-level meets and traveling all over the country to compete. At these competitions I was coming into contact with many of the swimming legends who'd graced my bedroom wall. I still recall my first junior nationals in Gainesville, Florida, in 1983. Two days into the weeklong meet, I spotted Craig Beardsley, then a student at the University of Florida, casually walking the pool deck. A member of the ill-fated 1980 Olympic team that missed the chance to compete due to President Carter's boycott of the Moscow Games, Craig was the reigning world champion in my specialty, the 200-meter butterfly. Undefeated in the event since 1979, he'd held the world record for more than three years running. To say he was my hero is an understatement. In awe, I followed him but was too afraid to approach. Sensing someone shadowing him, Craig turned around to see what I was up to. But I was much too overwhelmed to talk to him and made a quick exit—unfortunately, into the women's bathroom!

But I didn't care. *Holy cow, Craig Beardsley looked at me!* I felt that I'd arrived in the elite world of swimming.

During this time I began to excel academically as well, clawing my way up to the top of my class. In particular, I fell in love with biology, hatching a dream for a career in medicine. Out of necessity, my tight schedule focused my schoolwork, which translated into excellent grades. Socially, I left well enough alone at Landon and increased my time spent with my swim club teammates, forging long-lasting friendships with kids who shared my passion. All told, my master plan was working.

By my senior year, I was established as one of the top high school swimmers in the country. The only feather missing from my cap was a win at "Metros"—the D.C.-area high school championships. But I faced one major obstacle. I wasn't eligible to enter this meet because Landon lacked a swim team. No high school swim team, no high school championships. So once again, I made an unwelcome return to Athletic Director Lowell Davis's office, this time with a petition to form Landon's first swimming program. Maybe he resented that outside his control I'd become one of the area's best athletes, because once again he threw up a roadblock. No matter what I did, I just couldn't win with this guy. So it was back to Headmaster Coates for another appeal. With his help, I became Landon's "team of one." And by exploiting a few loopholes in the high school swimming league rule book, I qualified for the championship meet by piggybacking into a few high school dual meets. Essentially, I crashed a party I wasn't invited to.

At Metros, I was forced to strut my stuff in the shorter sprint distance, the 100-yard butterfly; the 200-yard butterfly is not a high school event. The 100 wasn't my specialty—with butterfly, as well as with triathlon later in life, the longer the distance the better— but I was determined to win anyway. Unfortunately, once again I came up a hair shy, finishing second to my Curl teammate Mark Henderson (who would later win gold at the 1996 Olympics, swimming the butterfly leg of the United States' world-record-setting 4×100 medley relay). Coming in second was becoming a habit.

I may not have won that race, but I proudly represented my school that day, even though some there had been reluctant to support me. And what was most gratifying was that my persistence, buttressed by a top performance, set the stage for Landon to found an official swimming team the following year—a team that exists to this day. I may have been exempt from Landon's sports program, but my athletic legacy there nonetheless remains.

CHAPTER THREE

COLLEGE CURRENTS

Fast Water, High Times, and California Cool

My Metros results, combined with my national rankings, were more than sufficient to catch the attention of top university programs. And with A's across the board and enrollment in every advanced placement course available, my chances of college acceptance were nearly bulletproof. Even so, I worked hard on my applications, crafting an esoteric essay on my knack for persistence and love affair with water, and I even included an underwater photo of me, my smile distorted by the turquoise current. Soon the coaches began calling, and I quickly got a taste of college life as I jetted around the country on all-expenses-paid recruiting trips.

First up was the University of Michigan, a top-notch university and home to a swimming program with a legendary history, then led by my favorite coach in the sport, the popular and über-talented Jon Urbanchek, who'd later go on to coach the 2004 and 2008 U.S. Olympic swimming teams. As a native of the state, my Wolverine roots run deep. Not only had my mother and father both attended U of M, so had many of my cousins, aunts, and uncles. As a family, we bleed maize and blue.

But by far the most important person in my extended family to attend Michigan was my grandfather on my mother's side, Richard Spindle. During the late 1920s, Richard had led the University of Michigan swimming team to an array of Big Ten Conference championships and countless individual victories under the tutelage of venerable coach Matt Mann, who noted at the time, "The

University of Michigan swimming team of 1926–27 is the greatest team ever organized by any college."* And my grandfather was a standout that season, setting the national record in the 150-yard backstroke. That feat made him an Olympic hopeful for the 1928 Summer Games in Amsterdam, along with the most famous swimmer of the day, Johnny Weissmuller—who would later achieve *Tarzan* fame on the silver screen. Ultimately, my grandfather came up short, missing his Olympic berth by one place when he finished fourth in the trials. But he remains one of the great swimmers of his time—a true legend, who completed his career as captain of the Michigan squad during his 1929 senior year.

Adorning the hallways of the world-class Matt Mann Natatorium on the Ann Arbor campus are many team photos dating back to my grandfather's time. And if you look closely at the photo from 1929, setting aside the sepia tone of the weathered image and the sleeveless wool body suits, my resemblance to my grandpa is beyond eerie. Unfortunately, Richard Spindle died years before I was born, the victim of a genetic predisposition to heart disease that took his life during my mother's college years, at the relatively young age of fifty-four. But despite his never having met his namesake grandson, he's influenced much of who I am today. Though I must rely on my mother's memories to fill out my knowledge of him, it's clear that we shared many things, including most obviously a fascination with water, a competitive fire, and a passion for fitness.

It was my mother's love for the father who was too early taken from her that motivated her to name me after him and imbue my life with the things he loved. It's why she threw me in the pool that

* Bruce Madej, *Michigan: Champions of the West* (Urbana, IL: Segamore Publishing, 1997), page 63, accessed at http://books.google.com/books?id=KAGAwpROdW4C&pg=PA63&lpg=PA63& dq=richard+spindle+michigan+swimming&source=bl&ots=R9YWEqDxqU&sig=xb2YhwXSXN dsKctR_1IcXm_cLrw&hl=en&ei=RBR5TcGtEsTYrAGR7fnOBQ&sa=X&oi=book_result&ct= result&resnum=1&ved=0CBUQ6AEwAA#v=onepage&q=richard%20spindle%20michigan%20 swimming&f=false.

fateful day when I was an infant, and it was a huge factor in her devoted support of my own swimming dreams. I often joke that I'm the reincarnation of Richard Spindle. But in many ways, it's no joke. I feel a spiritual connection to this man; I'm convinced that I'm here to carry on his legacy and complete his unfinished business.

Upon my graduation from college, Mom gave me framed prints of those team photographs. They hang above my desk. For my birthday several years later, she gave me his Michigan letterman's blanket, a dark blue woolly drape with a block "M" in bold maize and his name in elegant cursive embroidery. To this day it lies spread across our bed. Both these gifts are daily reminders of where I came from, who I am, talismans to represent the rationale behind my decision to change my life.

And it was my grandfather's image that came to mind on the eve of my fortieth birthday as I nearly passed out climbing the stairs. I didn't want to die like he did. I *couldn't.* I knew it was my mission to somehow correct in my own life what had gone terribly awry in his. It's because of Richard Spindle that I recommitted my life to expanding the boundaries of health and fitness.

But back to my recruiting trip to Michigan. The visit kicked off with a Friday evening dual meet, where I sat quietly intimidated in the bleachers, watching the team compete as swimmers came by to introduce themselves. I was painfully aware of my undeveloped social acumen, that my conversation was forced and that I failed to make eye contact. Away from my friends at Curl Swim Club, I felt like an utter misfit. I may have loved swimming, but interacting with people had always been difficult for me—especially *new* people. Others my age seemed to display an ease with themselves that left me baffled. As yet, I hadn't realized that very soon I'd find a solution to my problem, albeit one that came with a cost.

After the meet, I was shuffled off to a swimmer party at a local house. The team had won the meet, and spirits ran high, literally and figuratively. Before I could even remove my coat, a gigantic plastic mug of beer was shoved in my face, a first in my young life, courtesy of Bruce Kimball.

Aptly named the "Comeback Kid," Bruce was Michigan's top diver, fresh off winning a silver medal at the 1984 Olympic Games in the 10-meter platform. But just three years prior, Bruce had been struck head-on by a drunk driver, breaking his leg and fracturing every single bone in his face. His liver was lacerated and his spleen had to be removed. The scars he wore on his face told the tragic tale well. Everybody knew who Bruce was—his story was legend. And now he was giving me a beer. My first beer.

"Chug it!" Bruce yelped, followed by his teammates. "Chug! Chug! Chug!"

Although I wasn't a diver, I idolized Bruce and what he had overcome to achieve greatness. So there was no way I was going to let him down, despite my hesitation about this strange brew. I'd always prided myself on my teetotaler nature and was apt to be judgmental toward classmates who spent weekends wasted. But this time was different. This time a true sports legend was exhorting me to imbibe. I obliged, tipping the Big Gulp–sized cup back and sucking down all thirty-two ounces until nary a drop was left. Not bad for my first beer ever.

My gut distended, I buckled over, trying to keep it down. But after a moment, my stomach settled. And what I next experienced would change the direction of my life forever. It started with a flush to my head. Then a deep warmth began to course through my veins, as if the softest blanket ever had suddenly enveloped my entire body. And within a heartbeat, all those feelings of fear, resentment, insecurity, and isolation just vanished, replaced with the rush of comfort and belonging.

My only thought? *Get me more. Now.* And before you could blink, to the delight of the Michigan swimmers, I'd drunk the better part of a six-pack, with plenty more lined up. And the more I drank, the better I felt. For the first time in my life, I experienced what I thought it must feel like to be *normal*—to walk into a group of people and just start a spontaneous conversation, to look someone in the eye and crack a joke, to flirt with a girl, laugh, and just plain feel good about myself. I found myself engaging—funny even, holding court. Truly, I'd found my answer. Could it really be this easy?

Early data indicated that yes, it really was that simple. Within an hour, Bruce Kimball had become my best friend. We chugged more beers together, and I watched in awe as this rare athletic specimen performed what to this day is the greatest party trick I've ever seen. With a full cup of beer firmly in one hand, from a still position he launched himself several feet in the air before tucking his knees and jerking his head back, completing a perfect standing backflip, nailing his landing square on his planted feet with nary a wobble. The kicker? Not one drop of beer spilled from the full cup he held. Whatever this guy had, I wanted it.

But Bruce's future wouldn't become the brightly lit success story I then imagined. Three years later, and just two weeks before the 1988 U.S. Olympic Diving Trials, he would plow his car into a crowd of teenagers at close to ninety miles per hour, killing two boys and injuring four. Drunk at the time, he was sentenced to seventeen years in prison and ultimately served five.

Of course, I couldn't foresee this future, or how my own life would later devolve because of the seeds planted that night. No, that night my horizon was limited to only my quickly blurring vision and the growing ecstasy I felt. I was deliriously happy not just because I'd at last blended into a group of strangers and had discovered I could be charming with girls, but because I'd found a remedy for everything that ailed me. Only one thought looped through my mind: *When can I do this again?*

I returned home to Bethesda thinking only about when I could take my next recruiting trip. And over the next several months I repeated my adventures up and down the Eastern Seaboard. I hob-nobbed at Princeton, touring the famous eating clubs and sipping vodka tonics with the academic elite. After that, I journeyed to Providence, where I hit the best house parties Brown had to offer, eating clams and oysters over countless beers. Attending classes, learning about what each school had to offer, and evaluating the swimming programs all took a backseat to rooting out a good time.

Then it was on to Harvard—for obvious reasons my top choice. *The dream school.* Up in Cambridge for Harvard-Yale weekend, I kicked things off playing tailgate touch football with the Harvard swimmers. Swilling beers from a keg seemed to work miracles on my hand-eye coordination deficit. With my head buzzing, we headed over to the Harvard-Yale football game, where I kept warm by tast-ing my first bourbon, elegantly poured from a monogrammed sil-ver flask. At halftime I left Harvard Stadium with swimmers Dave Berkoff and Jeff Peltier and snuck into nearby Blodgett Pool, Har-vard's top-notch natatorium. The facility was utterly empty save for the three of us and a twelve-pack. We changed into our Speedos, climbed atop the ten-meter diving platform, and took turns chug-ging beers before launching our drunken bodies off the high ledge in an impromptu belly-flop contest. Before long, we were joined by the rest of the swim team and the other visiting recruits, who rolled a shopping cart containing a freshly tapped keg onto the pool deck for a game of "beer polo." With the natatorium all to ourselves, for the next two hours we played a drinking-game version of water polo that was pure hilarity.

Now completely drunk, I had to shower, dress, and head over to a local restaurant to meet with Coach Joe Bernal. I did my best to appear sober, but I stumbled through my dinner "meeting," slurring my speech and embarrassing myself by repeating my questions, talking nonstop and fighting the urge to nod off. My memory of the encounter is vague at best, but I knew well enough that I'd blown it. So much for attending Harvard. Clearly Coach Bernal could tell I was hammered. I was terribly disappointed in myself for behaving this way. I'd worked so hard, come so far. How could I have jeopardized the opportunity of a lifetime by acting in such a manner? It wasn't me. Yet it *was*. I'd hit the first speed bump in my drinking career.

Before departing Cambridge, I made sure Coach Bernal knew where I stood, with all the humility I could muster,

"First off, I want to apologize for the other night. It was inexcusable," I said, trying to maintain eye contact.

"Apologize for what?" he responded, giving me a blank look.

Had I dodged a bullet? Or did he just not care? I decided to let sleeping dogs lie and leave it alone. "I just want to make sure you know how much I want to go to Harvard. If I get in, I'm definitely coming. Definitely."

"Great, Rich. That's what I like to hear. At this point, it's up to the admissions folks. But we'd love to have you. I'll be in touch."

When the dust settled, I'd been accepted to every single college I applied to: Princeton, Amherst, University of Michigan, University of Virginia, Cal Berkeley, Brown, Stanford. And yes, *Harvard.* A perfect eight-for-eight. In fact, I was the only student at Landon who'd been accepted to both Harvard and Princeton. The future was looking bright indeed. I was going to Harvard—just as I'd promised Tom Verdin, that swimmer I held in awe back when I was eight.

But I had a nagging feeling I just couldn't shake. It was late April 1985 when I delved into the newly arrived edition of my beloved *Swimming World* magazine. On the cover was a photo of the Stanford University team, grouped atop the podium at the 1985 NCAA Division I Championships and celebrating victory with broad smiles and proud fists raised high. I couldn't help but wonder, *What would it be like to swim with those guys out in mysterious California?* I couldn't shake the fantasy. Yet I couldn't imagine it a reality either. Sure, I was a decent swimmer. But make no mistake, I was far from *great*. So I shrugged it off as an impossible dream, turned the lights out, and tried to sleep. But I couldn't.

The next day I set aside my fear, doubt, and insecurity, picked up the phone, called information, and procured the number for the office of Stanford's notorious drill sergeant coach, Skip Kenney. Sweat beading on my brow, I nervously dialed. Then someone picked up on the other end.

"Stanford Swimming, Coach Knapp speaking." Ted Knapp was Stanford's young assistant coach, a recent graduate himself and a fine swimmer in his day. I introduced myself, explained my interest in Stanford and the fact that I'd been accepted, and I relayed my swimming times.

"I'm not sure I'm fast enough. You guys have so much talent. So much depth. Just tell me if I'm wasting your time." I prepared myself for the inevitable letdown.

"Not at all, Rich. When can you come out and visit?" I couldn't believe my ears.

I'll never forget the first time I laid eyes on Stanford's Palm Drive, an absolutely gorgeous boulevard lined with palm trees and punctuated by the Spanish sandstone of the Stanford Quad at its terminus, with the Stanford Church gleaming in gold relief against the low sun setting radiantly behind the Palo Alto foothills in the background. I instantly knew I would not be attending Harvard.

"It's spring break, so campus is going to be pretty quiet," Knapp had told me on the phone. "Most students are gone. But many of the swimmers are still around. I'll make sure you meet everyone."

Good enough. For once, this trip wasn't about partying. This trip was about connecting with a place that felt like home before I'd even really seen it. Over the next few days, I toured the campus and spent casual time with students in flip-flops and tank tops, playing Frisbee and riding brightly colored motor scooters. I met my swimming heroes and visited the impressive athletic facilities, including DeGuerre Pool, Stanford's world-class outdoor swimming stadium—a far cry from the dreary indoor facilities I'd grown accustomed to. *I could swim outdoors under the sun every day!* I thought. Most important, I was made to feel welcome. The message I got from the coaches and swimmers was that even if I wasn't a world champion, or even a scholarship athlete for that matter, there was a place for me on this team. But what was most striking about Stanford in contrast to my Ivy League experiences was just how happy and positive the students appeared. Everyone I met enthusiastically shared with me how much they loved Stanford. Everywhere I looked, happy students milled about, studying outside in the sun, windsurfing in Lake Lagunita, and riding beach cruiser bikes.

It was everything that Landon wasn't. And I loved it.

When my parents picked me up at the airport, they could see it written all over my face. "Uh-oh," my mom declared, fearing that her only son would head out to California, never to return again. Of course, they wanted me to go to Harvard. What parent wouldn't? But more important, they wanted me to be happy. So Stanford it was. Later that week, gripping my Harvard acceptance letter in my hand—a heady diploma-like document on ivory parchment with my name written in bold calligraphy—I called Coach Bernal to tell him that I'd changed my mind. *Who am I to say no to Harvard? Are you nuts?* I thought to myself. But I stuck to my guns and broke the news. He wasn't happy. In fact, he never spoke to me again. I felt bad, yet I knew I'd made the right choice. I was following my heart.

That fall, my dad and I packed up the green Volvo station wagon and headed west for a cross-country drive en route to college. It was a wonderful father-son bonding experience. We took our time, visiting big-sky country and staying at Yellowstone Lodge, where my dad once spent a summer washing dishes when he was in college. We arrived at the "Farm," a colloquialism for the pastoral Stanford campus, a couple days before registration to get familiar with this foreign environment. It would be a few weeks before swim team training would even begin, but I was determined to show up in shape. So while my future teammates acclimated to campus, I opted to join legendary swimmer Dave Bottom at the weight room each day and at Stanford Stadium for gut-busting sets of running stadium steps.

Registration Day arrived, and Dad took me to Wilbur Hall to check into my dormitory room.

"Name, please?" asked the teaching assistant charged with signing in the new freshman residents.

"Rich Roll," I announced, my reply meeting with smiles and snickers from the dormitory staff. *Great,* I thought. *Am I being made fun of already?* It pushed all the insecurity buttons that Landon had so adroitly installed.

"Right this way," a teaching assistant quipped with an unsettling smile as he walked my dad and me down a first-floor hallway to a door adorned with a label announcing the names of its soon-to-be occupants: Rich Roll and Ken Rock. The staff gathered close, watching for my reaction. It took a moment, but the joke finally settled in. That's right, "Rock 'n' Roll" would be bunking together. The infamous pairing was vintage Stanford tongue-in-cheek, matched only by the four "Johns" who were purposely placed in one large room across the street in Banner Hall, Stanford's largest freshman dorm. Word spread fast, giving me instant campus notoriety that would shadow me for the next four years.

With Landon in my rearview mirror, I was determined to have a social life, and I didn't waste any time making my mark. My first night at Stanford I hit many a party, meeting as many people as I could, including all of the freshmen swimmers. And unlike at Landon, where football was everything, at Stanford swimmers occupied a special place in the social strata. For the first time, I had a chance of fitting in. And I wasn't about to blow it. Classes started, and so did swimming.

Despite my no-scholarship "walk-on" status, I resolved to make an impression on the team and the notoriously hard-nosed coach, Skip Kenney, an intimidating figurehead who ran his squad of aquatic warriors like General MacArthur commanded troops in the Pacific theater during World War II. So I did what I did best, going the extra mile at every opportunity. During workouts, I shared the butterfly lane with world record holder Pablo Morales and Anthony Mosse, an Olympian from New Zealand—the two fastest 200-meter-butterfly specialists in the entire world. *Was I dreaming?* Sure, they were much faster than I. But who better to learn from? Together in the diving well, we'd throw down gut-busting sets: twenty sets of twenty yards butterfly on the twenty-second interval, no breathing, followed immediately by twenty times twenty yards butterfly on the fifteen-second interval. At Curl, I had learned how to jump into the shark tank and rise to a new level, and I was un-daunted in my attempt to do it again. So what if I wasn't a scholar-ship athlete. I'd show them.

In addition, I was determined to assume a leadership role among my freshman teammates. Accordingly, I made a habit of dropping in on a different swimmer each night in their respective dorms, on my way home from studying at the library. I soon came to care deeply about my new friends and was hopelessly devoted to the team. And during each evening's dorm visit I'd also meet my teammates' dorm friends. In that way my social horizons began to expand exponen-tially. Within a month, I had more friends than I knew what to do with. And I was truly happy. I was attending one of the best uni-versities in the world, swimming with the best athletes in the world, and fitting in socially for the first time in my life. Life wasn't just good—it was great.

A week before our first big dual meet against the Texas Longhorns, then the second-ranked team in the nation behind Stanford, I at-tended my first Stanford football game, an evening match in the warm October breeze. Hitting a variety of tailgate parties with my swimming buddies, I enjoyed a nice head buzz before heading into the stadium with fellow freshman John Hodge and senior John Moffet, a twelve-pack in our grips. At the time, Stanford had no restrictions on alcohol in the stadium. Students would haul kegs right up into the stands, and you could carry in as much booze to the bleachers as your heart desired.

That night, the two Johns and I made our way up and down the stands from one keg to the next, our frivolity slowly escalating. As the game wrapped up, our merriment devolved into a wrestling match in the stands. Laughing hysterically, I watched the two Johns go at it, both impossibly strong, matching might and muscle.

Then the rain started to fall. Jogging our way laterally across the slippery aluminum bleachers under the dark sky illuminated by the halogen stadium lights, we realized it was time to depart in search of the next party. And that's when it happened. Leaping from one bleacher to the next across the aisle, my flip-flop slipped on the wet surface, sending my drunken body downward. *Crack!* My chest made impact with the sharp metal corner of the next bleacher bench, and I went down. Lying on my back, I knew I'd broken my first bone ever—a rib, maybe two. I couldn't believe it. Just one week away from my first meet against our biggest rival, and I'd injured myself in my drunken stupor. *How could I be so stupid!?* As I lay on my back, I opened my eyes to the rain falling down onto my face and the hysterical laughter of the two Johns. Resolved to not let them see my pain, I snapped up. And fueled by alcohol, I shrugged it off.

"Where to, boys?"

But the next day, I could barely inhale, let alone swim. Each stroke sent bolts of pain through my chest and up my spine. X-rays confirmed that I'd fractured two ribs. It was my first true negative repercussion from drinking, but not my last. And not anything that would motivate me to modify my behavior. I was just getting started. What happened to me could have happened to anybody, right? After all, it was wet and dark—who said my slip had anything to do with drinking? At least, that's the story I told myself. But the fact remained that just one week from the day we'd be challenging the mighty Longhorns, I couldn't even take a stroke. With no alternative, I was forced to take the entire week off of training; not ideal, but my only hope to heal up somewhat in time for the meet. Come Saturday, I was still in a lot of pain. Yet there was just no way I was going to kick off my Stanford career by sitting out my first meet. So I somehow convinced Skip I was fine, and he allowed me to compete, never the wiser about how my injury had actually occurred.

As I mounted the blocks for the 200-yard butterfly, I looked to my right. There was Longhorns standout Bill Stapleton, who'd later compete in the 1988 Olympic Games before achieving acclaim as Lance Armstrong's longtime agent. But at the time, I knew him only as one of the world's greatest butterfliers. And another lane over was teammate Anthony Mosse, then ranked second in the world in this event.

The starting gun exploded, and we were off, my rib pain made bearable only by the adrenaline of the moment. After the first 50 yards, I already trailed both Bill and Anthony by half a body length. I tried not to panic, knowing I always excelled on the back half. But after 100 yards, their lead increased to a full body length. Time to throw in the towel or double down. So I put my head down and got to work, determined not to let this moment pass without my best fight. Each stroke felt like a sword being thrust into my side, but I ignored the pain and just accelerated, my lungs screaming for air. At 150 yards I'd actually narrowed the gap to almost even, pushing off for the final 50 yards with abandon. *Now is the time,* I thought. I'd come so far. And here I was, in this moment I never dreamed would happen, matching stroke for stroke with two of the best swimmers in the entire world. As I turned for the final 25 yards, I'd actually pulled ahead of both Bill and Anthony. *I was leading the race! I can win this! Is this really happening?!* But the thought removed me from the moment. For an instant, I'd taken my head out of the game—the death knell in a sport where hundredths of a second make all the difference. Or maybe I just didn't feel I deserved to beat these guys; after all, I was just an unknown "walk-on." Then again, it could just have been the pain in my rib cage. Or my body seizing up from making my move too soon. Anthony had just barely nudged me for the victory. Once again, second place.

And yet I'd beaten Bill. And taken everyone—my teammates

and Skip included—by complete surprise. Nobody, and I mean nobody, had thought I had the ability to perform as I had—especially with two broken ribs. Leaning over the lane lines to shake hands— both Longhorn orange and Cardinal red—I looked to the pool deck to witness the raucous cheers of my new teammates, thrilled by my underdog effort.

By unanimous vote, I was awarded "Outstanding Performance" of the meet. And later that week Skip would call John Hodge and me into his office to declare that we were the team's future leaders. Come senior year, he anticipated that we'd co-captain the squad, so we'd better start assuming the role now.

I couldn't believe it. Just a few months before, I'd held out little hope that I could ever compete with the best. And now I'd done it. And my freshman season had only begun. I was blinded by the bright light of the future that lay within my grasp. But little did I know then that this moment would be the highlight of my entire swimming career. It was the beginning of the end. Alcohol would soon take it all away.

CHAPTER FOUR

FROM UNDERWATER TO UNDER THE INFLUENCE

From the moment Bruce Kimball handed me my very first beer that snowy Michigan night, I knew subconsciously that alcohol just might pose a problem for me. Maybe not right then, but somewhere down the line. Although a miracle salve to my social inadequacies, I just liked it *too much*. I wasn't raised in an alcoholic household—far from it, in fact—but I knew enough to know that this magnetic attraction could not be good. My fall on the stadium bleachers only sealed that subliminal conviction. It didn't mean I was going to do anything about it; it was just an early sign of the evidence soon to come. So I filed the thought away. *If I pretend it's not a problem, then there's no problem.*

But it didn't take long before one drunken night a week morphed into two. By spring of my freshman year, I was partying four to five nights a week. But wasn't that what college was supposed to be all about? So what if I shirked studying in exchange for a Wednesday night kegger at the Phi Delt house? I still maintained mostly A's. And when you're young and strong, it's no big deal to shrug off a hangover, put in a morning workout, and show up for class prepared. Sure, I had a little alcohol on my breath when my bare feet hit the concrete DeGuerre Pool deck at 6 A.M., but I wasn't the only one. And I never overslept.

At the Pac-10 Championships during the spring of my freshman year, I managed to clock my best swimming times. But I still fell just short of meeting the minimum time standards required to attend the NCAA Division I Championships. I was disappointed. But on some level, I also didn't believe I deserved to make the cuts. The following month, Stanford secured its second consecutive NCAA Championship victory in Indianapolis. But I stayed home, denied a coveted championship ring. To top it off, I'd never again clock a best time.

During my sophomore and junior years, I continued to swim, but the love dwindled, fading until it was lost entirely. For the first time in my life swimming was a chore. I was sick of feeling exhausted all the time. I remember "Christmas Training" my sophomore year—an annual event during which the team would return to a dormant campus early from winter break, cohabiting in a vacant fraternity house to do nothing but train, day in and day out, for two weeks straight, until our eyeballs hurt. Other than eat, I did nothing but sleep between sessions, only to awake to one singular emotion—*dread.*

And hence began a slow abandonment of my many lofty goals, both in and out of the pool. As my interest in swimming waned, so did my regard for essentially everything else aspirational— everything besides staying out late, getting drunk, and having the best time possible. I even dropped out of my declared major, human biology, mysteriously discarding my medical school ambition. The only recollection I have of my rationale is, *Who needs the hassle?* My focus narrowed to only that which was right in front of me. In other words, *Where is my next good time?* Alcohol will do that.

Sophomore year, my swimming times reflected my loss of focus, a pattern that escalated in my junior year. Predictably, I would continue to fail to qualify for NCAAs, missing out again on the opportunity to participate in Stanford's championship win (their third consecutive) and collect a ring. In preparation for the Pac-10

Swimming Championships held during the spring of my junior year, I pledged to myself and to my swimming peers not to drink for a month leading up to what would be my biggest meet of the year, and I had high hopes of finally making the NCAA squad. Sadly, I couldn't even make it a week. Needless to say, my Pac-10 performances that year were woefully poor—pathetic, in fact. Despite the thousands of miles I'd swum since my arrival at Stanford, I'd swum faster in high school than I did at that meet. But rather than address my escalating dependence on alcohol, I just quit the sport altogether.

I can't say the decision was easy. I labored over it for weeks.

During the spring off-season, I stopped by Skip's office. "I've decided to hang it up, Skip. I just can't do it anymore."

I'd expected him to fight me on my decision, talk me off the ledge and convince me to stay—tell me how much the team still needed me. Instead, he just shrugged his shoulders, barely lifting his gaze from the newspaper he was reading.

"Okay, Rich. Good luck."

Then, silence. I had no reply for his unexpected nonchalance. Was this some sort of passive-aggressive tactic? A Jedi mind trick? As a former marine who voluntarily enlisted his services as a crack sniper in Vietnam, Skip is a take-no-prisoners badass, renowned for his mastery of the mind game and penchant for fits and tantrums—he's a legend in the annals of college swimming. But the truth was, he knew I didn't care anymore. So why should *he*? For the last three years he'd watched from the pool deck as I squandered the countless opportunities presented. He had better things to focus on than my pity party—things like a coveted fourth consecutive NCAA title. And real athletes devoted to their sport and determined to be the best. I just wasn't one of those guys anymore. He knew it as well as I did. *Good riddance.*

Looking back, I wonder what might have become of my swimming career had I decided to address my drinking back then. But hindsight is always 20/20. And at the time, I had little capacity for introspection. A scrupulous look in the rearview would have required a courage and capability I simply lacked. And thus began my nosedive into the grips of denial—the defining characteristic of the alcoholic. I blamed my failures on everything but myself—on Skip for his attitude, on a program that left me overtrained, on my parents for being overprotective, on the studies that took priority, and on a God I didn't believe in for letting me down.

After my brief conversation with Skip, I was overcome by a deep sense of sadness and loss—it was a kind of mourning. For as long as I could remember, swimming had been all I cared about. And now—just like that—it was gone. I was unprepared for the emotions that welled up inside me, causing not just confusion, but vertigo—as if I was in free fall. *What now?* I thought, realizing I'd never really put any reflection into who I was, what truly interested me or what I wanted to pursue outside the pool. Disoriented, I got into my old green Volvo and headed alone up to Marin County—beautiful countryside north beyond San Francisco's Golden Gate Bridge. Sitting atop a hillside above the port of Sausalito, I peered out toward Alcatraz and realized that I was lost. The tears welled up. And I cried my eyes out for the better part of an hour.

I wish I could say that was a moment of clarity in which I realized that alcohol had killed my swimming career and it was high time I addressed my problem and pulled myself together, before things got really bad. Unfortunately, that's not what happened. When the tears dried up and the catharsis passed, I felt only relief—a sense of being liberated from the chlorine prison that had shackled me for as long as I could remember. Funny how the mind works, that I could so quickly forget the love I had for my sport and how far it had taken me. But at that moment, it represented little more than an impediment to my good time. And so I returned to campus, where I wasted no time immersing myself in anything and everything associated with fun. Fun, for me, meant getting drunk. Very drunk.

Senior year was a blur. One continuous blinding light of late nights, parties, girls, and hangovers. I won't lie; I was reckless. But it was also fun. I followed the party and happily went wherever it would take me.

But I knew I needed to find some kind of job before graduation. What do you do when you're just not sure which turn to take? You start considering law school, that's what. At least, in my case this was true. For the most part, my dad seemed to genuinely enjoy his career. I can't say I had any passion for jurisprudence—I had no idea what it even meant to practice law—but it seemed like an acceptable and respected route to go. I'd get to wear a nice suit and maybe a cool pair of glasses. Work in a stylish office with a view. Debate the issues of the day over long lunches at fancy restaurants. And without too much risk or expenditure of energy, fit into the approved stream of urban society. In other words, my interest had no substance. But it was too late to apply to any law schools for the following year. Maybe a short stint at a law firm would be a good way to spend a year seeing what this world was all about. I figured I'd get my foot in the door, support myself, and put my parents' minds at ease.

So I began paralegal work the following fall at Skadden, Arps, Slate, Meagher & Flom, a gigantic New York City–based firm that had made a name for itself papering the mergers and acquisitions boom of the 1980s. It was hardly a high-paying job, but the program offered tuition reimbursement to legal assistants who matriculated to law school—a good deal if I ended up heading in that direction, I told myself. Before this, I'd only visited New York very briefly in my youth. It seemed so exotic and, although only a few hours north of D.C., a world apart from the city of my upbringing. New York, I reasoned, was the exciting trade-off I needed to counterbalance what would likely be a descent into drudgery. But the primary thought that began to loop continuously in my mind was *In New York, I won't have a car. I won't drive. And then I can drink as much as I want without worrying about getting a DUI.* And so I headed to Manhattan primarily because it seemed like a world-class place to drink. And it was.

I fondly refer to New York as Disneyland for the alcoholic—a fast-paced zone of escape where nothing is out of bounds. Moving into a tiny midtown apartment with Stanford swimmer Matt Nance, who'd landed an analyst job at Morgan Stanley, I couldn't wait.

But as work at Skadden began, my predictions of drudgery were confirmed. I'd underestimated just how mundane, tedious, dysfunctional, and unpleasant the position would be. For hours at a time, I hunched over a photocopier until my back ached. Weeks went by during which I was imprisoned in a windowless conference room filled floor to ceiling with hundreds of boxes of paper. There I organized documents in file folders by date or subject matter. If I was lucky, I'd be put in charge of "redacting" information from the documents. This heady task entailed covering up privileged information with strips of white tape from dawn through the wee hours of the night, day after endless day. But there was an assignment even more mind numbing—something called Bates stamping: a means of cataloging massive amounts of paper for purposes of litigation discovery. Today this chore is accomplished with computer scanners. But in 1989, it entailed hand-stamping consecutive numbers on each and every page of a document with an archaic prewar heavy metal hand stamp machine. Simple enough—unless you have to stamp hundreds of thousands of pages. *Someone* had to do it—why not a Stanford graduate?

The hours were long. Forget about making evening or weekend plans. Most of my waking existence was spent at the firm, where I traded my life for an annual salary of $22,000 and the privilege of being exploited by overstressed and sleep-deprived attorneys taking their many personal frustrations out on the underlings. On countless occasions I witnessed grown men reduced to tears or throwing tantrums in fits of exasperation. Once, an attorney even threw a heavy federal code book at my head.

I'm not trying to elicit pity—I was hardly working in a coal mine. It's just a snapshot of big New York City law-firm life in the late 1980s—a reality far different from what is portrayed on television or pitched to unsuspecting law students, and certainly far different from the more gentlemanly practice my father had enjoyed. I wish I could say that I knew then that law school wasn't for me, that I would seek out a more meaningful life. But that's not really what happened. This was my first real job. And so I just assumed that my experience was normal—that this is what it meant to work in corporate America. *It's what men with educations like mine are supposed to do.*

That said, I didn't want what these attorneys had, a life that appeared to be misery placed atop piles of money. And I had no real desire for their approval. I simply didn't care. I knew that a job well done would be rewarded with nothing beyond an increase in demand for my services.

And so when my phone rang, I just let it ring. Then I'd wait an hour or so before returning the call, knowing that by then the attorney seeking assistance surely would have found someone else to do his or her bidding. On many an occasion, I'd nurse a hangover by locking the office door, turning the lights off, and taking a nap. Other days, I'd leave the office for hours at a time, lingering over long lunches, strolling the streets of Midtown, or catching a movie, no one the wiser. If anyone asked where I was, I could just make up some story. But nobody ever asked. It was just too big a place to keep tabs on a low-level employee like me. And I took every advantage.

As my friend and office-mate Adam Glick was often fond of saying, "Dude, you are officially the worst legal assistant in Skadden history." I can't argue with his assessment, a perception he wasn't alone in sharing.

But my other prediction also proved true. The banality of my professional existence was compensated for by a robust social life. I made great friends with fellow legal-assistant colleagues, falling into a tightly knit troupe of fun-loving, like-minded late-night party hoppers. We dubbed ourselves "Kings of the Low Budget Social Scene."

A drunken wanderlust sent me deep down into the Manhattan nightlife underbelly, routing out as many downtown bars, avant-garde clubs, loft soirees, and degenerate after-parties as I could find. On one occasion I ended up in the basement of some decrepit and half-vacant downtown building watching midget bowling, otherwise known as "dwarf tossing"—a horrific and now outlawed relic of the fashionable 1990s New York party scene in which little people in padded Velcro costumes were literally hurled onto Velcro-coated walls by partygoers competing for the farthest throw. I'd read about this in Bret Easton Ellis's book *American Psycho* but assumed it was literary license. Then I saw it with my own eyes.

Around this time, my roommate Matt Nance began training for the Manhattan Island Marathon Swim—a 28.5-mile circumnavigation of the entire island of Manhattan.

"You should do it with me, Rich," Matt urged.

Swim all the way around Manhattan? Including the Harlem River? Yeah, right. Not only did it seem impossible, I had zero interest. No, I was too busy emerging from drunken stupors in strange apartments, wandering empty downtown crevasses in the dead of night, and subsisting on nothing more than booze, Gray's Papaya hot dogs, McDonald's, and Ray's Pizza. Though I lacked the self-awareness to realize it at the time, I was adrift in mayhem, slowly destroying myself.

Then came the call. One day before classes began, I was informed that I'd been the last person accepted off the wait list for Cornell Law School. After a slew of rejection letters, it was my final opportunity to pursue a career in law. Given my less than stellar experience at Skadden, I'm often baffled that I chased this particular carrot. But at the time, it seemed like the right thing to do. Maybe some protective instinct had me realizing that it might save me from disappearing down the rabbit hole altogether.

Less than twenty-four dizzying hours later, I found myself transplanted to the curious rural hamlet of Ithaca, New York. Walking into a lecture hall to hear portly Professor Henderson regale a group of eager and wide-eyed "One L's" on the less than fascinating tenets of tort law, I felt my sleep-deprived head spinning. As I scanned the room, it was beyond obvious that all the other students had spent the better part of the summer preparing for this day. While I was busy losing myself in the bizarre lower depths of Manhattan, my fellow classmates had diligently completed a robust reading list, arriving beyond prepared. The only thing I was prepared for was happy hour. Six thousand applications for only 180 spots. And I was the very last person permitted entry. The absolute bottom of the barrel. I couldn't help but wonder if I'd just made a big mistake.

As it turned out, though, I genuinely enjoyed law school. I felt a sense of relief to be on a solid trajectory, any trajectory. I can't say Cornell's professors instilled in me a love for the law, but I relished the return to an academic environment and the challenges it presented.

I've always been sensitive to the weather, my moods taking their cue from whether the sun is shining on a given day. Call it "seasonal affective disorder" or just a lack of vitamin D, but at first the cold Ithaca weather precipitated as much depression as snowfall. Good thing I had a cure for this malaise. You guessed it. Alcohol.

At the time, I held out hope that getting out of New York City would be the perfect way to put my drunken exploits behind me. Not that I consciously admitted I had a problem. Rather, what I had was an impulse *to control and enjoy my drinking.*

But of course no matter where I went, I always brought myself with me, so it wasn't long before I resumed my old ways. Things were exacerbated, in fact, by adding a car to the mix. It led to a few brushes with the law and the specter of a DUI arrest, which I narrowly dodged on more than a few occasions. And when my pastoral environs began to bore, I hightailed it back to Manhattan—the four-hour drive a small price to pay for a lost weekend soaked in booze.

Yet somehow I maintained decent grades. Nothing like straight A's, but a solid B to B+ average. Okay, so I got a few C's. But not many, even an occasional A thrown in from time to time to balance it all out. Not bad, I thought. Considering I was the last person admitted to my class, anything better than last place was a win as far as I was concerned. So much for the unbridled ambition of my youth. That fire in the belly that had defined me in younger years wasn't just dormant, it was all but extinct.

On one occasion, I swallowed a six-pack of Beck's beer in my Volvo en route to presenting a paper on Russian constitutionalism. My class began at two o'clock in the afternoon. I might be an idiot, but I'm not stupid. I knew full well disaster was the most likely outcome. *Then why?* There's no satisfactory explanation. Really no point in even asking the question. All I recall is a feeling of power-lessness to stop myself. After my fifteen-minute oration, the visit-ing professor from Moscow pulled me aside.

"May I have a few minutes with you after class?" he asked calmly, his thick Russian accent right out of a KGB spy movie. Al-cohol coursing through my veins, I quietly drew my breath in deep and held it. *Prepare for the gulag.*

When the classroom emptied, I approached, braced and terri-fied, and he placed his hand on my shoulder. An odd smile spread across his face.

"Richard. This is a brilliant paper. A+. With your permission, I would relish the opportunity to present it to the Russian special constitutional convention in Moscow."

Say what!? This special body of seven hundred comprised some of the world's most savvy political leaders and legal minds, who'd been recruited to assist in redrafting of the Russian Constitution. Far from the inevitable humiliation, discipline, or even expulsion I was prepared to suffer, I was actually being rewarded. The mes-saging was, of course, exactly what I didn't need: *Drinking is the solution to your problem, not the culprit.*

In the spring of my third and final year I received an offer to work as an associate at the law firm Littler Mendelson, a labor and em-ployment outfit in San Francisco. Did I have a passion for labor law? Hardly. But the office was really nice and the salary decent. Good enough. And landing the job put my mind to rest about where I'd head next, allowing me to set aside any concern about grades and live out the rest of my law school days in a carefree alcohol haze.

On graduation day, I decided to commence my drinking within moments of waking up. Eight or so beers disappeared down my throat as I donned the elegant black and maroon cap and gown of the newly anointed Juris Doctor and drove to campus to greet my beaming parents and several of my friends. Welcoming the rare warm sun, I spent the early afternoon cocktailing through a variety of soirees, before heading to commencement at a beautiful outdoor amphitheater. During the procession I enhanced my already significant buzz by sneaking hits from a silver flask a friend had thoughtfully smuggled in.

As I watched my classmates summoned to the stage to receive their diplomas, it struck me just how much everyone seemed identical, part of an assembly line of newly minted lawyers issued by the Cornell factory. Despite the festive environment, warm weather, and every reason to feel nothing but gratitude, joy, and pride, I was struck by a sense of suffocating desperation. *Is this all I am?*

In that moment, I felt compelled to stand out in the crowd. So when my name was called, I kicked off my shoes and socks and walked to the stage to receive my diploma in front of three hundred or so students, faculty, and family—*barefoot.*

In my semi-stupor, I thought it was a stroke of genius. I'd shown how groovy and laid back I was. *Pure California cool.* What an idiot.

My friends and classmates cheered, or at least that's how I interpreted their response at the time. But the professors on the dais were quietly unimpressed. And my parents were traumatized. When I joined them after the ceremony, I was caught completely off guard by the look of horror, embarrassment, and disappointment on their faces. The image is forever seared in my brain. What

I utterly failed to grasp was that graduations are just as much for the proud parents as they are for the student—probably more so. The day was intended to memorialize a tremendous amount of sacrifice on their part. And so my mockery of the pomp and circumstance was more than injurious—it was devastating.

Over dinner that evening, they did their best to put on smiles and place the event in their rear view. But the damage was done. That night they bid me a muted good-bye, their departure laden with overtones of dismayed finality that seemed to say, *You're on your own now, big man.* As I laid my head on the pillow, I wept until my stomach ached with grief, remorse, and regret.

Back in Palo Alto, where I planned to spend a quiet summer studying for the California bar exam, I shared an apartment off bustling University Avenue with Pablo Morales. Yes, the hero of my adolescence whose image adorned the walls of my bedroom was now my roommate and bar prep study partner. Still licking my wounds from graduation, I pledged to stay dry the entire summer. And I meant it. Focus on my studies, pass the bar, and begin anew. Unfortunately, I'd once again brought myself with me. And with Stanford playing host to the 1994 World Cup Soccer Tournament, and the around-the-clock revelry that came with it, staying sober became impossible. Needless to say, I failed the exam.

Though I was deeply embarrassed at having to retake the bar that February, being a young associate lawyer at Littler Mendelson was something of a solace. Unlike at Skadden, the people were nice—they respected the need for employees to have a life. And the pay was decent. I spent my days in a plush downtown office, with a spectacular view of Alcatraz and the Golden Gate Bridge, handling a very manageable caseload. Still, I just couldn't summon much interest in labor and employment law, and I spent hours wistfully gazing through my window at the afternoon fog rolling in across the bay. Miraculously, I'd survived law school and managed to land on my feet in a pretty darn good place. *I should be happy,* I told myself. *So why do I feel this way? What is wrong with me?*

San Francisco isn't New York. But I was back living in an urban environment. So it was time to pick up where I left off. I moved in with Gavin Holles, a banker and former LSU swimmer whom I'd once competed against in the 200-butterfly. Gavin is a great guy and made for a good roommate. And if I had to choose one word to describe him, it's *tolerant.* Together we had plenty of good times enjoying the San Francisco nightlife, barhopping our way across the Marina. But when it came to me, Gavin would soon discover that he got more than he bargained for.

Here's a typical weekday snapshot of how I rolled in 1995. Honing the skills I developed at Skadden, I'd generally perform the least amount of work possible, fulfilling only the bare minimum of expectations. On many occasions, I'd leave the office with no goal other than to aimlessly walk the streets alone. Leaving my jacket draped on my desk chair gave the appearance that I might just be down the hall, working in a quiet conference room or perhaps meeting with a client. Around five o'clock, I began staring at the clock and evaluating my environment in an effort to determine exactly how early I could duck out. En route to the Marina from the financial district, I'd generally stop by my favorite liquor store, where I'd pick up four large twenty-two-ounce Sapporo beers and one bottle of Sauvignon Blanc. For the drive home, I'd usually drink at least two of the Sapporos, hiding the empties under the seat. The remainder of my stash I concealed in my soft leather satchel. That way, if Gavin was home when I arrived, I could sneak the booty into my room without notice. In other words, *I began to hide my drinking.*

After drinking another Sapporo in the shower, I'd head to my bedroom. Door closed, I'd turn the television up loud to obscure the sound of my wine cork popping and proceed to finish my stash in privacy as Gavin ate dinner alone in the kitchen. With my head now fully buzzing, I could finally embrace the night and all the adventure it might hold.

I convinced myself that Gavin had no concept of just how depraved I'd become. Of course, he was well aware. In later years he confessed that he knew just about everything. He just decided to keep it to himself.

Ironically, during the two-year period in which I shared an apartment with Gavin he competed as an avid Ironman triathlete and open-water swimmer. So while I lay passed out in the next room, Gavin would generally awake before dawn to train. On the weekends, he'd leave town to compete in this race or that, often winning or placing in a variety of long-distance ocean swims or other multisport events.

Gavin would cajole me: "Come on Ricky, you should do this stuff with me, I bet you'd be pretty good." He liked to call me Ricky, a nickname I earned one night after overdoing it on Sambuca liqueur. Sambuca, rocker Richie Sambora—similar-sounding words, you get the idea. I hate that nickname. But it stuck.

During a long weekend spent with friends in a house on Lake Tahoe, I remember waking up one morning around 10 A.M., wildly hungover, to find Gavin, along with his buddy Greg Welch—an Ironman world champion—and a bunch of other triathletes hanging around the kitchen in their cycling attire.

"Wow, you guys are up early. Headed out for a ride?" I asked.

"Just finished, mate," Greg replied in a friendly Aussie drawl, taking in my pallid appearance with a wry smile. While I was passed out, the crew had already logged a ninety-mile loop around the lake. Part of me wanted to vomit just thinking about it. But the other part felt an entirely different emotion. Shame. *Why can't I be more like that?*

CHAPTER FIVE

WHITE SANDS AND RED STRIPE

Hitting Bottom in Paradise

In the spring of 1995, while I was still living with Gavin in the Marina, I fell in love with Michele, a native of Palo Alto with green eyes, long legs, and equally long, dark hair. Of course, we met in a bar. And predictably, I was drunk.

I still have no idea how we met exactly, or what I might have said to draw her attention. But it didn't matter. All I recall is her inviting smile, and the fact that I liked her immediately.

Michele worked as the executive director of a newly founded and experimental middle school called the San Francisco 49ers Academy, located in impoverished East Palo Alto and designed to provide individualized attention to at-risk underprivileged youth. I respected her commitment to service—something I lacked entirely in my own life. Soon I was spending most of my time with her down on the Peninsula and commuting each day up to the city for work. Her friends became my friends. And her family became mine. Best of all, I was in love. Or at least, I thought I was.

Meanwhile, I was growing increasingly restless at work. It would be years before I understood that the hole in my spirit had nothing to do with my job—that it required a different remedy. But at the time, I was convinced a career reboot would do the trick. And so I began to look around for a new job. Since I loved film, I thought

I'd enjoy the practice of entertainment law. I pictured my law degree as a lever to insert myself into the Hollywood machine.

So I started sending my résumé out, slipping it to everyone I knew with even a tangential connection to Hollywood, including my old Stanford swimming friend John Moffet, who was then a producer on the daily entertainment news show *Hard Copy.* But nothing seemed to materialize. Then, out of the blue, I received an interview invitation from a law firm called Christensen, White, Miller, Fink & Jacobs—one of the top entertainment litigation houses in Los Angeles. Sure, it was litigation—not the transactional deal-making practice I sought—but it was better than nothing. Curiously, I had no idea how this firm even knew about me, since I'd never sent them my résumé. *Better not even ask,* I thought.

A few days later, I called in sick to Littler and hopped a flight to Los Angeles to interview with the Christensen firm. As I plopped down in my assigned aisle seat, I was amazed to discover my friend John Moffet sitting in the window seat right next to me—the same John I was partying with that fateful night I cracked my ribs at Stanford Stadium. *What are the odds?* A happy coincidence, for sure. But nothing more, I thought. It wasn't until years later that I would divine greater meaning in John's presence not just on that flight, but in my life. The truth, I'd later realize, was that John was the only reason I was even on this flight to begin with.

I'd eventually learn that some months prior John had passed my résumé to a young lawyer I'd never met named Chris Green,* then in-house counsel at *Hard Copy.* Chris was impressed with my credentials and, utterly unbeknownst to John and me, had passed the document along to Christensen, *Hard Copy*'s outside counsel. In a

---

* Actual name fictionalized out of respect for the principles of anonymity that govern addiction recovery.

stroke of great ironic harmony, many years later I'd have the pleasure of working closely with Chris, and ultimately I'd play a large
role in helping him discover sobriety. John and Chris, through a
few tiny gestures, managed to completely change my life. And in
turn, I was later placed in a position where I could share with Chris
what had saved my life so he could save his own.

I got the job. And within a few short months, I'd packed my
bags for what would be my final move. Destination: Los Angeles.
Michele and I were still going strong at this point, and despite the
distance, I was determined to make our relationship work. A few
months later, I even popped the question at sunset on the beach in
Santa Barbara, during one of our many romantic getaways. She said
yes. *We were getting married.* The plan was that we'd host the ceremony in her hometown of Palo Alto, but that she'd soon relocate
south so we could build a life together. Things were looking up.

From the word go, my work at Christensen was all-consuming—
beyond intense. "The Firm," as I like to call it, was home to some
of Los Angeles's most elite "super lawyers" and ground zero for
some of Hollywood's most high-profile disputes. It had its finger-
prints on everything from the famous O.J. Simpson and Rodney
King cases to top-level city politics and major movie studio disputes. No, this wouldn't be the relatively polite and gentlemanly
practice of Littler. This was hardball. Roll up your sleeves, get dirty,
and in the case of some employees, even push the ethical envelope.
In 2006, for example, name partner Terry Christensen was indicted
on charges that he instructed famous Hollywood private investiga-
tor Anthony Pellicano to unlawfully wiretap a litigation opponent.
The drama played out in the halls of Christensen was the stuff of
Hollywood lore, the métier of Dominick Dunne and the pages of
Vanity Fair. And I was dropped right in the middle of the action.

My first day, I was summoned to the office of Skip Miller,
one of Los Angeles's most feared attorneys. As I sat across from

him to receive my first assignment, the irony of once again voluntarily submitting my life to the whims of a powerful overlord named Skip was not lost on me. That marine sniper turned swim coach had now morphed into a tenacious litigator. And I was his submissive pawn.

My first assignment was to draft an appellate brief for a prominent client. The junior partner assigned to the task had just taken maternity leave, and the matter fell entirely into my hands to handle. Alone. The only problem? I'd never written an appellate brief—a task usually reserved for a small team of lawyers, not one clueless associate whose only area of legal expertise involved protracted disappearances from the office. But I couldn't let Skip see me sweat. Not on my first day. As I swallowed the terror and accepted the charge, he left me with one final remark: "Don't drop the ball."

I didn't. For the next few weeks, I immersed myself in the matter, combing through boxes of documents and poring over case law to deliver a brief that proved instrumental in winning the appeal. And so from that moment on, I belonged to Skip. *I was his boy.* Sure, he was demanding. He expected much from me. But behind the intimidating mask, there was a devoted family man and a mentor who pushed me hard. Most important, when I eventually struggled through the most difficult time in my life, he stood steadfastly by me.

Outside the office, there was one thing I learned quickly. When it comes to drinking and driving, Los Angeles doesn't screw around. From the moment I started getting wasted at eighteen, I'd been pulled over by the police for suspicion of drunk driving no fewer than nine times. It seems like a lot. But when you consider how much I drove while inebriated, I should have been pulled over far more often than I was. Either that or maimed, dead, or responsible for someone else's maiming or death. Yet each and every time the red and blue flashed in my rearview, I somehow managed to wiggle free without arrest. Sometimes it was fast-talking. Other times, just blind luck. I prefer to believe something outside myself was looking out for me—call it God, my Higher Power, my Guardian Angels, or the Universe. The label matters little.

But my luck was about to finally run out.

It was a particularly warm October evening when I began to detect that all too familiar sense of restlessness starting to throw me off my already precarious sense of balance. As the eerie, hot Santa Ana winds blew wide through the open windows of my apartment, I could feel my dormant demon stir. *I should go to bed,* I thought. *I have a lot of work tomorrow.*

Minutes later, though, I was wending my way through the urban morass from Westwood to Hollywood, a tumbler of vodka between my legs. With the music blaring, I was firmly saddled in that sweet spot of distorted perception where everything finally makes sense. *I was in the groove.* Several nightspot stops later—and after further fortification from beer, vodka, and shots of Jagermeister— I was doing a liquid fade into beautiful oblivion. That's when it happened.

Bam! My next memory was the sound of crushing metal, cracking plastic, and a broken horn. Somehow, I'd just decimated the rear end of a small sedan. *Shit.* It took less than two minutes for the cops to arrive, but only seconds for them to haul my goose limbs out of the car and handcuff me to the bus stop bench on the corner. In L.A., the cops don't mess around. If you get pulled over, the assumption is *always* that the car is stolen, there's a warrant out for your arrest, you have a shotgun under the seat, and you're high on crack. And until proven otherwise, you're treated accordingly. In my case, harsh treatment was warranted. On the Breathalyzer, I blew a 0.29 percent—more than three and a half times the legal limit. Most people would be passed out at this level. In fact, anything above 0.30 percent is considered lethal. But drive a car? Not just a bad idea, but close to impossible.

I was uninjured. Unfortunately, I can't say the same for the elderly woman I rear-ended. She was taken to the hospital and ultimately suffered from severe whiplash and chronic neck and back problems. I wish I could say that the moment caused my heart to swell with shame, remorse, and compassion. But mostly what I felt was the fear that comes from contemplating going to prison—that and the painful pinch of the steel handcuffs that were cutting off blood supply to my hands. I spent the better part of the night in jail before my allotted phone call roused Adam Glick—my friend and former Skadden office mate now working as an entertainment lawyer in Los Angeles. He was kind enough to come to my rescue, post bail, and get me home in one piece, just as the sun began to rise.

A day of reckoning? Not so fast. A scare, for sure. But a failure when it came to modifying my ways. *Everyone gets a DUI,* I told myself. *What's the big deal?* I gave little thought to the condition of the poor woman I hit, pushing the painful image deep into my unconscious. *Let the insurance company handle that one.* To truly consider my actions would require a change in behavior—something I wasn't yet ready for.

In fact, not two months later, I was driving home after the firm's Christmas party when the cops once again pulled me over—this time for driving the wrong way down a one-way street in Beverly Hills. *The wrong way!* It was 3:30 A.M. on a Friday night. And this time I blew a 0.27 percent. After a stern lecture, it was back to jail for the night. My second DUI, just weeks after my first.

Come Monday morning, I was summoned to Skip's office. I knew something was terribly wrong when he shut the door behind me and looked me right in the eye.

"Take a seat. We need to talk."

Uh-oh.

"I got an interesting call yesterday from my friends over at BHPD. Driving the wrong way down a one-way street? A blood alcohol level of 0.27 percent? And from what I understand, this isn't the first time?"

Skip handled a lot of work for both the Los Angeles and Beverly Hills Police Departments. And these people weren't just his clients, they were his friends. In fact, Skip had a personal relationship with the very officer who arrested me. When I was booked, the officer lifted my business card from my wallet, noticed I worked at Skip's firm, and promptly gave him a heads-up call. *I'm screwed.*

"Are you firing me?"

At the time, Skip and I were knee-deep in preparing for trial in defense of the general manager of the Rose Bowl, who was being sued for sexual harassment. I'd devoted myself entirely to this case, spending countless hours with the client at the Rose Bowl, interviewing witnesses, taking all the depositions, and drafting all the pretrial briefs and motions. In classic Skip form, we had declined all plaintiff attempts to settle and were just weeks away from the jury trial I was meant to second chair. *My first trial.*

"I thought about it. But no. I don't take pleasure in getting into your personal life. But you have a problem. A big problem. I don't want to get any more calls. And I don't want to talk about it anymore. Just deal with it."

He handed me a card for a top criminal defense attorney friend of his named Charlie English and made it abundantly clear that I'd be hiring him immediately.

"We're about to go to war. I can't have you in jail. I need to know that you can show up and do what's required."

"I won't let you down."

True to his word, that was the last we ever spoke about what happened.

I'd never been so scared in my entire life. And so I was determined to live up to my promise. The next day, I paid Charlie my first visit.

"You're probably going to jail," he told me straight off. Intimidatingly tall, he was a silver-haired old-school hardass who pulled no punches.

"I *can't* go to jail," I replied, quaking, my armpits drenched in sweat. Just thinking about it made me want to vomit.

"Why not? You're a criminal," he replied. They'd do what they could, but with two DUI arrests looming, dodging jail time was a tall order, even for the best attorney. And he was the best.

While he was serving up the truth, he also pointed out that I was a straight-up alcoholic.

Of course, I *knew* I was. On some level I'd always known. It's why I never tried hard drugs. If I tried cocaine or heroin, I knew instinctively that I'd love it immediately. I was susceptible to the pull of anything that would take me out of myself. Yet Charlie was the first person to attach to me the label I deserved. *Alcoholic . . .* It was jarring. But on some weird level, a relief to finally hear. No more innuendo. All the cards were on the table.

"Get your ass to an A.A. meeting. Today," Charlie commanded, and I was ready to oblige. But then I received an unimaginable stroke of good fortune: the West Los Angeles Courthouse had somehow misplaced the file on my first DUI arrest. *They simply lost the docket.* Thus, I was never prosecuted for that offense. "I don't know who is looking out for you from above," Charlie said, shaking his head, "but this never happens. Ever."

As for the second arrest, well, let's just say that the Beverly Hills court never discovered my October arrest. I ended up pleading guilty to the December DUI as a first-time offender and avoided jail time in favor of probation and mandatory drug and alcohol counseling. As for the poor woman I rear-ended, I was sued. But my insurance settled the case.

In other words, I dodged a serious bullet. But more important, I was finally ready to face my demons.

I didn't know anything about the real A.A. My only point of reference was rooted in bad television: that image of chain-smoking old men in trench coats sitting semicircle in a damp basement, heads hung low in endless lament about the sorry state of their broken lives. *Weak* was all I thought. Part of me just wanted to handle my problems on my own. But I vowed to Charlie I would go. And anyway, there was a pesky court order mandating my attendance.

My first meeting was at noon in a whitewashed, fluorescent-lit, windowless conference room in Century City's ABC offices. The plan was to arrive late, avoid eye contact, and just quietly take a seat under the radar. Preferably in the back. Grit it out for an hour, get my court card signed, and bust a move. So I awkwardly shuffled through the door just as the meeting was about to commence. Mission accomplished. But my first glimpse of the group shattered my preconceptions. Far from the bad breath and curmudgeonly scowls I expected, the room was bright and alive with smiling, mingling professionals: men of all ages in snappy suits, and chatty attractive women catching up on their lunch break over healthy salads and Starbucks lattes. Everything about it said, *Welcome. Take a seat. We're here for you.*

Oddly, my first thought was *Why are these people so happy?* I was utterly terrified.

Conspicuously keeping to myself, I naively assumed nobody could tell I was "new." Later I would discover just how painfully obvious my act was. Judging correctly that I was a rookie, Eric, a young, bespectacled lawyerly-looking guy, handed me a tattered blue book and requested that I read aloud a passage entitled "The Promises." Not exactly what I had in mind. *Gulp.*

With hands trembling and voice cracking, I began to spit it out. "If we are painstaking about this phase of our development, we will be amazed before we are halfway through. . . ." But before I could cull even the slightest bit of meaning from the passage's first sentence, there was an interruption.

"Who are you?" more than a few people called out in an overlapping imperfect unison; a disruption that sent bolts of panic up my spine.

"Uh, my name is Rich," I managed to stammer.

"And what are you?" asked Eric. *What am I? What kind of question is that?* I flashed once again to my only point of reference—television—searching for the appropriate response.

"My name is Rich. . . . And I'm, uh . . . *an alcoholic?*"

It was the first time I'd ever spoken those words aloud. And if you'd told me I'd ever utter them before a group of complete strangers, I would have said I was more likely to undergo a sex change. But the effect on my psyche was instantaneous, and unexpectedly profound. Even more curious was the group response that followed: "Welcome, Rich! You're not alone."

It felt like a fifty-pound backpack had suddenly been removed from my shoulders, replaced with a warm blanket that deflected shame and enveloped me in a protective shield of community. *Maybe they do understand,* I thought. *Is it possible?*

For the remainder of the hour, I listened attentively as people shared their stories. *What it was like; what happened; and what it's like now,* as it's called. Some people were a lot like me, and others were so radically different it was hard to imagine we shared one iota of common ground. Yet I was struck dumb by how much I identified with what each and every person had to say. Not necessarily the *facts* of their experience, but the *feelings*. That sense of feeling apart. Different from.

But that doesn't mean I was suddenly struck sober. Yes, I began attending this meeting somewhat regularly. But I remained unwilling to jump in with both feet; instead, I resorted to my default modus operandi: skate through on the least amount of effort possible. I was what you'd call a *tourist*.

In A.A., it's repeatedly said that "half measures will avail you nothing." But I thought I had them fooled on that one by stringing together a few solid respites from drinking. Thirty days here; ten days there. Even six months at one point. But these dry intervals were exactly that—dry, but far from *sober*. At the time, I didn't understand the difference. I assumed it was normal to suffer uncomfortable teeth-grinding periods during which I'd resist my powerful urges while simultaneously plotting the day that I'd inevitably drink again. Unfortunately, that day appeared at regular intervals. Time and time again I relapsed, often in dramatic fashion, picking up not just where I left off but sometimes in a place that was far worse.

They say the best way to ruin your drinking is to have a headful of A.A., and I can say that's true. Drinking was no longer fun. In truth it was awful. But it remained a necessity. I was beginning to grasp just how powerless I was when it came to fighting this demon.

A few months before the wedding, I came clean to Michele about my sordid adventures in the southland. Well, maybe not entirely clean, but I painted the general picture. I told her I'd been arrested for DUI. *True.* I left out the other arrest and spared her the painful hairy details. Things like hiding my drinks. Missing work. And an occasional blackout-fueled dalliance. Then I dropped the bomb.

"The DUI made me finally admit that I'm an alcoholic. But this is a good thing, Michele. I've been going to A.A. meetings, and I've been sober now almost sixty days." *Also true.* I was sober at the time and had every intention of staying that way. Even if it was *my* way.

"Uh, that's a lot to take in, Rich." She was a good sport about all of it. She put on a smile and tried her best to be enthusiastic, but eyes don't lie. It scared the crap out of her. Of course, I'm sure she knew on some level that I had a drinking problem. After all, I was tanked when I met her and drunk on almost every occasion we went out together. But who wants to suddenly discover they're about to marry an alcoholic? Her trepidation was more than understandable.

But I was in love with her. And determined to prove that I could stay sober and earn back her quickly dissolving trust. Clarity became my priority. I decided to set aside my reservations about A.A. and give it an honest go. Because I finally had a reason outside myself to remain sober. The introduction of another person—someone I cared deeply for—made the stakes that much higher.

Meanwhile, the wedding plans proceeded, and with the big event a mere month away, I became more and more excited. But things started to take an odd turn a couple weeks before the ceremony. Up in San Francisco one Friday taking a deposition on a case I was working on with Bob Shapiro (the famous attorney who'd defended O.J. Simpson), I booked a nice hotel room that I extended for the weekend. The plan was for Michele to make the forty-five-minute drive north from Palo Alto so we could share a romantic evening. But when I called her late Friday afternoon to check on what time she'd be arriving, her tone revealed a change of heart.

"I'm not going to make it up tonight," she said, her voice distant.

"What? Why not? I have dinner reservations and everything."

"I'm just tired. All the wedding planning has me stressed out."

"I understand. I know it's been a lot. What can I do to ease your stress?"

"Nothing. It's fine." But I could tell there was more on her mind.

"Why don't I come down to you and we can just hang out?"

"No. I just need sleep. Go out. Have fun. We'll talk later." Not the response I was looking for.

Clearly something was amiss. But despite my instincts, I refused to believe it was anything serious. So I decided to chalk it up to a simple case of pre-wedding nerves. But the interlude stuck in my brain like a splinter in the foot. It was a slow ache I just couldn't shake.

A week later, I took off from work and drove my green Ford Explorer up from Los Angeles to Palo Alto to get settled in a couple days prior to the big weekend. Friends and relatives slowly began arriving from all across the country. On the evening before all the group activities were to commence, I took Michele out for a quiet dinner in San Francisco. I'd picked a romantic restaurant near Telegraph Hill with a gorgeous view of the San Francisco Bay beyond. But Michele fidgeted in her seat, clearly uncomfortable. Finally, she began. She wanted, she explained, to wait until we got back from the honeymoon to sign the marriage certificate. She needed time, she explained. To decompress from the stress.

To say that her request made no sense to me is an understatement. In fact, I couldn't believe we were even having such an insane discussion. But I was desperate to mend the intimacy crevasse that was quickly expanding between us. I wanted her to be happy, excited about the wedding—and relaxed. And so, after distraught reflection, I relented. With everything I'd put her through with the move, the DUIs, the lying, and the struggle with alcoholism, I figured it was the least I could do for her. In retrospect, I should have never agreed. And looking back now, it's unbelievable to me that I did.

And yet this ludicrous arrangement failed to bring her closer. In fact, she only grew more distant. During the rehearsal dinner at a beautiful winery high atop the foothills above Palo Alto, Michele avoided me entirely. Refused to hold my hand even. To the casual observer, everything seemed fine. But I was in my own private hell. Man, did I want to drink that night. *Just one strong drink to numb this misery.* But I knew I could never have just one drink.

The next day, as I mingled with my groomsmen getting dressed in the wedding venue anteroom, I put on a smile and did everything in my power to enjoy the moment, choosing to believe that all would be right in the world and refusing to accept that I was about to make the mistake of my life. I hadn't seen Michele since the previous evening when she ducked out of the rehearsal dinner with her friends, leaving me to venture back to the hotel alone with my parents—so I couldn't help wondering what her current mind-set might be. Was she even going to show up?

She did, and before I knew it, the "I do's" were said and we were pronounced married. After, when it came time to sign the marriage certificate, Michele rushed through a lie that somehow the judge who married us believed, and as crazy as it sounds, we did not, in fact, sign the certificate. In a sober but painfully confused daze, I stumbled through the reception, during which Michele was as chilly and unavailable as ever.

Our wedding night was even worse. From the threshold of our penthouse suite, I demanded answers for her inexplicable behavior. But Michele was unresponsive, retreating to the next room and refusing to even acknowledge the elephant looming between us.

As for our honeymoon, I have never had a more awful time in

such a beautiful place as I had in Jamaica. Privately, I decided I'd back off, give Michele the requested space to decompress. So for five days, we shared a room yet barely spoke. Forget making love— mere eye contact was a challenge.

On the morning of the fifth day, I went for a swim in the ocean. Since my days at Stanford, I rarely got wet unless I was taking a shower. But as I stroked offshore that day and enjoyed the warm Caribbean current, muscle memory took over. Suddenly, I was summoning my deep love for the water and lamenting how long it had been since I just *swam*. I reflected on how disconnected I'd become from this huge part of my core being, and without thought, I began paddling faster until I was flat-out sprinting. For that brief moment, I felt entirely comfortable in the world. Because out there everything made sense. I knew who I was.

Minutes passed. As I swung my left arm overhead to begin my next stroke, I suddenly felt my wedding band slip off my ring finger. In seconds it had sunk to the seafloor thirty feet below. I immediately dove down to search for it, but it was too deep. And too murky to even see, let alone retrieve it. No, the ring was gone. *Perfect*, I thought. Like something you'd expect to see in a cheesy movie.

I swam back to shore, walked up the beach, and stood before Michele, who was quietly tanning herself.

"I lost my ring," I reported matter-of-factly.

"Oh, well. Probably for the best," she replied, completely unfazed by the news.

I couldn't take her nonchalance one minute longer. With a deep breath, I girded myself for a reckoning.

"I'm done, Michele. It's time to get real."

I pulled a large smooth stone out of the sand and plopped it down in front of her. "See this rock? That's you. An island. I thought if I gave you room to decompress like you asked, that you'd eventually open up to me. But it's just gotten worse. You don't talk to me. You won't even let me touch you. I don't know who you are anymore. You have to tell me what's going on. Because I just can't handle this silence one minute longer."

"I don't have anything to say," she responded. I doubt her heart rate increased one bit.

How is that even possible? I thought, altogether dumbfounded. But it was obvious this would go nowhere. My plan had failed. It was over. Before it had even begun, this "marriage" was kaput. Despair turned to anger. My move. "Time for you to go home. Pack your bags. I want you gone by tonight."

"Fine." And without any emotion other than possible relief, she raised herself up, calmly collected her things, and decamped to the room, leaving me alone on the beach without a single clue to explain how something that had once been so good had ended so terribly.

She was gone, and to this day, I've seen her only one time since, a brief and highly unpleasant occasion after my return from the honeymoon in which I visited her to retrieve the wedding gifts bestowed by my friends and family members so that they could be promptly returned.

But that night, just moments after Michele left, an old acquaintance showed up. My demon. Picking up the phone, I dialed.

"Room service? Yes. I'd like a twelve-pack of Red Stripe beer, please."

Six months of sobriety out the window.

Somehow, after some several rough days deep into the bottle, I made it back to Los Angeles, and once there, I wasted no time seeking out Michele's friends to see if I could extract from them what had *really* been going on with my almost bride. I'm afraid I reverted to full Perry Mason mode, grilling these blameless people as if they were on the witness stand. Finally, though, one of Michele's friends broke down crying.

"She's been having an affair. I'm so sorry."

As it turns out, during our engagement, when I was down in Los Angeles, Michele had fallen in love with her next-door neighbor in her apartment complex. She wanted to call the wedding off but just couldn't summon the courage. So she did the next best thing, pushing me away in the expectation that I'd have enough spine and self-respect to do what she couldn't. But the whole thing backfired. And then it was too late. I should have seen it coming, I suppose. It was the one explanation that made sense out of this baffling mess. Yet I'd been utterly blind.

Armed with this new information, I hopped in my truck that night and drove north until dawn, arriving in Palo Alto to confront Michele and retrieve the wedding gifts. Her only remark?

"It was just a party. I don't see what the big deal is."

Did she seriously just say that? As I pulled my truck out of the cul-de-sac, all I felt was rage. All the feelings of betrayal, anger, and confusion that I'd begun to put behind me came rushing back. *I needed a drink.*

CHAPTER SIX

INTO THE LIGHT

Certainly I wanted to be sober. But taking the necessary actions required not just to achieve but to maintain sobriety proved a task I was simply incapable of. During the nine months following my wedding fiasco, I rubber-banded in and out of recovery, but I couldn't make it stick. And with each successive relapse, my spirits sank lower, and I began to despair of ever managing to lead a "normal" life.

With my increasingly frequent absences, it was only a matter of time before I was fired. And my parents weren't just fed up; they were scared to death. During one painful visit from my father in January 1997, I was completely unable to show up for him sober. I had to drink two vodka tonics during my morning shower to calm my nerves enough to walk down the street with him to grab a simple cup of coffee.

"I know what's going on, Rich," my dad sternly informed me when we returned to my apartment. "You know we love you more than anything. And I'm so sorry about everything that has happened. But your mom and I just can't continue to watch you destroy yourself like this. If you get sober, give us a call. But until then, we don't want to hear from you. You're on your own. Good-bye."

Just like that, my family was gone. And so, too, my sanity. I'd become just another wet-brain, hopeless alcoholic certain to wither and die a slow, lonely death.

But unbeknownst to me at the time, back in D.C. my parents had sought out counseling to better understand not just the disease of alcoholism, but how to insulate themselves from the pain of my downward spiral. They began attending Al-Anon meetings, finding solace in this support group for people suffering from the alcoholism of loved ones. And a couple months after my father's fateful visit, I received an unexpected call.

"I'm going to say this once. And then you're not going to hear from us anymore," my dad said on the other end of the line. "We found a psychiatrist. He's helped a lot of alcoholics. What you do with this information is up to you. But we think it would be a good idea for you to go see him."

Great. A shrink. *That's all I need.*

Maybe it was because despite all my screwups, I still desperately wanted his approval. With stinging remorse I recalled his loving words of support in the immediate aftermath of the wedding debacle. *We love you, Rich. And we will get through this . . . together.* Or maybe it was because deep down I still harbored a dim pilot light of hope that I could somehow beat this thing. *You can be a victim. Let this destroy you. Or you can be strong. . . .*

Only after another painful relapse—opening up a brief and narrow window of willingness—did I book the appointment.

As I pulled into the parking lot of a nondescript two-story office building just beyond the perimeter of Los Angeles International Airport, in my battered Ford Explorer, its front end still decimated more than a year after my DUI collision, all I could think was *Same old shit, different day.*

But from the moment I sat down across the desk from Dr. Garrett O'Connor, a gray-haired Irish gentleman in tweed jacket and tie, I could tell this wouldn't be business as usual. Over the course of our first hour together, he wasted no time in taking me apart piece by piece, with laser precision.

"You're what I call terminally unique. You think you're special. Your problems remarkable and singular. People like you die."

So much for easing into things. He continued, "But you're just a garden-variety alcoholic. Nothing more, nothing less. Just like me." Garrett told me he'd been quite the drunk back in the day, but had been sober for decades. "What you need is treatment. And until you embrace this fact, you're never going to get sober."

By "treatment," Garrett meant rehab. A minimum of thirty days away, with nothing to do but focus on my problems in a highly controlled environment. All I heard was *mental institution*. And I wasn't buying.

But I agreed to see him again. And for the next two months I visited him weekly. Until one day I didn't, missing my appointment because of yet another relapse. The following week I told him what had happened, with a vulnerability and level of raw honesty that I'd been unable to muster in any of the A.A. meetings I'd attended over the last fifteen months.

"So, are you finally ready to talk about treatment?"

"I still think I can handle this without rehab. One more chance. If I relapse again, I'll go. You have my word."

"Last time I heard that excuse the guy died choking on his own vomit. You sure you want to risk it?"

I nodded. And Garrett assented. Not because he thought it was a good plan. It wasn't. But only because he understood one crucial fact: *You can't help someone who doesn't want help.*

So I returned for another spin around the A.A. merry-go-round. Primarily because I was scared to death of rehab. But I was a ticking time bomb. And sure enough, a couple weeks later I once again fell off the wagon.

I called up Garrett from my office to let him know my plan had predictably failed.

"I can have a bed ready for you at Springbrook tomorrow," he replied. Springbrook Northwest was his treatment center of choice. Not the sun-soaked holiday spa of my rehab dreams, but a hard-line recovery program deep in the farmlands of rural northern Oregon. The immediacy of it all was terrifying. But a deal's a deal. And I knew if I didn't take instant action, my willingness would vanish. So I marched to Skip Miller's office to take the news to him directly.

"I need to take some personal time."

I didn't have to say anything more. He knew exactly what I meant.

"Do what you need to do. Take as much time as you need. And we'll still be here for you when you're ready to come back." It was unbelievable support from a man who didn't suffer fools lightly, and whose patience I'd tested to the limit.

Armed with Skip's hall pass, I walked outside 2121 Avenue of the Stars to meet the bright sun wash and headed straight to the liquor store. I had one night of solitary drinking left, and I wasn't about to squander it. Because despite all the misery, I still didn't want to let this life go.

Sloshing about my apartment in the wee hours of the night, I was half-committed to backing out on my deal with Garrett when that damn photograph caught my eye. The 1929 University of Michigan swim team photo of my grandfather given to me by my mother, recklessly lying upside down on the floor of my barren living room. It had sat there for months with nary a glance. But suddenly it was speaking to me, calling sharply through the glaze of my inebriation. Picking it up, I carefully rehung it on the naked wall above. And just stared. The sepia-toned maize and blue glory of my doppelgänger Richard Spindle peered back and spoke to me from the beyond: *Why are you doing this to yourself? This is not who you are, Rich.* The shame was unbearable.

Located about twenty-five miles southwest of Portland, Springbrook Northwest is an addiction treatment center (acquired by

Hazelden in 2002) tucked in the pastoral woody farmland of the Willamette Valley. Comprising several low-slung post-and-beam dormitories, meeting halls, offices, and a communal cafeteria, the campus is reminiscent of a small boarding school set against a backdrop of rolling green fields. A thick forest surrounds its perimeter like a protective moat.

But that dark night of my sodden arrival I saw nothing, my vision glazed and my balance compromised as I stumbled out of the van and apprehensively found my way up the steps to the main hall entrance, pushing through the double doors to the impossibly bright fluorescent-lit intake desk within.

"Rich Roll here. Checking in for duty," I cracked wise to the unamused nurse.

She averted her glance and wasted no time zipping open my duffel bag and rifling through my belongings.

"Hey, that's my stuff!" I slurred smugly, a good twelve beers under my belt for the day's travels. But without offering a response, she continued to toss my clothes about the countertop, rummaging for drugs in every pocket and crevice, uncapping the lids of my various toiletries, scavenging even the inner lining of my bag. Addicts can't be trusted. And attempts to smuggle contraband are routine.

Luggage frisk complete, the nurse pointed me to a small bedroom just behind the desk: hospital drab meets boot camp chic. Shutting the door behind me, I hit the plastic pillow fully dressed and promptly blacked out.

The next morning, I awoke in a complete fog. Rubbing my eyes and breathing in deep, I raised my aching bones out of the cheap, damp bedsheets and stood at the window. The drizzly gloom of the Oregon skies stirred a foreboding that began to rhythmically pound the temples of my throbbing head. And then I remembered. The day was June 7, 1998. *Holy shit. I'm in rehab.*

Hence began the first day of a self-imposed incarceration shared with inmates from all walks of life—people who would other-wise never in a million years comingle. Doctors, poets, professors, priests, students, pilots, drug dealers, bartenders, soccer moms, salesmen, and bankers. Many with wreckage more heartbreaking than you can imagine.

My problems seemed small in comparison. *I'm not like them,* I repeatedly told myself.

But the walls of separation I built would soon come down. One of my first assignments—*Step 1,* as it's called—was to prepare a detailed written account of my top ten most catastrophic drunken escapades. Then I was compelled to read the twenty-page overview aloud before the entire Springbrook regimen of patients and staff.

Shortly thereafter, I was summoned to the office of Spring-brook's executive director; out of respect for anonymity, let's call him Paul. Paul was a recovering addict who years before had traded in a promising magazine publishing career in favor of Colombian white. But he'd come out the other side intact. And along the way, Paul had heard every story, fielded every excuse, and didn't suffer any bullshit.

"You remind me a lot of Jay Maloney."

Once a Hollywood talent agent and the youngest of the infamous "Young Turks" of CAA, Tinseltown's most successful agency, the charismatic Maloney had represented superstars like Martin Scor-sese, Leonardo Di Caprio, and Dustin Hoffman before succumbing to the free fall of drug addiction. And despite several rehab sorties, including a stint at Springbrook a year or two prior, Jay had been unable to achieve lasting sobriety. Fifteen months after this conversa-tion, he would hang himself in the shower. Dead at thirty-five.

"We think you should consider a protracted stay. You're young. But your alcoholism has progressed to that of a sixty-five-year-old lifelong chronic drinker. And unless you make this your absolute top priority, you're going to end up just like Jay."

At the time, my plan was to spin-dry the mind for a short spell. Three weeks tops. I was already suffering acute anxiety from the confiscation of my cell phone. And haunted by the idea that back home, the world was passing me by. But Paul's words helped me realize that my top priority, much like Jay's, was my career—not sobriety. And that unless I made this final stand, there would be no career. No, if I didn't do this now, and do it right, I had no future.

And so I agreed. *I became willing,* ultimately staying one hundred days.

"You only have to change one thing, Rich. Everything."

Daunting words from Stan,* the Springbrook counselor assigned to lord over my rigid and admittedly pathetic butt. Once a successful trial lawyer, Stan's love of the needle had left him disbarred and homeless before he found sobriety and reinvented himself as a drug and alcohol counselor. *Let's get to work.*

Every morning, the alarm went off promptly at 6:30, reveille for the first of several group and private counseling sessions of the day. Some days it was painful. Other days, hilarious. And often confrontational, like the time I got busted sneaking out to give Jen— a young college professor with a nasty heroin habit who decided to head back to New York City "AMA," or against medical advice— a lift to the airport. That move almost got me tossed out.

Then there was the dreaded family weekend. Two days of group-therapy torture with my parents and sister in which I was pounded with a litany of my failures. They all ganged up to provide an exhaustive recounting of how their cherished son/brother had humiliated them, abused their trust, and otherwise disappointed them.

---

* Personal names in this chapter all changed to protect anonymity.

It was tough, to say the least. But with Paul's words ringing in my mind, I decided that if I was going to be here, I would let go of my misapprehensions and simply do as I was told. *Willingness.* And in time, I began to open up, eventually coming to understand that I was absolutely powerless not just when it came to alcohol, but with respect to most things in life. And my persistent belief that I could find a way to control my drinking had left my world not just completely unmanageable, but in ruins.

But most important, I learned that it wasn't my fault. I had a disease. And like a diabetic who needs insulin, I, too, needed a treatment protocol. It's just that the treatment for alcoholism doesn't come in the form of medication. *The solution is spiritual.*

I'd never been a religious person, let alone spiritual. In fact, I can't say I even knew what that word meant. As a youth, I briefly attended Presbyterian Sunday school, but it never stuck. Yet I wasn't an atheist either. The fact that I was still alive was potent testimony that something beyond my awareness just might be looking out for me. But I never found answers, let alone solace, in church. No, religion was not for me, I'd long ago decided. And from that point forward, the only time you'd find me seated at the pew was for a wedding or the occasional Christmas Eve service with my parents.

But lasting recovery, I was coming to understand, is purely spiritual, premised on the conviction that only a power greater than yourself can restore you to sanity.

"Let's face it, Rich. Your best thinking has you institutionalized. The time has come to set aside your self-will. Because that barometer is broken. If you look at it objectively, it's an attribute that has essentially destroyed your life. And you simply cannot solve this problem with your mind. So let it go, already."

I couldn't fathom it at first. Without self-will, who was I? *Doesn't that mean giving up?* But Stan seemed to know what he was talking about. He'd helped hundreds before me get sober. Who was I to challenge his methods? So I agreed.

My immediate reaction? Relief. A huge burden lifted. A realization that by making a simple choice, I no longer had to be solely responsible for solving all my problems. That's not to say that I abdicated all control over my life. Just that I became willing to do what had always been so difficult for me: *not just ask for help, but be willing to receive it.* And as payback, I began helping others—because it turned out that a cornerstone of recovery was *service*.

It's said that alcoholism is a disease of perception. *Change your perception, change your reality.* As the Springbrook weeks blurred into months, I began to replace my distorted perspective with a finely ground lens of objective clarity. The first step was compiling a written account of all my resentments, fears, and harms to others in an attempt to uncover my "character defects." The project took weeks to complete, ultimately totaling more than one hundred pages. For example, I resented my father for his success and for placing expectations on me that I felt I could never quite meet. And I resented myself for never being quite enough in his eyes. But the inventory helped me to understand that my emotions were primarily fabricated; misdirected and ill-placed. Behind them lay a deep insecurity—a desperate need for approval rooted in poor self-esteem.

And that all these confusing feelings boiled down to one singular emotion. *Fear.* Fear of people. Fear of situations and institutions. Fear of economic insecurity, the unknown, and events that hadn't yet and possibly never would transpire. All told, fear of everything.

And there's only one cure for fear. Faith.

Bridging that gap started with another irksome assignment in which I was compelled to share—*out loud!*—the entirety of my encyclopedia-sized moral, or should I say *immoral,* inventory. It's one thing to concede the nature of your wrongdoing to yourself. On some level we *all* do that. But expose every dark corner of your soul to a stranger?

"What on earth does this preposterous activity have to do with quitting drinking?" I asked Stan.

"If you don't haul the garbage out to the curb, your house is gonna stink like holy hell. And that rotten stench always leads back to using."

And so for the next five hours I recounted to a friendly neighborhood priest (hardly my person of choice) the resentments I held against essentially every person I'd ever met, everyone from my mother to the mailman. But even as I recalled some of the most embarrassing and horrific episodes of my life, he never once flinched. And when it was over—my depleted body and exposed soul having been turned inside out—he left me with just one question.

"Are you ready to let all of this go?"

"Yes."

"Good. For the remainder of the day, I want you to refrain from speaking to anyone. Find a quiet place. Reflect on the work we've done today. And when you're ready, ask that these character defects be removed."

I knew just the place to spend a quiet day. Hopping in my car, I headed west to Cannon Beach, a small weekend getaway of a village nestled along Oregon's rugged and barren Pacific Coast. No radio, no music. Just me and my thoughts. When I arrived in this salt-stained postage-stamp hamlet, I parked along the blustery shore and made my way down to the beach. With the sun and tide low, the beach was expansive, the orange glow of dusk casting long shadows across the glassy sheen of the flat wet sands.

Barefoot, inventory in hand, I walked the beach until I found a private spot. And for a long while, I just sat, taking it all in as I pondered not only the events of the day but all the decisions, emotions, and actions of my decimated past.

And when I was ready, I did the unthinkable. *I prayed.* Not to the Sunday school God of my youth. Or to the God of any church I'd ever visited. Instead I prayed to a God purely of my own understanding, asking that I be delivered from the character defects that had precipitated my demise.

Then I took out a match and, just like that, burned my inventory until all that remained was ashes in the sand. No, I didn't just "haul the garbage out to the curb." I incinerated it. *Finally, I let it all go.*

To this day, the funeral pyre of ashes that was my inventory sits in a Tibetan singing bowl on my bedside nightstand as a constant reminder of that day that set in motion a new way of living.

One of my most profound realizations in this process of baggage purging was discovering I no longer harbored any anger or resentment toward Michele, or a sense of victimhood with respect to the marriage that never was. Miraculously, I could now see that it was I, rather than Michele, who'd caused our relationship to falter, that it was I who set in motion every event that culminated in that mockery of a wedding. I was the selfish one. I was the one who repeatedly lied, who strayed from being faithful when under the influence, and who abused her trust until it faltered altogether. Looking back, it's amazing she permitted the relationship to last as long as it did. Liberated from resentment, I now see her and our relationship with nothing but love.

I have come to appreciate that great beauty lies in destruction. Looking back, it is undeniable that the wedding that almost destroyed me was necessary to my ultimate salvation. And for this, I am—and will always be—eternally grateful.

––––––––––

It was September 1998 when I left Springbrook and somewhat un-easily began to find my way. I knew with certainty one crucial fact. Big corporate law firm life was not for me. Nonetheless, I returned to my job at Christensen—I owed Skip at least that much. But during that time, sobriety was my career. In fact, my life outside the office was completely consumed by recovery. I attended three meetings a day, followed by meals with new sober friends.

Ultimately, the new clarity I was enjoying told me that I needed to make a choice about my career. I could continue to pursue what was expected of a man of my education, a path I'd seen many follow, but which I now knew all too well would lead back to despair. Alternatively, I could choose to believe that my life was worth more than the name of my firm or the car I drove, and have faith that something more meaningful awaited if I could summon the courage to break free. I desperately wanted to believe in the alternative, and finally, with the help of others, I found the courage to take the leap.

"I'm not going across the street for more money," I told Skip, breaking the news. "I don't have another job. I just know I need to do something else with my life."

Surprisingly, Skip was remarkably unfazed. "Well, it's too hard if you're not having fun." *Having fun? Who in the world finds this stuff fun?* Apparently, Skip does. More power to him. "So what are you going to do?" he asked.

"I don't have the slightest idea." And that was the truth.

I've never felt more free—or more terrified—than I did that day.

And yet an opportunity did arise, almost immediately: part-time legal work on behalf of an old Christensen client. Hardly ideal, but a good baby step. It was soon followed by calls from friends in the entertainment industry seeking counsel on this deal or that. Faith, it seemed, was paying off.

It was around this time that I began taking yoga classes. And one day, there she was. Julie.

Standing out among the many beauties who crowded the bright and airy Brentwood studio, she had my eyes riveted on her olive-toned skin as she flexed her lean arms to the rhythm of the poses. Her long dark hair with its groovy orange and blue extensions flowing in sync with the soundtrack. What most captivated me, though, was her warm, inviting smile and the sparkle in her eye that captured the focus of the few straight men bold enough to show up at a yoga class.

It would be weeks before I'd summon the courage to even speak to her, but nonetheless, I boldly announced to my friend Mike Minden, "I'm gonna marry that girl." I don't know where my sense of conviction came from. But in the same way that I knew leaving Christensen was the right move, I just *knew*. It wasn't hope, or some throwaway comment. It was fact.

Sure enough, a few months later I found myself on a yoga retreat in Ojai, kissing Julie for the first time, in the kiva, an underground cave-like sanctuary reserved for spiritual ceremonies. We've been together ever since.

I had assumed that my next girlfriend would be much younger than I was—living a simple life and unencumbered. To borrow a pejorative term, *no baggage*. But love doesn't work that way. Newly divorced and more than four years my senior, Julie happened to be a mom to two young boys—Tyler, age four, and Trapper, three. Hardly a simple setup. I would never have imagined that I'd insert myself into such a complicated equation. And let's be honest, I was hardly without my own baggage. *Tread lightly,* more than a few friends warned me. But the heart wants what the heart wants, and I wanted Julie.

I couldn't keep my eyes off of her. But what I fell in love with went far beyond her beauty. She was strong, opinionated, and wise, to be certain, but she never took herself too seriously. If someone asked how long it had taken her to paint a gorgeous canvas, her reply was always "My whole life." And she seemed free from the fear that for too long had controlled my path. A master of many trades, she's an artist, yogi, sculptor, musician, builder, designer, and healer—in other words, a powerhouse. To this day she's the coolest woman I've ever met.

Within a year we were living together. Professionally, I'd begun— without any grand design—building my own solo entertainment law practice. And I was finally having the fun Skip talked about, representing screenwriters, directors, and producers in their various transactions in film and television.

Around this time, Julie decided to take a huge risk and outright buy a three-acre parcel of raw land in rustic and beautiful Malibu Canyon—a move many cautioned against. We took out a large construction loan and, over the next three years, put absolutely everything we had into building our dream home.

Everything seemed to be clicking into place. And soon Julie became pregnant with our first child. With construction on our home finally complete, we celebrated by getting married on our land. Upon a backyard stage adjacent to a tepee that had been our winter abode, we hosted a veritable world music concert for one hundred of our closest friends and family. The event featured gospel singers, West African drummers and dancers, and rock musicians, including Julie's brother Stuart, a professional guitarist. Aside from the days my daughters were born, it was the happiest day of my life.

I was finally sober, and while I was hardly a poster child for recovery, I was a far cry from that shattered soul who'd arrived thoroughly soused at Springbrook just a few years prior. Too, I'd learned what it meant not only to love, but to receive love.

CHAPTER SEVEN

MY SECRET WEAPON
Power in Plants

It's 1984, a Tuesday, 7:15 A.M., and two high school students stand in line at Montgomery Donuts, out Old Georgetown Road in Bethesda, Maryland. Marking time, my swimming buddy Brian Nicosia and I consider the merits of ordering chocolate-covered custard versus jelly-filled with powdered sugar on top. In the end, we split the difference: "Six custard-filled, six jellies," I say, and Brian forks over some crumpled bills. We tread lightly across the icy parking lot, eating mouthfuls of doughnut as we make it to Brian's car. Brian starts the engine, and as the car warms up we devour our super-high-calorie meal like lions lunging at prey, interrupting ourselves only to share a laugh over whatever just came out of Howard Stern's mouth on the radio.

We've come directly from morning swim practice, where we knocked out four miles in the pool before most people had even woken up. Our chlorine-damaged hair is still wet, the tips frosty icicles courtesy of a typical subfreezing February weekday, but in our sugar haze we don't even notice. In less than fifteen minutes, all twelve doughnuts disappear. After that, we drive to McDonald's, where we order two bacon, egg, and cheese biscuits plus two Sausage McMuffins for me and two orders of pancakes, eggs, and bacon for Brian.

It's just one morning like any other in a string of similar mornings: an insanely early swim practice followed by various iterations of sugar, flour, meat, and fat, taken in as quickly and in as large a quantity as we can manage. We're teenagers, we're logging four hours a day in the pool, and we can handle it—the more calories the better. We don't think about what the stuff is, what it contains, how it makes us feel, or what it can do to us. *We just eat.*

Unfortunately, in my case, the ingrained habits of a high schooler became the default dietary approach of a collegian, and after college, during my stints in New York and San Francisco, my appetite turned to even cheaper, faster food. Cook my own meals? Forget that. Instead, it was Gray's Papaya hot dogs (by the dozen) or Ray's Pizza (five slices for five bucks). Burgeoning alcoholism finally curbed my appetite—to a point. I'd go out drinking on an empty stomach, wanting the buzz to hit harder and faster—as it invariably did—with no food to cushion it. But the night would always end the same—in drunken gorging at whatever fast-food institution happened to be nearby and open at three o'clock in the morning.

And it wasn't a problem—until it was.

I barely lifted a finger—let alone a pair of swim trunks—throughout the nineties. Alcoholism left me too hungover to get off the couch, and then everything became about recovery, leaving me zero time to exercise. Or so I believed. Combine a new family to care for with ever-present financial pressures and, well, the state of my physique seemed very low priority.

For years, as I sought to excel as a husband, father, and entertainment lawyer, the idea of "eating healthy," hitting the gym, or even getting some fresh air for that matter, rarely occurred to me. *Who has time? There are just not enough hours in the day.* I was no different from so many men I know and respect. And just like them, I had a bulging waistline to show for it.

Admittedly, even at my maximum weight of 208 pounds, I

wasn't, for my height, obese by today's standards—but I was almost 50 pounds heavier than the 160-pound fighting weight I maintained during my collegiate swimming years. And what was worse, I didn't feel great. In fact, I felt horrible. As described in Chapter One, my casual disregard for my own health caught up with me on the night before my fortieth birthday. I found myself gasping for air while climbing a few stairs on my way to bed, my mind and body collapsing in a sudden and awful understanding of what I'd become—and, more important, where I was headed. The signposts up ahead spelled out words in big red letters that were truly frightening: "heart disease" and "death."

So what followed was what *had* to follow: a massive overhaul of diet, mind-set, and lifestyle. Those months were tough—days and nights of intense cravings, a body detox that left me dry-mouthed and shivering on the couch, and banishment of foods that I'd counted on for emotional comfort. But the clarity and wellness that eventually came made the process all worth it.

After that aha moment on the stairs in October of 2006, my do-it-yourself overhaul began with a seven-day herbal, fruit, and vegetable juice–based "cleanse" (for information on my recommended cleansing program, see Appendix III, Resources, Jai Renew Detox and Cleansing Program). Then came the uninformed six-month stab at vegetarianism, during which I reverted to my pre-cleanse lethargy. Discouraged, I was ready to throw in the towel and revert to my old eating ways. But in June 2007, I decided instead to launch an experiment, undertaking on a trial basis what is generically known as a vegan, or plant-based, whole-food diet. My program wasn't devoid of just *all* animal products, but most processed foods as well. In the five years since, I've tweaked and revised the regimen to maximize my athletic performance, stave off the onset of illness and disease, and ensure optimum long-term wellness for myself and my family.

I've dubbed the regimen the *PlantPower Diet.*

From the beginning, the PlantPower Diet—even in its untweaked form—brought me tremendous energy. I felt lighter. My energy levels escalated to that which I experienced during my cleanse and remained high throughout the day. My thinking became clear. Absent were those lulls I'd felt after meals, those food comas I thought I just had to live with. And any depression I felt began to subside. In short, I felt *amazing.* My strength and endurance levels increased quickly and my cravings for dairy—even my beloved cheese—slowly dissipated. I began working out more, and as the weight slowly came off, I felt better and better. Buoyed by the results, I deepened my study and understanding of plant-based nutrition, disease prevention, and exercise physiology. I devoured every authoritative text I could find on these subjects and felt more and more convinced that I was on the right path.

Six months into the experiment, I'd already lost *forty-five pounds,* lowering my body weight to a lean and mean 165 pounds. Not only was I ripped, I was hooked. And then I really put my regimen to work, testing my body's absolute limits.

I'm a forty-five-year-old man. A husband and a father who just five years ago crouched winded in my bathroom, fearing a heart attack. If you had told me back then that I'd be sitting where I am today, enjoying a level of fitness and vitality beyond anything I previously thought possible, I would have said you were a lunatic. I simply couldn't have imagined in my wildest dreams that my life would unfold as it has. And yet here I stand. How is this possible?

I can say with full confidence that my rapid transformation from middle-aged couch potato to Ultraman—to, in fact, everything I've accomplished as an endurance athlete—begins and ends with my PlantPower Diet.

Along the way, I've sought and been blessed with the support and wisdom of many others—medical authorities, professional athletes, spiritual guides, not to mention Julie, who was my very first mentor in finding a food lifestyle that worked for me.

And that food lifestyle has meant removing all animal products and most processed foods from my diet. No chicken, no eggs, no fish, no dairy. All plants, all whole foods, all the time. It's what I live on. It's what I train on. It's what I compete on. It's what I thrive on.

I'm not a doctor. I'm not a nutritionist. I'm just a guy who started paying really close attention to what he was putting into his body. A guy who undertook some study to better understand which foods do what and why. And a guy who liked the results so much that he started taking on challenges that he'd never even dreamed of before.

LET'S GET PLANTPOWERED!

When people ask me what and how I eat, I sometimes hesitate before I use the word "vegan." Of course, that *is* what I eat; my diet is absent of any and all animal products. But the word "vegan" is a loaded term, connoting not just a nutritional regime but a code of ethics and a sense of political activism. For better or worse, there's a stigma to the word, which all too often alienates those who could most benefit from embracing what the word represents.

As I talked about in Chapter One, I was at first quite skeptical about such a way of eating—simply because of the undertones that the word "vegan" brought with it. To me, "vegan" meant a far-fetched, hippie way of not just eating, but living. I imagined dreadlocked students at Humboldt State, kicking around a Hacky Sack in Birkenstocks and tie-dyed T-shirts to the melody of the Grateful Dead. Cool for them. But not my scene.

My turn from a dairy- and meat-based diet to a plant-based

diet resulted not so much from a desire to adopt a certain lifestyle as from a simple question: *What makes my body run the best?* And the answer turned out to be simple. Plants make it run the best. And so I prefer to call my own eating lifestyle *PlantPowered,* a term that gets more to the heart of my relationship with food. Plants are what I've used to repair my health. They've given me the strength to do what I do. My pro-plant bias is not about being liberal or conservative. It's about optimizing both short- and long-term wellness. My diet is PlantPowered, and therefore I am PlantPowered. Never in my life has the equation of food to body been more clear. The old adage is true: You *are* what you eat.

KEEP IT SIMPLE

In this day and age it can be hard for even the most "aware" consumer to know which foods are healthful. We're so inundated with conflicting advertising and marketing messages telling us what to eat. Low-fat, non-fat, low in saturated fats, high in omega-3s, drink this, eat that, grass fed, red wine, no red wine, eat chocolate, you need more protein, don't eat chocolate—it can make anyone's head spin. Just walk the aisles at any typical grocery store and read the packaging—almost every product is adorned with a banner slogan about why it's good for you. And then there are the supplements—vitamin tablets, protein powders, energy bars, weight-loss shakes, nutraceuticals, and cure-all smoothies. The totality of it all can literally cause vertigo.

What do I see? A preponderance of disinformation, artful misdirection, creative advertising taking liberties with the truth, and sometimes downright lies, all market-tested and carefully crafted to dupe and confuse.

But when you cut a wide swath through the blinding morass of obfuscation and advertising to boil nutrition down to the basics, it turns out that eating right—eating the *PlantPower* way—isn't complex at all, or all that difficult or expensive to adopt. What I've done is to get back to fundamentals. At times I *can* get fairly "scientific" about what I eat, because I'm aiming for specific athletic performance goals—but my approach is probably not as complex as you think. So if you're interested in the PlantPower way, you can jump in with both feet without a whole lot of thought or planning. There's no need to be intimidated. This kind of diet doesn't have to be rocket science!

In the most general sense, I eat and recommend plant-based, whole foods and advise staying away from many—but not all—processed foods. I don't like to overcomplicate the eating part of my life, and I don't obsess. I don't prepare elaborate or expensive dishes. I don't weigh my food, count grams, or overthink my proportion of carbohydrates to proteins to fats. Why? Because getting overly caught up in such minute details leads to burnout. And burnout always leads back to old habits. The name of the game is sustainability. And simply put, *if it's too complicated, it's not sustainable.* And if it's not sustainable, what's the point? Not only does it have to work, it has to be user-friendly, operating with relative ease within the framework of the modern busy family.

The general take-away is this: *eat plants.* Lots of different kinds. Vegetables, fruits, grains, seeds, legumes. Every meal. All the time. All colors, all sizes, and simply prepared, close to their natural state. Keep it varied. Stick to the perimeter of the grocery store and avoid the middle aisles, which generally feature processed and refined foods. Don't eat things with ingredients you can't pronounce or that aren't found in nature. Try to eat organic and locally grown produce when at all possible. Go easy on the sugar. And as for oils—one of the few technically processed foods I support in moderation—use sparingly or avoid altogether.

Eating this way doesn't have to be hard or complicated. And after you adjust to the change, you very well may find, as I have, that it's often easier to eat the PlantPower way than you imagined, since most of the foods are close to their natural state and thus very simple and easy to prepare. Keep in mind: The closer your plant-based foods are to their natural state, the better.

I didn't invent my regimen from whole cloth. It's built on a foundation of scientific data generated by leading medical professionals and other experts in the field: people like Dr. Neal Barnard, founder and president of the Physicians Committee for Responsible Medicine, and T. Colin Campbell, professor emeritus of nutritional biochemistry at Cornell University and author of *The China Study,* a groundbreaking book published in 2005 that examines the close relationship between the consumption of animal proteins and the onset of chronic and degenerative illnesses such as cancer, heart disease, and obesity. In one of the largest epidemiological studies ever conducted, Professor Campbell and his peers determined that a plant-based, whole-food diet can minimize and actually *reverse* the development of these chronic diseases.

Equally influential is Dr. Caldwell Esselstyn's book *Prevent and Reverse Heart Disease.* A former surgeon at the Cleveland Clinic, as well as a Yale-trained rower who garnered Olympic gold at the 1956 Melbourne Summer Games, Dr. Esselstyn concludes from a twenty-year nutritional study that a plant-based, whole-food diet can not only prevent and stop the progression of heart disease, but also reverse its effects.

You might have seen former President Bill Clinton in 2011's CNN special *The Last Heart Attack* speaking with Dr. Sanjay Gupta about his decision to adopt a whole-food, plant-based diet as a means to combat his own struggle with weight and heart disease. If you did, you know he cited Dr. Esselstyn, along with Dr. Dean Ornish, as key influencers in his decision.

Dr. Esselstyn's son Rip, a former swimmer and triathlete and later an Austin, Texas–based fireman, authored a book called *The Engine 2 Diet* that in plain English demonstrates the power of a plant-based diet by chronicling the astounding health improvements of his Engine 2 firehouse colleagues who undertook his regime.

And yet another influence on me was former pro triathlete and ultra-runner Brendan Brazier's *Thrive*—a go-to primer that details all the hows and whys of plant-based nutrition for both athletic performance and optimum health.

The irony is that, despite the consistent and unequivocal findings of these readily available books, from the moment I undertook my own personal experiment in nutrition and fitness, I met with resistance. Naysayers and critics, ranging from nutritionists and trainers to doctors to concerned family and friends, have tried to persuade me from this path. Whenever I advocate for the Plant-Power Diet, I'm pummeled with well-meaning but myth-based objections: *Aren't you anemic? What you're doing is dangerous. How can you stand all that bland food? You can't be an athlete without steak and milk. It's impossible to build muscle without animal protein. You can't get enough calories without meat and dairy. I've never seen a vegan who looked healthy. You're missing key nutrients. You're harming yourself. Man evolved to eat animals. It's not natural!*

It's crazy how emotional and threatened people can become when the subject turns to food and diet. Merely mentioning plant-based nutrition often prompts immediate debate. But I relish the dialogue. It's been a kick confronting head-on the arguments of the critics and dissenting voices and putting them to the test. I've done my homework. I know how I feel. And my results speak for themselves.

I should make one thing clear: The PlantPower Diet is *not* a fad diet. I like to think of it as a lifestyle. The word "diet" can have

a negative connotation and is almost always construed as something temporary, with health improvements and general wellness
almost always taking a backseat to the primary goal—weight loss.
But proper weight maintenance is only one aspect of living in optimum health. If you're overweight, you'll undoubtedly shed pounds
if you adopt the PlantPower way. Maybe not as fast as you would
on a starvation-based regime. But over time you'll achieve your
proper body weight. And most important, you'll keep it that way.
However, weight loss is not the focus of being PlantPowered; it's
the natural by-product of adapting to *a new perspective on food* that
is keenly focused on achieving balanced, long-term wellness.

But despite PlantPower's obvious benefits, I have no doubt that
many of you reading this are starting to feel a low-grade panic, en-
visioning all your favorite foods vanishing from the fridge and the
cupboard as you stare blankly at barren shelves. You're thinking to
yourself, *No way.*

Believe me, I'm sympathetic. But I can assure you that banish-
ing favorite foods from your diet doesn't mean sentencing yourself
to a life of humdrum eating. It's all about retraining your taste buds.
Also, remember: There's nothing wrong with starting slow. Let go
of trying to be perfect right out of the gate. Use as guideposts the
detailed nutritional information and additional reference materi-
als in this book's appendixes, and feel free to ease into it. Maybe
avoiding fast food is all you can handle the first few weeks. That's
fine. But after that, try incorporating more plant-based meals into
your daily rotation. For example, make that beloved chicken breast
a small side dish to a plant-based entrée until you're ready to let go
completely. Next step: Remove the most tempting and unhealthy
animal products and processed foods from your fridge and pantry. After that, replace dairy with almond and coconut milk. Small
steps such as these will help your mind and body to adapt.

Over time, as you begin to feel better, you just might discover, as I have, a growing appetite and craving for truly nourishing foods. And with the experience of positive results might come a resolve to expand the proportion of plant-based foods that make up your daily menu. Before you know it, you'll be a convert. The point is to change habits. Alter those and you'll create *sustainability.*

Believe me, if I can do it, so can you.

A FINAL THOUGHT

We live in the most prosperous nation on Earth, yet as a society we've never been more unhealthy. Obesity, heart disease, diabetes, high blood pressure, and a vast array of very preventable diseases plague us unnecessarily. But rather than address these ailments' underlying causes, our culture emphasizes pharmaceutical fixes. Just watch television for an hour and count how many ads you see for prescription medications.

If we want to heal—truly *heal*—and thrive, then we must embrace preventive medicine. A plant-based, whole-food diet has been shown, for example, to prevent and actually reverse heart disease (America's number one killer) and impede or even arrest the development of a litany of other maladies, including the growth of cancer cells. Even erectile dysfunction is often symptomatic of circulatory disease. Overall, eating a plant-based diet is the easiest, most cost-effective—and environmentally conscious—way to vastly improve not just your own health but that of America and the world at large.

I'm not alone in my advocacy of this alternative approach to eating. In fact, plant-based nutrition has begun to go mainstream. Practitioners of veganism range from martial arts fighters such as Mac Danzig and Jake Shields, to Georges Laraque of the Montreal Canadiens, to Dave Zabriskie, who made headlines in 2010 as the first professional cyclist to ride the Tour de France as a vegan. And it's not just professional athletes who've caught the fever. Among the converts to plant-based nutrition: Twitter founder Biz Stone, real estate magnate Mort Zuckerman, and Vegas hotelier Steve Wynn. The list is growing daily.

Still wary? Then here's my challenge to you. Using the information in this book's appendixes, adopt the PlantPower Diet. Stick to it religiously for thirty days straight and you'll feel dramatically better. Your energy levels will rise. You'll feel lighter. Your focus will increase. Your mood and sleep will improve. Your blood pressure and cholesterol levels will normalize. You'll feel motivated to exercise. If you're an athlete, your recovery time, and thus your performance, will improve. And yes, you'll lose weight. And if after a month you haven't experienced most, if not all, of the above drastic improvements, I'll happily wish you well as you return to your disease-provoking, artery-clogging, animal protein–based style of eating.

CHAPTER EIGHT

TRAINING AS LIFE

The year was 2007. I was a few months into my evolving experiment in plant-based nutrition. Nutrient-dense foods slowly replaced empty-calorie processed foods. Raw vegetable, fruit, and superfood smoothie blends prepared in my beloved high-powered Vitamix blender took the place of gluten-rich, high-starch refined grains. In fact, almost everything artificial was swapped for plant-based whole foods, my waist slimming in proportion to my expanding nutritional knowledge. With my energy levels skyrocketing to an unprecedented high, I began a routine of mild exercise. Then came "the run" that I described in Chapter One. And once that was accomplished, a yearning for a midlife athletic challenge took root.

On a whim, I signed up for the Wildflower Long Course Triathlon. A tough, very hilly half-Ironman test, the race is held in rural central California every March. I knew that competing in a full Ironman competition was not within my reach at that point. But given how I was beginning to feel, I thought, *No problem with this Wildflower thing. I got this.*

And without any inkling whatsoever of how to properly prepare for a triathlon, I got to work in my own half-baked, weekend-warrior style. Just as I'd launched into a vegetarian diet without any real investigation or understanding, I relied on my past experience as a swimmer as a baseline for how triathlon training should be approached and just threw myself into it. *My way.* My routine was nothing crazy, extreme, or even all that time-consuming. One or two morning trail runs a week. A quick swim or two at lunch should my work schedule permit. And one bike excursion every Saturday morning with my buddies Trevor Mullen and Chris Uettwiller.

I took the time my daily demands allotted and just pushed the pace as fast as I could—much as I'd approached every swim workout back in the day. If I had an hour to run, I ran as hard as I could until my lungs seared, my thighs screamed, and I buckled over. I blasted my short swim sets. And I pushed the pedals to the maximum until I bonked. *No pain, no gain, right?* Recalling my halcyon Stanford days when I used to routinely puke in the pool gutter, I did what I assumed any serious athlete would do in preparation for such a race. There was no reason to believe that what had served me well in the past would fail to reap results now. I might have been brand-new to this triathlon thing, particularly everything having to do with a bike, but how hard could it be? Wildflower was going to be a snap.

But I was wrong. Just 500 meters into the 1.2-mile swim, my lungs were searing. Hasty and overconfident, my body suddenly seized up in lactate paralysis from going out too hard, too soon. Not halfway through the swim, I actually had to stop, roll over on my back, and spend the next five minutes trying to catch my breath. What followed was a mighty struggle just to complete the swim. Stumbling light-headed into the "transition" area, I somehow became lost searching for my bike, and when I finally located my trusty two-wheeled steed, I bent over and threw up all over my cycling shoes.

The bike portion of the race only heightened my humiliation. No matter how hard I pedaled my Trek road bike, I seemed to go backward, helpless as countless cyclists effortlessly zipped by in their fancy time-trial chariots. Somehow I completed the fifty-mile ride, but it took everything I had. And when I bent down to remove my cycling cleats, I cramped so severely that I actually collapsed on the ground. It took eons just to get my running shoes on. Then I tried to run. I made it about a hundred yards before I realized it wasn't going to happen. I just couldn't move my legs. And that's when I quit. Not from a failure of will but from a complete failure of the body.

Next to my name on the race results appeared the acronym every endurance athlete dreads: "DNF"—Did Not Finish.

This triathlon thing had turned out to be much harder than I'd thought.

THE BIRTH OF ENDURANCE

Despite my less-than-stellar debut as a middle-aged endurance athlete, I was determined to improve. And so for the remainder of 2007, I kept at it. *I just need more time.* After all, I'd only been exercising a few months after spending the vast majority of adulthood in the prone position. *What did I expect?* So I crushed the trails when I could, continued with my all-out Saturday rides, and every once in a while jumped in the pool. By the time autumn rolled around, I felt ready for another competitive go. So I showed up at the starting line in Long Beach for my first official marathon.

Everything started out fine. But at mile 18, my legs completely gave out. And I walked the remaining eight miles.

It had been a full year since my staircase epiphany, a period of time in which I'd taken a giant leap forward in improving my health. But it was pretty clear that a future in endurance sports held little promise.

So what? It was this new lifestyle—not race results, finishing times, or age-group rankings—that captivated me. I reveled in the simple purity of the outdoor experience that washed over me in the midst of a trail run, the feeling of calm that enveloped me while engaged in a hard swim, and the satisfying camaraderie I discovered while pedaling with gung-ho fellow bikers.

Fast or slow, it mattered little. I was in with both feet. Hooked.

That first year taught me a few important lessons. First, you can't build Rome in a year, let alone a day. Second, I had absolutely no clue about what I was doing; it was time to get educated. And third, deeply aware of what makes me tick, I knew I needed a goal to better focus both my energy and my time.

And that goal boiled down to one word: *Ironman.*

Ironman is considered by many to be the ultimate test in endurance, a race that entails a 2.4-mile open-water swim, followed by a 112-mile bike ride, and culminating with a full marathon—26.2 miles of running. All in one day. Long before NBC began winning Emmys for its Hawaii Ironman World Championships broadcast, and decades before triathlon grew to become one of the biggest participation sports in the world, Ironman was born from one hotly debated question: Who are the fittest athletes—swimmers, cyclists, or runners? In 1978, U.S. Naval Commander John Collins resolved to answer this question once and for all by combining the essence of three Hawaiian Island of Oahu–set events—the Waikiki Rough Water Swim, the Around-Oahu Bike Race, and the Honolulu Marathon—into an informal one-day slugfest among friends. That year, fifteen athletes undertook the challenge. Twelve finished.

The rest is history. With tens of thousands of athletes participating in dozens of races across the globe, today Ironman isn't just huge business; it's a phenomenon. And a year and a half after my age-forty epiphany, the Ironman seemed, to my push-it-to-the-max self, the obvious choice to test my abilities. Forget the fact that I'd yet to even finish a single triathlon or complete a marathon without stopping.

In April of 2008 I was on the phone with Gavin, my former roommate from my San Francisco days, grilling him about his past

Ironman experiences, when he suggested that I get in touch with his friend Chris Hauth.

"Everybody needs a coach, Rich. And he's the guy who can take you there."

Not only had Chris swum in two Olympiads for Germany, he was a top Ironman professional triathlete with a thriving business coaching many successful amateur athletes—people with full-time jobs and families, like both Gavin and me. So on the strength of Gavin's endorsement, I made the call.

"Which Ironman do you want to do?" Chris asked me early in our conversation. I was stumped. "Well, let's just work on some base fitness for now, until you figure it out."

Base fitness? What does that mean exactly? And don't I already have that? Apparently not.

Before he would even begin to train me, Chris insisted that I undertake what is called a *lactate test*—a torturous procedure scientifically designed to identify a person's level of fitness with relative exactitude. So the first week of May 2008 I visited Phase IV Scientific Health and Performance Center in Santa Monica. My bike was rigged up to a machine called a CompuTrainer, which used a computer to calculate my cycling cadence and watts—the measure of power my legs exerted with each pedal stroke. After a brief warm-up, watts—or pedal resistance—were progressively increased every four minutes until failure. And with each successive four-minute interval, my heart rate was recorded and my blood tested—all to evaluate the level of lactate in my system, an indicator of physiological fatigue.

I felt good, and figured I'd rocked the test. Chris's response? "Just as I thought." Translation: I couldn't have been more wrong. Despite all my self-styled "training," the test results were dismal, reflecting the farthest thing from a truly fit endurance athlete.

"If you want to work with me," Chris lectured, "you're going to have to throw out the window everything you learned as a swimmer. We start over. And do it my way. It will take patience, time, and discipline. And you're going to get even slower before you get faster."

"I'm in." The date was May 7, 2008. Just one month shy of my ten-year anniversary in sobriety.

What ensued was a training program focused entirely on building the capacity and efficiency of my endurance engine. Our bodies have two basic energy-burning systems. The first is the "aerobic system," which utilizes oxygen and fat for fuel. It's your "go all day" mechanism that fuels activity up to a certain level of intensity. But when the intensity of exertion exceeds what is called the "aerobic threshold"—the point at which my lactate test curve began to escalate skyward—then the secondary system known as the "anaerobic system" takes over. Used to power more extreme efforts, such as sprint bursts, heavy weight lifts, and fast running, the anaerobic system utilizes glycogen, or sugar, for energy. And it can only be turned on for about ninety minutes before it shuts down, depleted.

Proficiency in endurance sports, explained Chris, is all about building the efficiency of the aerobic, "go all day" system. To accomplish this, I needed to focus on training that system specifically—which meant staying in the second of five specific training "zones" that are established by the lactate test. For a guy like me, that meant slowing down. Way down. No more gut-busting trail runs. Forget about battling my buddies up the Santa Monica Mountains on the bike. From that minute forward, I was to never escalate my heart rate above 140 beats per minute on any run. And on the bike? Cap it at 130. Zone Two. All day. Every day.

"But if all I do is go slow, how will I ever get fast?" I asked Chris.

"The prize never goes to the fastest guy," Chris replied. "It goes to the guy who slows down the least." True in endurance sports. And possibly even truer in life.

Doing a bit of corroborative research, I discovered a consensus that consistent Zone Two (aka Z2) training for the endurance athlete will, over time, stimulate an increase in mitochondrial density in muscle cells. And a proliferation of these mitochondria—the cells' power generators—in turn enhances both the efficiency of the aerobic engine and the duration for which one can perform endurance exercise. Do it long enough and Z2 training will lead to an increase in aerobic threshold—the maximum level of intensity at which the body continues to process oxygen and fat for fuel.

Up to this point, I'd been spending the vast majority of my running, cycling, and swimming sessions in what is referred to as the "gray zone"—a dreaded no-man's-land where the effort exerted exceeds that which is required to properly develop the aerobic engine, yet falls short of the intensity necessary to significantly improve speed or increase anaerobic threshold. It's that level of effort that leaves you feeling nice and winded after a brisk run but yields little in terms of performance improvement. In actuality, such training undermines true progress. It leaves you tired, with little to no gains in either endurance or speed. It creates plateaus that stunt athletic development, and often leads to injury. *And it is by far the most common mistake made by amateur endurance athletes—myself included.*

In other words, the typical amateur endurance athlete trains far too hard on the aerobic and active recovery days. But not nearly hard enough on the intense days. A certain level of proficiency can be achieved this way, but full potential is never realized.

Beyond the scientific mumbo-jumbo, I still struggled with just how counterintuitive it all seemed. All I ever knew was *No pain, no gain. Go hard, or go home.* And now I was being told the exact opposite. It defied everything I'd ever believed about how to condition the body.

"You're just going to have to trust me," Chris said. "And get a heart-rate monitor. Because it's going to be your new best friend."

So with my newly purchased Garmin GPS watch on my wrist and the heart-rate monitor strap awkwardly bound across my chest, I headed out for my first official workout under Chris's tutelage, a brief forty-five-minute Z2 run on nearby Victory Trail, on Ahmanson Ranch, a three-thousand-acre open-space preserve smack in the middle of the San Fernando Valley. *Forty-five minutes? That's it? Doesn't Chris realize I've been banging out two- to three-hour runs for a year?* I felt like he was treating me like a child. I resisted embracing the truth—that when it came to endurance sports, I was less than a child; I was an infant.

But that denial was about to morph into acceptance. I began with a very light jog to warm up, and after five minutes or so, I checked my heart rate to make sure I was in the proper zone—in other words, heart rate below 140 beats per minute. *150!* It must be a glitch, I thought, since I was barely moving. The GPS signal on my watch bounced off an invisible satellite overhead to register my pace at a slovenly ten minutes per mile. No, it was accurate. My aerobic system, it seemed, was simply so undeveloped that even the slightest jog had pushed my heart rate above my aerobic threshold into verboten *gray zone* terrain. I couldn't believe it. In fact, I had to slow to almost a shuffle just to settle in the 140s. And when I hit even the slightest hill, I had to walk just to keep it in check. Meanwhile, I suffered the humiliation of allowing more than a few less-than-svelte joggers fly past me on the trail. Chris said it would take discipline to rebuild. I was now starting to understand what he meant.

At this rate, the idea of competing in the Ironman suddenly seemed all the more impossible. But I trusted Chris. And I stuck to the plan.

THE ULTRAMAN DISCOVERY

But what's a plan without a goal? A road to nowhere. I still needed to find that Ironman I'd sheepishly avoided committing to. My enthusiasm ran high, and I didn't want it to wane. Unless I soon found a race to zero in on, I knew I'd lose focus.

So after a month under Chris's wing, in early June 2008 I logged on to the official Ironman website, naively assuming that I'd have my choice of the twenty-five-odd Ironman-branded races offered throughout the year and across the globe. What I failed to realize was that these races sell out a full year ahead of time. Entries open the day after each race and generally sell out before day's end, often in a matter of hours. Needless to say, every race from 2008 through May 2009 was completely sold out.

Damn. I knew Ironman was popular. I'd watched the Ironman World Championships in Hawaii on television many times and seen the thousands of bodies strewn across Kailua Bay and the famous lava fields of the Queen K Highway. I just had no idea it was *that* popular.

What now? For the next two weeks I was depressed. I'd come so far. I ached for an endurance challenge to celebrate my life overhaul. But the door to the dream suddenly seemed closed. To be sure, there were plenty of other races out there. Shorter-distance triathlons. Century rides, trail runs, and open-water swims. But none of them had that Ironman mystique.

"Why not just start with a local half-Ironman this year? We can always do a full Ironman next year," said Chris. But his comment left me unsatisfied. No, a half-Ironman wasn't going to cut it. And I didn't want to wait a full year to do an Ironman, either. But I'd essentially left myself with no options. In retrospect, it's ludicrous that I would scoff at a challenge I'd yet to conquer. My only attempt at a half-Ironman had resulted in a DNF. And my lactate test proved that my aptitude for endurance sports—if any—was at best embryonic, more likely just a pipe dream. I was in no position to be haughty. Yet much like that moment I walked out on a secure corporate career, or the first instant I laid eyes on Julie, I just knew that the proper objective would soon present itself.

And sure enough, it did. Only a week later I found myself at Jamba Juice, awaiting a large carrot-and-orange concoction after a morning run, when I casually picked up a copy of *Competitor* magazine lying on the countertop. One of those free multisport-focused periodicals with race schedules and obligatory running-shoe reviews found in most large cities, a piece in the magazine featured a picture of a large and impossibly muscled African-American man running shirtless in Hawaii. Entranced, I began reading the amazing story of a Navy SEAL known as David Goggins.

A former football player and power lifter who once tipped the scales at 290 pounds, Goggins decided to honor the tragic death of several of his fellow SEALs and raise funds for the Special Operations Warrior Foundation by competing in some of the most difficult endurance challenges in the world. "When I joined the military, I couldn't run to the mailbox," he once famously said. Yet in 2006, he nonetheless completed an event I'd never heard of called Badwater—a 135-mile jaunt through Death Valley in heat so intense that it melts the rubber right off your running shoes.

And three months after Badwater, he participated in a mysterious event called the Ultraman World Championships. A three-day stage race circumnavigating the entire Big Island of Hawaii, which is roughly the size of Connecticut, the event entailed swimming 6.2 miles, cycling 260 miles, and, on the third day, running 52.4 miles. *More than twice the distance of an Ironman!* And despite having never before competed in a single triathlon or cycling event, and riding much of the course on a borrowed bicycle in his running shoes, Goggins finished second overall. Unbelievable.

"I'm nobody special," he often repeats. And his mantra isn't false humility. He believes it. Yet his story struck a major chord with me. The farthest thing from a born runner or triathlete, I identified.

But what really captured my imagination was Goggins's vivid description of Ultraman. No prize money. No closed roads and entirely self-supported (by your own crew). Nary a shred of media coverage, let alone television time. More spiritual quest, it seemed, than spectacle race.

Ultraman. No question about it, I'd found my goal.

I must be mentally ill was my next thought, a waterfall of self-doubt working overtime to douse my fragile flame of inspiration. The idea of completing an Ironman was lunacy enough given my current state of endurance acumen. But Ultraman? Even considering it was over the top. Yet for the next week, I could think of nothing else. What most worried me was the implausibility of someone with my utter lack of credentials ever securing entry. Limited to just thirty-five carefully vetted international competitors each year, Ultraman was, and to this day remains, invitation-only.

Nonetheless, against all logic and reason, I knew with utter conviction that somehow, someway, I'd be lining up to participate in the event come November—then just six short months away. The first step was picking up the phone. I called Jane Bockus, Ultraman's grande dame and chief gatekeeper.

After I introduced myself and explained my fascination with the race, I received the predictable inquiry: "So what have you done?" Jane asked.

"Nothing." I couldn't lie. "But if you can find it in your heart to let me in, I'll be ready. I promise."

There is earnestness. And then there is idiocy. My words fell somewhere in between. Jane made no promises, but she didn't say no, either. It was all I needed. By hook or by crook, I'd find my way into the race.

First, though, there would be the distressing business of breaking this secret news. Julie's response was predictably optimistic. "I think it sounds awesome!" But that didn't mean she knew anything about undertaking a challenge of this magnitude.

Then came the terrifying call to Chris. "I found my race," I began, my voice trembling in expectation of the inevitable reality check. "Ultraman."

"Whoa!" he responded with a gleeful chuckle, followed by an interminable silence. I braced myself for the stern rebuke. *You are way out of your league. . . . It will never happen. . . .* But to his great credit, Chris swallowed what had to be prodigious doubt and left me with one simple comment: "Okay, let's do it!"

Now a man possessed, I continued to pester Jane over the next several weeks, making sure she understood just how serious I was. Later, Chris even e-mailed her in support, letting her know he'd have me ready. And finally, she relented.

I was in.

THE ROAD TO ULTRAMAN

So it began. With fewer than six months to steel my body, mind, and soul for this seemingly insurmountable adventure, I had absolutely zero room for error.

Chris and I began by building my training volume slowly to ensure against injury, no small possibility given my body's previous dormant decades. At first, it was around ten hours a week. A couple one-hour swims. Two or three Z2 runs of only an hour to ninety minutes maximum. A longer bike ride on Saturday morning, anywhere from three to four steady hours. And a longer run on Sunday, generally about 90 to 110 minutes in length.

In a perfect world, I would have supplemented my rotation of swimming, cycling, and running with a wide variety of cross-training and rehabilitative pursuits: a modicum of weight lifting to improve overall strength, which wanes with age, particularly past forty; weekly massage and use of foam rollers to remove scar-tissue buildup and enhance blood flow to aid in muscle recovery and further ensure against injury; yoga for flexibility; core workouts to improve body stability and enhance my swim, bike, and run form; and spinal adjustments to correct body alignment. These are all things I now incorporate into my regime. But there are only twenty-four hours in a day. And back in 2008, I simply didn't have the time. With that six-month clock ticking, I was compelled to devote all available training hours to one of the three specific race disciplines. And I almost never missed a workout. Not because I sought Chris's approval. But because I was terrified.

By mid-summer, my body was beginning to acclimate to the volume, and the hours increased—up to fifteen hours on average, with the occasional eighteen- to twenty-hour week, always followed by a light rest week of easy workouts and reduced volume. It wasn't until September that the volume escalated to a ceiling of twenty-five hours. But the approach always remained the same—a prescription of steady Z2 medicine. The midweek rides and swims just got a bit longer. I never ran two days in a row—a key reason I was able to avoid a run-related injury—but Tuesdays turned into double-run days. That Saturday ride just got longer and longer. And the same for the Sunday run.

True to Chris's word, unwavering adherence to the plan began to pay significant dividends. I found myself able to run quicker without my heart rate escalating. What started at a 10:15-minute-per-mile run pace at 145 beats per minute was soon a 9:30 pace. Before long, an 8:30 pace morphed to 8:00—all within the sacrosanct Z2 range. But the bulk of my training was spent on the bike. Because the body can ride many more hours than it can run or swim, it's the optimal and most time-efficient way to build endurance fitness without risking leg and shoulder injuries.

And by sticking to the ethos of Z2, I was surprised to never experience the debilitating fatigue I'd grown accustomed to as a collegiate swimmer. Escalating volume very incrementally gave my body time to adapt without suffering exhaustion, the idea being that aerobic zone training allows the body to train day in and day out without heading into that black hole of fatigue that can bury an athlete for weeks, sometimes months, and destroy a season.

Then there was this bizarre training approach called *periodization.* It stipulated that a block of heavy training weeks should always be followed by a rest week. Further, it declared that every week should include at least one rest day in which I did absolutely no training. The objective was for my body to repair itself in between heavy loads. Seen another way, all my improvement was slated to take place in those periods *between workouts.* Fail to properly recover, and I'd limit my overall potential. But set periods throughout the season when my body could heal—*absorb the training*—and I'd lay the groundwork for maximum performance gains. The concept seems self-evident, and, in fact, it's the current operating system for most endurance, track, cycling, swimming, and triathletes today.

But to me, these ideas were anathema. *Go slow to go fast? Rest to improve? What is this craziness? I can't spare the time to rest!* During the heyday of my swimming career in the 1980s, conventional wisdom called for pushing oneself to one's absolute limit for up to eight months straight. *Aerobic zone? What's that?* Before I hooked up with Chris, I'd never heard of a rest week, let alone anything resembling active recovery.

But armed with these insights, I soon became a geek for performance technology and data. For example, I grew to love my Garmin bike computer, a device latched to my bike's handlebars that received important data points wirelessly and via satellite—everything from heart rate to pedal cadence, location, speed, elevation, grade, and more. Perhaps the most important contraption I acquired told me what level of power I was generating—or, more specifically, the force exerted by my legs with each and every stroke of the pedals. By contrasting my legs' watt and kilojoule output with my heartbeats, the road incline, the air temperature and elevation, and the miles per hour I was traveling, I was able to set what was for me an optimum training intensity.

I grew to love the numbers. After every workout, I looked forward to uploading the data accumulated from my various training devices to the analytical software on my laptop. Eventually, I utilized Web-based services like Strava to keep track of my progression on local climbs and share my rides with friends. And I began to rely on programs like TrainingPeaks, WorkoutLog, and Golden Cheetah, which lend meaning to the numbers by producing a dizzying array of graphs and metrics. Always, I scanned the data for insight into how I could improve, which I'm sure has contributed greatly to my ability to enhance my performance with each successive year.

RUNNING SHOES AND INJURY

Only as I began to understand how to train optimally did I realize how little I knew—and how much there remained to learn. This was particularly evident when it came to running, something I enjoy but that has never come easy. I am the farthest thing from a natural-born runner. In fact, I don't really consider myself a runner at all. Any success I've achieved on foot is more a matter of fitness and discipline than innate ability. And in 2008, the only subject I knew less about than cycling was running. I was downright clueless—particularly when it came to shoes. Utterly naive and susceptible to bad advice, I haplessly went through a dozen pairs of running shoes trying to find a model that would suit my maladroit stride, keep me erect, and prevent my knees from buckling under the stress of my impending double-marathon attempt. But nothing seemed to fit quite right. Seeking counsel at my local running-shoe chain retailer, I had my gait videotaped on a treadmill. Then it was "analyzed" by an "expert," who informed me that I required a shoe with a big foamy raised aft section and very firm custom-molded insole inserts to further raise my heel and arch. This predated the minimalist running craze ignited by Christopher McDougall's bestselling book *Born to Run,* and I was in no position to argue. Thus, through the remainder of 2008, I found myself clodhopping in shoes that were seemingly more suitable for snow skiing than running.

But in the years that followed, I took it upon myself to quest more aggressively after the perfect running shoe. Influenced by *Born to Run,* in 2010 I steered away from the big-heeled shoes that were quickly falling out of favor and sought out the new, less supportive, flatter-soled varieties that were suddenly all the rage. The idea was to gain a better feeling of connection with the ground, and to foster a more natural stride in which my forefoot—and not my heel—would strike the ground first. According to McDougall and others, the cause of many injuries is the nefarious heel strike promoted by the typical big-heeled running shoe. At one point, I even went to the minimal extreme, trail running in Vibram FiveFingers—essentially, covered sandals with individual toe sleeves. I still wear them, albeit sparingly, but prefer a bit more support for longer efforts. The search continues, since I've yet to find the ultimate shoe.

It was not until 2011—long after that early Ultraman training—that I suffered my first running injury ever, preparing for the Boston Marathon. It was during a training period in which I was running far more often and intensely than ever before. A sharp pain in my lower left calf began to develop that simply wouldn't quit. I figured nothing much could be done other than to hang up the shoes for a spell and rest. That, and maybe some ice and a compression sock to reduce inflammation. Two months went by without running, yet the pain persisted. It was suggested that I explore some proactive therapy options, but such therapies seemed like a false promise. *I just need more time off,* I told myself. But my friend Greg Anzalone insisted I see Dr. Shay Shani, a chiropractor in Westlake Village, near my home, who was known for working miracles. I was very reluctant to allow anyone to touch my spine. I'd never suffered back pain, and the idea of someone twisting my neck and back until it cracked just seemed like a bad idea. Besides, why would someone go to a chiropractor for a calf injury?

Ultimately, though, I yielded to Greg's urging. And X-rays of my spine proved immediately revealing. A close look at my pelvic area showed why every time I suffered any kind of pain, ache, throb, or injury—be it passing, mild, or severe—it *always* appeared on the *left* side of my body. Due to scar-tissue buildup, a mild spinal displacement known as spondylolisthesis, and slight muscular asymmetry, my left leg was actually four millimeters longer than my right. This disparity in length, compounded by years of pounding and countless hours running, was the underlying cause of the calf injury. It also helped to explain why my left hand always went numb after hours on my bike, despite an endless array of professional bike-fit adjustments undertaken to resolve the dilemma. In other words, the calf injury was merely a symptom of a more congenital infirmity. Most orthopedic or podiatry specialists would have gone no further than prescribing an insole for the right foot to even out the length differential. But that's like treating erectile dysfunction with Viagra. It may resolve the symptom, but it ignores the root cause.

Within a week after having my spine adjusted—and the scar-tissue buildup around the calf injury dispersed by laser therapy, active release therapy ("ART"), and massage—I was astonished to be running again pain-free. By maintaining this treatment protocol on a periodic basis, I got the injury to all but disappear. And with my muscle tightness alleviated and my problematic connective tissue subtly altered, my legs were once again even in length. In other words, Dr. Shani treated my injury the same way I treat my body—with preventive medicine. Having learned my lesson the hard way, I now make time for what I formerly overlooked in my training: massage and electrical stimulation (to improve blood flow and expedite the repair of small muscle tears), ART (to continually correct my imbalanced musculature), chiropractic adjustments and core exercises (to maintain spinal alignment and strengthen body stability), and laser treatments combined with the consistent use of foam rollers (to break up the accumulation of scar tissue in worn muscles, which can lead to injury).

NUTRITION EVOLUTION: BEYOND WELLNESS TO PERFORMANCE

Throughout 2008 and beyond I continued to deepen my plant-based nutrition knowledge, experimenting with new foods and paying close attention to their impact on my training and recovery. I discovered, for example, that a raw vegetable and fruit–based Vitamix blend pre-workout seemed to give me more energy for my training than a traditional grain-based breakfast of cereal, oatmeal, or toast. Performance increased further when I began adding endurance-boosting foods like beets, maca powder, and chia seeds.

I also noticed that the more quickly I replenished myself with certain whole foods post-workout, the more rapidly I could rebound for the next session. For example, I added apple cider vinegar to my water to quickly alkalize my system, and I also drank coconut juice, which is high in electrolyte trace minerals lost in perspiration. To replenish glycogen, I made sure to eat plenty of complex carbohydrates in the form of sweet potatoes or brown rice. That seemed to work far better than nutrient-poor sources of carbohydrates such as pasta or bread. (Even the gluten-free varieties are processed and leave me feeling heavy and lethargic.)

Prior to more fully understanding the finer points of subsisting on plants, I was worried about not getting enough protein in my diet to meet the rigors of training. And so large canisters of hemp, soy, brown rice, and pea protein powders began to proliferate in our pantry—along with an array of other muscle development supplements such as L-glutamine, creatine, and branch chain amino acids (BCAAs), countless scoops of which would find their way into my post-workout Vitamix blends. But over time—and as I furthered my study of the specific protein content of plant-based foods as well as the unique protein needs of the endurance athlete—I began to consider the possibility that I might be overdoing it. I didn't like ingesting so many processed items, many of which are laced with chemical-based coloring and artificial flavoring. And realizing that nutrients in whole foods are always better and more easily absorbed by the body than nutrients in supplement form, I began upping my intake of plant-based whole foods high in protein until I eliminated the majority of these supplements from my diet altogether. I began eating things like quinoa, beans, lentils, peas, and tofu, a product I ultimately swapped for its more nutritious fermented soy-based cousin, tempeh. I also ate a lot of raw almonds, walnuts, cashews, and Brazil nuts, the latter a natural testosterone booster due to its high selenium content. Also on my dietary plate: spirulina, a blue-green algae that is 60 percent protein, complete with all essential amino acids, the highest per-weight protein content of any food. In taking in all these whole foods, I discovered absolutely no protein-related impediment to my recovery or to building lean muscle mass. In fact, I continue to improve.

I still opt for a scoop of plant-based protein powder from time to time—after a particularly brutal workout, if I'm feeling overly fatigued from training, or when I know I haven't sourced quite enough whole food protein from my meals. I prefer to combine a variety of plant-based proteins for this purpose, such as hemp, pea, and sprouted brown rice, to ensure maximum bioavailability and assimilation of all the essential amino acids our bodies can't produce themselves. In fact, I recently formulated my own plant-based protein recovery supplement, in cooperation with microbiologist Compton Rom of Ascended Health, called Jai Repair. Infused with a proprietary blend of additional reparative nutrients like Cordyceps mushroom extracts, L-glutamine, vitamin B_{12}, and antioxidants such as resveratrol, Jai Repair is scientifically devised to enhance rapid recovery from exercise-induced stress and is a formula I've come to rely on as a key component in my training regime. For more information on this and many other products in my nutritional rotation, please refer to Appendix III, Resources.

The selection of foods I ingest *during* training has similarly evolved. In the early months of my Ultraman buildup, I ate what almost every endurance athlete I know eats in the midst of a challenging workout: a lot of sugary, electrolyte-laced, artificially colored and flavored drinks and gels. Popular brands like Gatorade, Cytomax, GU, and PowerBar are ubiquitous in the athletic and multisport world. Aside from some varieties, most of these products are *technically* vegan. They're hardly whole foods, though, and yet I was quite reluctant to steer away from them. They seemed tried and true—the go-to source of training nutrition for so many athletes. I needed the calories to fuel my efforts, yet there didn't appear to be adequate natural alternatives. One day, while out training with my friend Vinnie Tortorich, a hard-core endurance athlete and veteran of ultra-cycling races such as the Furnace Creek 508, a 508-mile nonstop bike race through Death Valley, he chastised me as I sucked on a gel. "Rich, you gotta ditch that sugar crap. You can't go all day on that stuff."

He pointed out the harm I was inflicting on my system by consuming so much artificial flavoring and coloring, and suggested replacing the simple sugar content of these products with a complex carbohydrate source: a more slowly metabolized energy that maintains and stabilizes blood sugar over a longer period of time. This is critical in ultra-distance training—which routinely involves eight- to ten-hour rides, for example. So I took Vinnie's advice and ditched the gels and colorful powders in favor of electrolyte sources such as simple table salt, coconut water, SaltStick tablets, and Endurolytes capsules by Hammer Nutrition. For calories, I began to experiment with non-GMO maltodextrin-based concoctions, such as Perpetuem by Hammer Nutrition, and *actual food*—for example, yams, sandwiches spread with almond butter or avocado and Vegenaise, as well as rice balls and baked potato wedges. Such foods might not produce the immediate burst of energy provided by a gel, but you'll be hard-pressed to suffer a blood-sugar crash. And my routine of taking in about two hundred calories an hour of such foods is one I've stuck to, since it keeps my strength high throughout even my longest training sessions.

At some point in my experimentation with nutrition I noticed that the more nutrient-dense raw vegetables—particularly dark leafy greens—that I incorporated into my regime, the more energetic and steady was my mood and disposition. So a certain leaf called kale became my new best friend, along with spinach, Swiss chard, and mustard greens. Also making their way into my daily green smoothies were chlorophyll, marine phytoplankton, beet greens, and spirulina. And as I began to add healthy fats such as avocados, coconut oil, and hemp oil to my blends, salads, and vegetable stir-fry dishes, I found my energy further increasing and stabilizing without any negative impact on my waistline, which was nonetheless continuing to shrink.

I'd assumed that with all this training, my appetite would be enormous, just as it had been throughout my swimming career. In fact, I expected to be at war with my cravings, given that I'd ditched the meat and dairy. But I was astonished to discover that as my body continued to adapt to the training load, and the nutritional density of my foods continued to increase, I became less hungry. My appetite actually went *down*. I no longer craved the "empty calorie" foods I'd relied on early in my transition to plant-based eating, foods that were technically vegan and admittedly tasty yet devoid of significant nutrients and, in my case, quite addictive. "Vegan junk food," as I like to call it. White bread, processed snacks (such as potato chips and french fries), and "fake" meats such as Tofurky faded from my program. And the less gluten I consumed, the better I felt, slept, and performed athletically. For the many recipes I have relied on over the last four years, see Appendix III, Resources, Jai Seed Vegan eCookbook.

With each successive week, I watched my body change. I became stronger, leaner; my face even changed—until I was almost unrecognizable, in the best way.

In August 2008, I returned to the sports training medical center in Santa Monica, Phase IV, for another lactate test and was proud to discover that I'd made a significant leap in aerobic capacity. My numbers were hardly elite. But my improvement was significant. By eating plants, I was getting stronger. And by going slow and rest-ing, I was getting faster. The irony wasn't lost on me. "Speed," I was learning, is an elusive concept in endurance sports, particularly when it comes to ultra-endurance, a discipline in which maximum velocity and effort are values of little importance. Instead, the criti-cal charge is to improve the ratio of exertion to relative speed; some-thing that in my case was improving rapidly and quite dramatically. *Efficiency*—that was the prize I was questing after. Or as Chris liked to call it—*true endurance*.

MANAGING LIFE

As the training volume increased, it inevitably encroached on every other area of my life. I was forced to make some serious adjust-ments in the way I managed my daily routine in order to meet my professional responsibilities, devote the appropriate amount of time to family, and maintain some level of life equilibrium—*a sense of normalcy.* To be certain, the challenge of completing Ultra-man had become very important to me—a *mission.* But I'm not a professional athlete. Time training meant time not earning. And it also meant, of course, precious hours away from my family. In other words, this mission—even if completed successfully—would be a failure if it came at the cost of my livelihood or intimacy with my wife and kids. No, I wasn't going to become an absentee hus-band or father. I'd heard too many stories of amateur endurance athletes who became obsessed with their training, only to end up divorced or disconnected from their children. And after all the pain I'd suffered to build the life I was so grateful to have, there was no way I was going to let that happen.

It was time to honestly evaluate how I spent every minute of every day. I scanned for wasted time, inefficient hours, and

activities that failed to meet the litmus test of *mission critical.* Utiliz-
ing many of the tools set forth in Timothy Ferriss's *The Four-Hour
Workweek,* I made some drastic cuts, eventually creating a lifestyle
template that forms the underpinnings of how I live and manage
time today. On the professional front, I did away with all nones-
sential networking and business-development lunches, events, and
meetings, a favorite Hollywood pastime that always sucked up precious hours and rarely led to new business. Unless it was crucial, I
politely declined meeting with clients in person, forcing conversa-
tions to the phone. And anything that could be done via e-mail
replaced lengthy conference calls. High-maintenance clients who
represented low revenue were let go. Hours spent on the freeway
commuting were traded whenever possible for the home office or
the local Starbucks. I went digital on all fronts, untethering my
business from location and always having handy my laptop or
iPhone.

And because I was self-employed—admittedly, a crucial component in my success equation—I could make creative decisions
about when and where I worked, giving me the flexibility to train
into the late morning and sometimes mid-afternoon without suffering professional consequences. It was a bargain I generally repaid
by drafting deals late into the evening, sometimes pulling all-
nighters. And come "rest day" Monday, I typically used the extra
time to cram three days of work into one.

Because we live in a very remote and rural area far from the locus
of my profession, my base was—and to this day remains—my
truck. In the run-up to my first Ultraman, my old orange Land
Rover Discovery doubled as a mobile office, traveling multisport
training unit, and wandering vegan commissary. With a precision
that bordered on compulsiveness, each day I packed the vehicle's
rear with all of my work and fitness equipment—my bike attire;
a plastic cabinet stocked with cycling parts; a tool kit for repairs;

a few pairs of running shoes and my swimming gear; a duffel of clothes to meet any professional, social, or training occasion; a cooler stocked with all the food I needed to fuel my training; plus large jugs of water and sanitary wipes for an impromptu shower after a trail run. Some days it appeared as if I were headed out of town for a week. And I can't tell you how many grungy gas station bathrooms I used for a quick post-workout wash, changing clothes like a fugitive in preparation for a work meeting.

On the mental and spiritual front, implementing a consistent meditation practice became paramount. Whether early in the morning, during a free half hour during the day, or even while out on a run or ride, I strived to set aside a few daily moments—not a lot, often a half hour but sometimes just ten minutes—to go *inside.* Putting into practice tools I'd gleaned from yoga, as well as Julie's experience in such matters, I became increasingly adept at gaining the upper hand when it came to persistent negative internal chatter. Meditation became a powerful tool that calmed my nerves, relieved my anxiety, and diminished the fear and pangs of self-doubt threatening to capsize my fragile ship (for information on recommended meditation programs, please refer to Appendix III, Resources, Jai Release Meditation Programs).

Yet the challenge of governing my schedule nonetheless remained Herculean. Many days I felt like I was spinning plates while tenuously walking a tightrope. My phone could be counted on to ring repeatedly with urgent business matters while I was out on the bike or trail, forcing me to pull up and sit in the dirt for sometimes upward of an hour to hash out deal points with talent agents and lawyers on a client's movie deal. Sweat drenching the phone, I often thought to myself, *What would these people in their suits in Beverly Hills think if they could see me right now?* My clients had no idea what I was up to—and for quite some time, I encouraged their ignorance out of fear of losing precious business.

I soon came to realize, though, that as long as the work got done, properly and on time, nobody cared where I was or what I was doing. And as my meditation program continued to develop, I eventually mustered the courage to let go of the fear. Coming clean, I learned to speak honestly with colleagues regarding the reality of my shifting and ever-evolving focus.

With respect to family, on weekends it was typical for Julie to immediately hand me a crying baby or two just as I haggardly returned from a very long ride or run. "Your turn," she'd say, smiling as she headed to a yoga class or elsewhere. *Fair enough.* Several hours later it wasn't unusual to find me juggling children, awash in mayhem, my legs cramping and my still-unshowered body clothed in a sweaty cycling bib—not advisable if you're prone to saddle sores like I am.

When something had to give, it was usually sleep. And the rest of the time, more often than not, it was a workout cut short. In turn, Julie supported me by managing the lion's share of household responsibilities.

But let's be honest. Juggling twenty-five-hour training weeks while trying to work full-time as a lawyer meant more hours away from my family than I care to admit. Most Saturdays, hours into an absurdly long ride and often so delirious I'd actually lose mental track of which canyon I happened to be climbing, I'd think to myself, *You could be at the park right now with the kids like a normal dad.* On cold rainy nights when I ran drenched and corpse-like through the dimly lit neighborhood streets, that questioning voice would return: *Why are you doing this to yourself?*

I wish I could say I had the answer. Compensation for my awkward youth perhaps? An effort to manifest swimming dreams unrealized? I'd like to think I was taking middle age to the mat and pinning it into submission. Maybe it was all these reasons. Or perhaps none. The only thing I knew with clarity was that a voice deep in my heart continued to chant, *Keep going. You're on the right track.*

SPIRITUAL RECALIBRATION

Come autumn of 2008, four months into my training for Ultraman, I was amazed at just how quickly I was improving. Every Saturday now involved a ride of no fewer than one hundred very hilly miles, followed the next day by at least a marathon distance of running. Then came the first of four progressive race-simulation weekends in which I approximated the Ultraman distances Friday through Sunday, growing longer each weekend. In the first week of October, I completed approximately 80 percent of the Ultraman overall distance, culminating in a forty-mile run along the Pacific Coast Highway from Venice Beach all the way to Point Dume in Malibu. And back. *A forty-mile run!* It was, without a doubt, up to that point the greatest physical achievement of my life.

However, accomplishing these athletic benchmarks came at great cost. My butt ached terribly from saddle sores, undercarriage infections that became so painful I could no longer sit on my bike saddle. After Sunday runs, it took minutes to climb the stairs to my bedroom. And plenty of days I could barely drag my creaky bones out of bed.

But the biggest obstacle was only starting to come into focus. Despite my intense efforts to keep all parts of my life working in harmony, our finances began to suffer. Too much focus on Ultraman. Not enough emphasis on generating new business. For the first time in my marriage, the bills began to pile up. Mentally, I began to flog myself. *You're dropping the ball, Rich.*

The crisis crystallized during my final race-simulation weekend, in early November, just weeks prior to Ultraman. Setting out at 4 A.M. on Saturday for a 130-mile ride, I froze for four hours, until the sun came up, because I couldn't afford to buy the proper cold-weather gear. And miscalculating my caloric intake, I became delirious just outside Ojai, with no food left when I pulled over at a rickety hamburger stand on a country road in the middle of nowhere. Not only did I not have any cash on hand, my bank account happened to be overdrawn at the time, rendering my ATM card useless. *Idiot!* Sixty-five miles from home, starving and worse than penniless, I was forced to improvise, my shaking arms dumpster-diving in the garbage bins behind the restaurant for something, *anything*—to resuscitate my failing body. Rummaging, I inhaled a mélange of old french fries, half-eaten onion rings, and discarded cheeseburgers. A very rare stray from my vegan regime. But desperate times call for desperate measures.

In retrospect I should have just asked for some free food, but I was more than embarrassed. Mortified, in fact. The journey home was a meek crawl, requiring every synapse just to remain upright as cold darkness fell and the shakes resumed. But the intense fatigue was nothing compared to my sense of shame. I was in deep despair over how I could have let things go so awry.

I'm done with this ridiculous fool's errand, my brain shrieked as I inched my way home, depleted. I couldn't bear the thought of my family suffering so I could complete a silly race. We had real-world problems, and as the man of the house, it was up to me to solve them.

Then the oddest thing occurred. Pedaling in the dark just miles from home, I began to lose the feeling of the road beneath me. Suddenly my wheels spun freely, and as if Newton's law of gravity had been revoked, I felt my body effortlessly angle skyward until I was enveloped by nothing but an expansive darkness. At that moment I had a sense of unexplainable oneness with the universe and, also, a sense of joy and gratitude. More than that, actually: a sense of love. I was in a deep meditative state in which my mind became absolutely still, liberated from thought, at peace. It's what the yogis call *samadhi*.

Later, my gray matter convinced me the experience was nothing more than an exhaustion-fueled hallucination, a delusion precipitated by low blood sugar. It happens. I've since been regaled with similar stories from many an ultra athlete. But I couldn't shake the feeling that I'd experienced something more. Something profound, even. *But what did it mean?* Julie didn't hesitate with her perspective.

"Can't you see? *You're being called to step into who you really are,*" she whispered, holding my weary head in her warm hands that night. "Money comes and money goes. That's not the issue. We'll get through this. But you have to let go of old ways of thinking. Surrender your ego. Because the solution to our problems is in *faith*. Nothing else matters. Stay strong. And just keep doing what you're doing."

With those words, Julie gave me a rare and beautiful gift, a potent reminder that when purpose aligns with faith, there can be no failure and all needs will be met—because the universe is infinitely abundant.

The next morning I woke up and ran. Forty-five miles.

And the following week, more than enough money arrived to pay our bills and finance my excursion to Hawaii for the big race.

I'm ready for Ultraman.

CHAPTER NINE

THE ALOHA, KOKUA, *AND* OHANA *OF ULTRAMAN*

Just finish.

In 2008, this was my only goal for Ultraman. I'd pushed my body as far as it could go in the six months of prep time. And I'd trained my mind to overcome fear and welcome the suffering I'd soon face. But I was also a realist. *Remember, two years ago you struggled to make it up the staircase. Don't do anything stupid. Be conservative. This is just a celebration of your life-changing journey. Enjoy the ride.*

Nothing left to do but show up. So I arrived at Kailua Pier in the dark predawn to ready myself for the three most challenging days of my life, Day One kicking off with a 6.2-mile ocean swim followed by a rigorous ninety-mile bike ride. Absorbing the nervous energy of my competitors' final preparations, I felt the familiar butterflies that preceded the swim races of my youth. With the moment I'd worked so hard for finally upon me, suddenly finishing didn't seem enough. *I wanted to race.*

But I couldn't do it alone; my success relied heavily on my crew. Unlike most endurance events, Ultraman is a completely self-supported adventure. From a van that was packed floor to ceiling with spare bicycle parts, tools, food bins, canisters of race nutrition, coolers of ice water, overnight luggage, and enough race apparel to suit all weather conditions, it was up to my crew to not just cheerlead, but monitor my hydration and caloric intake, manage unforeseen obstacles like equipment failure, and navigate the many tricky turns necessary to keep me on course.

Of course, nothing ever goes according to plan. But I'd assembled a great team that was captained by my cyclist friend Chris Uettwiller. Also helping out: the Buddha-like L. W. Walman, and my dad, who'd flown in from Washington, D.C., and was thrilled to be handling driving duties.

Later, Chris would tell me that as my dad stood on the pier watching me ready myself for the 10-kilometer swim, he got choked up.

"Dave, are you okay?" Chris asked.

Wiping the tears from his eyes, my dad composed himself with a broad smile and a lighthearted chuckle. "I'm fine. It's just that, you see the way he's swinging his arms like that? It's what he always used to do as a little boy before every swim race."

Soon, I was wading gingerly into the water and lining up next to my thirty-four fellow racers for the impending start. And before I knew it, the gun fired and we were off. *Steady as she goes.* Managing an even and sustainable stroke cadence, I steeled myself to relax, making a point to enjoy the sunrise off my left shoulder and the colorful marine life peppering the reefs below. A tidal chop jostled me about, pushing me backward at times, but you can't fight the current—better to *surrender* to its overwhelming power.

Next up on the list of challenges were the jellyfish. Ripping through a swarm of them around the halfway mark, I suffered more than a few stings across my arms, shoulders, and face. The shocks to the system sent my heart rate soaring and forced me to harness maximum mental composure to avert panic. Luckily for me, my stings were relatively mild in comparison to those suffered by Australian Kelly Duhig, who was pulled out of the water and rushed to the hospital in anaphylactic shock.

Two hours and forty-one minutes later, I stumbled up the shores of Keahou—interestingly, the Hawaiian word for "new beginnings"—not just intact, but in *second place*—just three minutes behind race leader Marty Raymond. But more important, I emerged a full fifteen minutes to an hour ahead of all the race favorites. *Not a bad start,* I thought.

Granted, I was a swim specialist. I expected to fare well in my natural environment. But the bike was a different story. Questionable ability aside, I'd soon discover that I'd made a big mistake in stubbornly refusing to upgrade my battered Trek road bike for something more aerodynamic. *It's not about the bike,* Lance Armstrong famously said. But that doesn't mean you show up for a race with the wrong equipment. I'd soon pay for my naiveté.

Cruelly, the very beginning of the bike segment featured the steepest climb of the day—a fifteen-hundred-foot, five-mile ascent that left my lungs searing and legs screaming. Nonetheless, I maintained my second position for the next few hours, traversing the main highway south across an ever-changing landscape of rolling hills, coffee farms, and thick forest. I pedaled with nary a competitor in sight as my crew leapfrogged past, cheering loudly and pulling over every half hour or so to hand off new bottles of water, electrolyte tablets, and calorie-laden Perpetuem to fuel the effort.

The day's plan was to take in three hundred calories an hour, even if I wasn't hungry. In an event like this, you'll inevitably run a calorie deficit no matter how much you eat, because you burn more than your body can possibly digest. The key is to not fall too far behind, and to understand that you're also eating for the following day. Fail to take in enough calories on Day One, and you'll pay dearly on Day Two. Also, you'll most certainly falter on Day Three.

Reality soon set in. Facing strong headwinds about three hours into the ride, I was passed in rapid succession by three of the top overall race contenders. I knew, of course, that any of these guys was capable of winning the entire event. But there went my pipe dream of taking the Day One victory.

Comfortably in fourth position, I hit the final climb of the day—a twenty-plus-mile gradual but unrelenting 3,950-foot ascent into Volcanoes National Park. But with another dose of brutal headwinds that had me feeling like I was pedaling backward, ambition gave way to inexperience and fatigue as I was summarily passed by two more competitors in the stage's last five miles. And in a final insult I was nipped by Czech native and pro triathlete Peter Kotland with only two hundred meters to the finish line.

Seventh overall. Of course, it was disappointing. Particularly my last-minute fade. But nonetheless, I'd exceeded expectations tenfold, taking my competitors and the race organizers completely by surprise. Every athlete who bested me that day was a tried-and-true professional—a veteran of this race. Not only was I the fastest "first timer," I'd finished the day as the top American.

All right, Day One down. Two more days to go.

Day Two would bring the longest bike ride of my life—a 170-mile jaunt from Volcanoes around the eastern side of the island to finish in the little town of Hawi, which was nestled on the island's northwest tip.

During training I'm wary of eating too much before a long ride, but as I joined my crew and fellow athletes at the nearby Volcano Military Camp at five o'clock the following morning for a cafeteria-style breakfast, I made sure I ate as much as my stomach could hold, even though the food they offered was far from my Vitamix concoction of dark leafy greens, maca powder, chia seeds, and beetroot juice. Ditching breakfast wasn't an option. Calories would have to take precedence. And so I forced myself to eat things I'd ordinarily avoid—gluten-rich bagels, heavily processed peanut butter, sugary cereal, and fried hash browns. *I should have planned better,* avoiding this predictable scenario by bringing my own stash. *Next year,* I thought.

With heavily fatigued legs, I began the ride by pedaling conservatively. In front of me was 170 miles and 8,500 feet of climbing through the island's pristine southwest tip to the urban landscape of Hilo and the pastoral cattle farms of Waimea Valley—and beyond that, a little bit of everything: steep climbs, wicked fast descents, and long flat terrain with more treacherous headwinds. With the field of competitors spreading out across the vast landscape, I spent much of the day completely alone, accompanied only by my crew and totally unaware of where I stood in the rankings.

Just keep riding.

And so I did. My legs screamed for rest, and my hands were now so numb from the chill that I was barely able to shift gears or brake, but I soldiered on, maintaining a steady cadence and eating as much as I could: almond butter sandwiches, potato wedges, bananas, water, and electrolyte tablets to avoid cramps. Eat, pedal, drink, repeat.

The ride culminated in an epic ascent over the Kohalas, a grassy range of steep mountainous terrain that marked the final climb of the day. It was a five-mile piece of nasty business that would challenge even the most experienced cyclist, including Lance Armstrong, who trained in the Kohalas in preparation for his 2009 Tour de France comeback. With almost 150 miles already hammered into my legs that day, it was daunting. But I reminded myself that this climb was much like Stunt Road, my favorite training ascent back home. *You've done this climb a million times,* I repeated under my breath. *Relax.* Then I thought about that time I bonked in Ojai, limping home on the bike after dumpster-diving. I recalled the inspiring *experience* that followed—call it delusion or epiphany. I'd overcome so much. I could certainly survive this. *You know what to do.* And with that, I entered a deep meditative state, visualized success, and laid down the hammer, powering the last three miles of the climb with everything I had, knowing that when I crested, all that remained was a fast fifteen-mile descent to the finish line.

Reaching the summit, I was greeted by cheers from my crew and unreal views of rolling green pastures, grazing cattle, and the Kona coastline in the distance below. It was a well-earned high as I began the most perilous descent of my life, battling heavy cross-winds that threatened to blow my bike straight off the road. But it was also the best roller-coaster ride of my life, depositing me safely in the little hippie town of Hawi and, finally, across the finish line.

Having ridden in relative isolation most of the day, I had no idea where I stood in the overall rankings. But I was certain I'd dropped considerably. With so many strong riders, there was simply no way I was still holding on to a decent placing. Then my dad approached, smiling proudly. "You're in ninth place overall!" he crowed, and hugged me. *Still in the top ten!* I couldn't believe it.

A perfect day, made complete when the sun set and I sat on the veranda of the rural Kokolulu Farms Retreat Center—my accommodations for the night up in Hawi—marveling at the sky lit with a billion stars strewn across the Milky Way. It looked as if you could simply reach out and touch the beyond. And in that moment, I felt I had.

Two days down. One remaining. Fifty-two point four miles of running along the baking lava fields from Hawi back to where the journey began—Kona.

Weary beyond words when the 4:30 alarm bell sounded the following morning, I threw on my running shoes and inhaled another substandard breakfast—*next year will be different!*—before wending my way down the dark Hawi highway to greet my Ultra-man *ohana* (Hawaiian for family). Along with *aloha* (love) and *kokua* (help), it's a touchstone word that embodies the communal spirit, camaraderie, and spiritual quest that is the Ultraman experience.

Crowded along the side of the highway in the dark predawn drizzle, my fellow runners joined hands in a wide circle around race director Jane Bockus, fellow race organizer Sheryl Cobb, and a portly Hawaiian elder adorned in native garb, a crown of palm fronds atop his head. Arm in arm, we bowed our heads as the elder recited a ceremonial Hawaiian prayer blessing. He called on the holy island spirit kahunas to bless the journey and keep us safe—then bellowed a loud and resounding tone on a huge conch shell. It was a simple yet utterly beautiful gesture, reminding me that this was so much more than a race.

A few minutes later my dad offered a few special words that I'll never forget. "I'm so proud of you, Rich. I love you. Now, go out and finish this." Our relationship having come full circle, I was raw with gratitude. But facing the road ahead, I had to reel it in and focus on the task at hand.

Just seconds later, we were off.

Just finish.

Today was to be my tortoise moment. Slow and steady, cautious and smart. The plan hatched by Chris Hauth was to break the run into an extremely conservative interval workout. Run four miles. Then walk a full mile. Repeat. It was a strategy devised to prevent my core temperature from rising beyond the point of no return. No one wanted to fall prey to the dreaded "Ironman shuffle"—that arresting corpse-like crawl brought on by overwhelming fatigue.

But it was also a plan that required me to check my ego at the door. *Walk?* I'd specifically trained to run the entire distance. And having completed a forty-five-mile run just weeks prior, I knew I could do it. My pride revolted at a strategy that seemed to bespeak a lack of confidence in my abilities. Then again, Chris had taken me so far. And now was not the time to question his methods.

I ran the first segment breezily, coming up alongside Jason Lester, an accomplished endurance athlete with only one functional arm, who was now well on his way to achieving his goal of becoming the first disabled athlete to complete Ultraman, a result that would garner him national acclaim, including a coveted ESPY Award for Best Male Athlete with a Disability. We agreed to take the first marathon gingerly and together. That's because we both knew that by mid-afternoon the Queen K Highway en route back to Kona would punish with its boiling surface.

I was inspired by Jason's example, and yet the first mile that I walked, per Chris's strategy, virtually every competitor in the field passed me. Do you know how long it takes to walk an entire mile? By the time I reached the half-marathon mark, I was in thirty-second place with only three competitors behind me. It was by far my slowest half marathon ever.

"Can I please start running? This is ridiculous!" I pleaded with my crew, exasperated.

"No. We stick to the plan," Chris Uettwiller abruptly replied.

But it wasn't long before this strategy started to pay dividends. With each successive four-mile running interval, I began to pass runners, two to four at a time. When I walked, one of these athletes would again pass me, but not the others. And when I resumed the running, I would pass that person, plus two to three more. Again and again. Leapfrogging my way up the field. And that's when I started to believe.

By the time I reached the first marathon marker—the day's halfway point—I had negative-split the course. In other words, the last thirteen miles were covered much faster than the first. But more important, I felt fresh, my legs springy, my mood bright, my

The Doppelganger. A victim of heart disease, my grandfather Richard Spindle, a champion swimmer who narrowly missed a 1928 Olympics berth, died far too young. As his namesake and one who has carried on his athletic legacy, I feel his presence with me everywhere I go.

Too Sexy for My Eye Patch. Cross-eyed since birth and weak throughout my early years, I was never projected to be much of an athlete, let alone an Ultraman.

Where's the Power Meter on This Thing? Here, my dad teaches me how to ride my first bike in the Detroit neighborhood of my youth. But I wouldn't get serious about this odd contraption until I was ten years older than my father in this picture.

Looking Good! To put it mildly, my first ten years were awkward. But finally I found something I was good at—swimming. This shot was taken just after I set the "10 and under" summer-league team record in the 25-meter butterfly.

Welcome to College! This picture pretty much sums up my Stanford experience, and the decade that followed. Nothing got between me, my new best friend, and a good time.

Golden Boy. On deck at Stanford's DeGuerre Pool with my Stanford swim team buddies Hank Wise (LEFT) and Dave Schraven (CENTER), 1987. The world was my oyster.

Best Day Ever. Very pregnant with our daughter Mathis, Julie and I get married—yoga style. That day held a little bit of everything—rock & roll, gospel singers, African dancers, a Hindu fire ceremony, a Sioux tee-pee, and readings from my stepsons, Tyler and Trapper. (PHOTO BY STACIE ISABELLA TURK)

Seersucker in the Ashram. My parents played the role of good sports at my wedding to Julie, which was—to say the least—less than tradi-tional. I'll never forget my dad's expression when he set eyes on Bhagavan Das, the legendary yogi and musician who married us.

My New Bride, Julie. Not sure what I did to deserve this woman, but she would help me immensely in getting through the tough athletic ordeals ahead. (PHOTO BY STACIE ISABELLA TURK)

Doctor of Jurisprudence—or Maybe Lack Thereof? Here I am at Cornell Law School graduation with my buddies Paul Morris (RIGHT) and Pablo Morales (LEFT), 1994. You could say I had *too* good a time that day, and things ended badly.

Cheeseburger Heaven. My only decent "before" shot, this photo was taken when I was 38—on family vacation visiting Julie's relatives in Chile. I'm tipping the scales at about 190 here, around 20 pounds shy of my heaviest weight.

The Bad News Bears. At my first Ultraman in 2008, I depended on this trusty crew (FROM LEFT): Chris Uettwiller, my dad, and the irrepressible LW Walman. None of us had any idea what we were doing. And that made it awesome.

Hang Loose. Cruising during Ultraman 2008. Things were much simpler early in the race when I had just one simple goal: finish. (PHOTO BY RICK KENT)

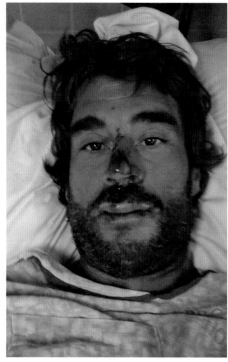

Post-Crash Face Bash. No, this isn't a Botox treatment. Rather, I'm in the ER after landing on my face during a training ride while prepping for Ultraman 2009. To this day, I have no feeling in my lower lip. But I still like kissing my wife.

Please Tell Me It's Over. Seconds after completing Day Two of Ultraman 2009, I collapse in pain and relief. After crashing my bike just 35 miles into the 170-mile bike leg, I somehow found the wherewithal to finish, despite a very battered and swollen knee. (PHOTO BY RICK KENT)

Trapper Sets the Pace. Crewing my run on Day Three of Ultraman 2009, my stepson Trapper works overtime to keep me hydrated and on pace.

Blessed. Celebrating with my family just moments after completing the Day Three 52.4-mile run at Ultraman 2009. Don't let the smile fool you. Moments later I was flat on my back.

Slow Down: This Is Molokai. Jason Lester (FAR LEFT) and I (FAR RIGHT) prepare to embark on the marathon leg of EPIC5 Day Three on Molokai along with locals Rodney Nelson (a schoolteacher, CENTER LEFT) and high schooler Akona Adolpho (CENTER RIGHT). (PHOTO BY REBECCA MORGAN)

How Many Did You Say? FIVE! On the fifth and final leg of EPIC5—attempting to complete five iron-distance triathlons on five islands—Jason Lester (LEFT) and I (RIGHT) ham it up with five-time Ironman Champion Luke McKenzie (CENTER), who dropped by the Kailua Pier to see us off to a good bike-leg start. (PHOTO BY REBECCA MORGAN)

Done Deal. Jason Lester and me in Kona, just moments after we completed EPIC5. No TV cameras, no real press, and nobody there to congratulate us, save our crew and a few good friends. (PHOTO BY REBECCA MORGAN)

Jai-loha! Julie with Jaya, Mathis, and Tyler, hiking the lava-encrusted beaches of the Big Island, 2011.

Hey Sanjay, Over Here! Sanjay Gupta (CENTER) visiting our home for a piece on CNN. He's supposed to be interviewing me, but of course all eyes are on Julie. She tends to have that effect on people.

Standing Tall. Genius photographer and friend John Segesta took this shot for the cover of Matt Fitzgerald's book *Racing Weight*. (PHOTO BY JOHN SEGESTA)

Body Evolution. For the cover of *3/GO* magazine, John Segesta re-created in the summer of 2011 the exact same image he snapped of me running two years earlier (the photo that graces the cover of this book). At the time, I honestly didn't think my body could possibly appear any fitter than it did in that picture. But when you line up the two photos alongside each other, it's not hard to see how my body continues to evolve—getting leaner, stronger, and faster with each successive year, regardless of age. (PHOTO BY JOHN SEGESTA)

Barefoot in the Barrio. Probably my favorite photograph, taken by John Segesta for *3/GO* magazine. (PHOTO BY JOHN SEGESTA)

vigor surging. With many runners beginning to falter, I thought, *Only twenty-six miles left? No problem!*

By mile 30, the plan had proved its merit. And then some. As predicted, athletes could be seen in the distance ahead, crumpled over and staggering. The Queen K Highway is so straight and long, I could spot runners a full half mile ahead, fuzzy oases of blurred color against the black backdrop of baking pavement and lava. I'd laser in on the next athlete in front of me, then challenge myself to pass before my four-mile spurt would end. And generally I'd do it. "Who's next?" I'd ask the crew. Then I'd reel my competitor in.

But fifty-two miles is still fifty-two miles. And the Kona heat is still the Kona heat. Just past the forty-mile marker, I began to falter. Even the slightest external stimuli proved too much. Something as simple as raising an arm to drink, or the sight of Chris or LW running alongside me, became overwhelming. The blinders came down and there were simply no energy reserves for a single thought or movement not mission critical.

With my systems shutting down, I was now reluctant to even slightly alter my running pace, let alone walk, fearful that if I broke stride, I'd be unable to resume—or, worse yet, that I'd quit. And so with eight miles remaining, I resolved to run straight to the finish or until my body gave out altogether, whichever came first. Every cell in my brain implored my body to stop. And so I tried to focus on the journey that had brought me here—everything I'd sacrificed for this moment. *All for naught if I quit now,* I thought. No, there was no way I was stopping. So I sped up, reaching into my deepest reserves for the physical energy and mental acumen to pick up the pace and finish strong.

Done.

Crossing the finish line along the craggy landing strip of Kona's Old Airport, I collapsed into the embrace of my crew, my dad right there to hold me upright, as exhilarated as I was exhausted. And I received a joyous hug from Jane Bockus, the gatekeeper who'd opened the door to make this dream possible.

"I told you, Jane. I told you I could do it," I whispered into her ear.

"Yes, you did, Rich. And I knew it, too," she replied.

"Thank you," I went on shakily. "Thank you for giving me a chance to change my life."

Nine hours even. Certainly not a time I could brag about to a true runner. But I took pride in knowing that I'd given this race absolutely everything I had to give. Not to mention that I was the only athlete who'd negative-split the course—my second marathon was actually faster than my first. At twenty-six hours, thirty-three minutes, and forty-two seconds, I was the fastest American male finisher over the full three days—and good enough to rank eleventh overall.

I'm nothing special. But I am *an Ultraman.*

The one thing missing from that perfect experience? Only the most important people in my life—the rest of my family. I'd thought having them there would be too much—both financially and emotionally. But as I stood on that finish line, I missed them all terribly. I couldn't believe they weren't there to embrace. A regrettable error in judgment I wouldn't repeat.

Next year.

I took the entire winter off to allow my body to heal—and also to restore some normalcy in my life. After training so relentlessly, I desperately needed a break. And I deserved it.

Unfortunately, our financial struggles resumed.

Determined to refill the family piggy bank, I canceled my dream of returning to Ultraman in 2009. That chapter was closed. I'd achieved my goal by just completing the event. I had nothing more to prove. It was time to focus on *real life. Forget all this time-sucking endurance nonsense and grow up,* I told myself. *Because what is a man if he can't make ends meet?* But as I woke one spring morning after yet another restless night, Julie took one look at my forlorn expression and sized me up with a simple sentence.

"It's time for you to get back on the bike."

It didn't make logical sense. Yet from her unique perspective, it was the *only* solution. *Pursue what's in your heart, and the universe will conspire to support you.*

So what can I say? I did as I was told. On a weekday morning that normally would have been spent chained to a desk, I mounted my bike for the first time in months and began pedaling toward the Santa Monica Mountains. Soon I was ascending Topanga Canyon, and as the sun rose into the clear blue skies above the ridgeline, I spotted a hawk. In a perfect symbiosis of air and wing, the majestic bird sailed its perfect arc across the morning sky. And that's when I understood. If I could summon the courage to pursue my passion with purpose and without fear, I, too, could experience such synchronicity. Somehow, everything would work out.

So with that insight to fortify me, and buttressed by the encouragement of Julie, I decided to resume training, with a keen eye on returning to Ultraman. No longer would the goal be just to finish, but, rather, to contend.

Meanwhile, I was starting to get noticed. Astonishingly, *Men's Fitness* magazine named me as one of their "25 Fittest Men in the World"—celebrating me as an everyman triumph. It was heady stuff indeed to be grouped with such athletic luminaries as Rafael Nadal, Usain Bolt, and LeBron James. The piece prompted a slew of interview requests. Even *The Dr. Oz Show* called. And Dr. Sanjay Gupta gave me a shout-out on CNN, noting my plant-based diet as a key to my athletic accomplishments. *How is this happening to me?* I thought. It all seemed surreal. *Maybe the universe had a plan for me after all.*

Just as precipitously, though, the rug was pulled out from underneath me. And I almost lost everything. Forever.

Just outside of Ojai, I was pedaling strong, about 70 miles into my first 130-mile ride of the season, energized by the power I was feeling in my legs and pondering excitedly what the season might bring. Then something went wrong. I have no memory of what exactly transpired, but my next recollection was of slowly awakening from a total blackout. Tangled in the spokes of my bike, bloodied and unable to move, I opened my eyes to peer up through blurred vision at two elderly ladies coming to my aid. *What happened?*

"Call an ambulance!" commanded a voice.

A crash, I realized. But how? Somehow I'd gone over my handlebars—hit an unforeseen bump in the road, perhaps. Or simply lost my balance. It doesn't take much. But I couldn't remember anything. And then everything went black.

My next impression was coming to in the hospital, confused by my surroundings and searching for clues until I slowly realized it was Julie and my then five-year-old daughter, Mathis, leaning over my bedside. Squinting up at them, I began tearing up, a frail sense of mortality coming into focus and overpowering my emotions. I'd suffered a severe concussion, but my disfigured face had borne the brunt of the impact. With my nose mangled and my lips split wide open and monstrously swollen, Mathis had to turn away. To this day, I still have no feeling in my lower lip. But I was lucky, the doctor said. I could have easily snapped my neck.

Convalescing in that hospital bed, I couldn't help but once again call into question the course I'd set for myself. Physically I was broken. Financial struggles continued to plague me. I was at a crossroads professionally. And spiritually, I suddenly felt lost.

Taking note of my distress, Julie leaned down, kissed my forehead, and presented me with a question. *The question.*

"So if that was it, would you be satisfied with how you'd pursued your life?"

I grew quiet, digging deep for a response. The bizarre mash-up of unexpected public accolades and private struggles exacerbated my disorientation. On the one hand, I seemed to be risking death—though prior to the crash I hadn't thought of it that way. Yet when the crash occurred, there was no doubt that I was doing what I loved. As I lay there, looking into Julie's eyes, I knew the answer.

"Yes."

Most spouses probably would have pleaded for a return to a more secure existence: life with a nine-to-five husband, two weeks of annual vacation, and barbecues on the weekend. There's nothing inherently wrong with that. But that's not Julie. And I wasn't ready to accept that either.

"I'm so happy to hear you say that," she murmured.

Because she understood what I was only then coming to realize—that safety isn't just an illusion, it's a cop-out. I know it sounds trite, but there's simply nothing like a near-death experience to remind one of the impermanence of everything. And living imprisoned by fear only to die with regret over dreams postponed was a life neither of us was interested in.

The crash was a blessing, forging in me a redoubled determination to push my body to new levels of strength and endurance. And as the story of my middle-aged transformation began going viral, I realized that it was inspiring positive change in others. That especially came into focus in July 2009 when I was asked by Dr. Sanjay Gupta's producer Danielle Dellorto to write a short article on my metamorphosis for CNN.com. No big deal, I thought. But to my amazement, the piece became the most e-mailed health story on the network's website for a few days running. Overnight, my little blog—which I'd thought of as a private confessional—went from getting close to zero traffic to garnering more than 200,000 unique page views. But what changed everything for me were the 400-plus e-mails I received from people all over the world, many of them intimate accounts of their own health struggles.

Newly focused, Julie and I—and even the kids—cut extraneous expenses and used creativity to meet our needs. The expensive Volvo was replaced by an old Ford Bronco and a dinged-up mini-van. Whole Foods excursions were discarded in favor of purchasing foods in bulk and from local farmer's markets. Julie began selling her photographs and paintings, and little Mathis even offered up her proud creative offerings. Increasingly, as a family, we began to tackle obstacles more as a fun board game than an ominous burden, with the overall tone set largely by Julie.

What's the worst thing that can happen? she'd ask. *We're healthy. In love. Living life according to our own rules. And that's all that matters. Everything else is just stuff.*

Putting this philosophy into action worked. Each successive week I broke new ground in training, surpassing every strength and fitness benchmark I'd set the previous year. And as summer turned to fall, our fragile economic state seemed on the mend. Perhaps most remarkable of all, without taking my eye off my primary mission, my law practice actually expanded. Come October, I was ready, focused, and prepared for the next opportunity to push the boundaries of endurance.

CHAPTER TEN

EPIC5

Rookie Mistakes, Burning Skies, Kahuna Spirits, and a Drunken Angel in the Pain Cave of the Real Hawaii

When I was training in Hawaii with my Ultraman brother Jason Lester in the weeks leading up to the 2009 Ultraman, he let me in on a project that he'd been developing over the past year.

"Four letters, Roll-Dawg. Four small letters, but one big word: E-P-I-C, *epic*. Five iron-distance triathlons. Five islands. Five days. E-P-I-C, *epic* . . . The EPIC5 Challenge!" A broad grin worked its way across his face as he spread wide five fingers on his left, and only functional, hand.

I let this sink in before I spoke. "Wait a minute. Let me get this straight, are you saying—"

Jason cut me off. "I'll start with an iron-distance triathlon in Kauai, then head to Oahu, where I'll do the original Ironman course. Then to Molokai, followed by Maui, and I'll finish up on the Ironman World Championship course on the Big Island."

I shook my head and chuckled. Nothing even close to this had ever been done before—not even attempted. The logistics of inter-island travel alone were exhausting. But an iron-distance triathlon a day? Every day, five days in a row, on top of flying from island to island each evening? Impossible. Still, I knew Jason well enough to know that once he set his sights on a goal, there was no stopping him.

Maybe that's because he'd never met an obstacle he couldn't overcome. He'd been taken from his drug-addicted mother at age three, been paralyzed in his right arm after being struck by a car in his early teens, and only a few years later he'd suffered the death of his beloved father, leaving him entirely alone in the world. But he'd come out the other side a champion. These days he cobbled together just enough funds to train and race full-time. Living a nomadic life, he was on a mission to inspire the best in others.

"Sounds like a party," I replied sarcastically. "But in all seriousness, let me know how I can help. Whatever you need, Jason. Just as long as I get to watch from the sidelines. Preferably the nosebleed seats."

As I described at this book's outset, in the fall of 2009 I returned to the Ultraman World Championships, leading the race pillar to post for almost eight straight hours to seize the Day One victory with authority—by a full ten minutes, in fact. For the first time in my athletic life, I was no longer the also-ran—that second-place guy who just couldn't quite get on top. Finally, at age forty-three, I'd shed that burden and won something. Something big.

But Day Two found me bloodied and battered, flat on my face, limbs strewn across Hawaii's Red Road. My bike was trashed. I was entirely alone. And I could barely move, my knee immobile. It seemed a given that the race was over for me. But it wasn't.

Lifted by the *ohana* of fellow crews, a first-aid kit, the miraculous donation of a brand-new pedal, and the encouragement of Julie and Tyler, I got back on the bike. At that point, I wasn't in a race against my competitors, but rather myself. It was a hard-fought battle just to complete those 170 miles with a raw, throbbing shoulder and a knee that screamed in agony with each successive stroke. When I finally pedaled into the town of Hawi to mark the end of Day Two, I collapsed in a heap on the warm dewy grass just past the finish line, in tears not just of pain but of powerful emotion at having found the wherewithal to somehow see the day through.

And even at that, I had one more ordeal to overcome.

It was on the last day of the race—a double marathon run that I doubted I could even attempt, let alone complete, given my horribly swollen knee—that I experienced the most suffering I'd ever felt on a run up to that time. Baking in the irrepressible heat of the Kona lava fields, dehydrated and body failing, I cursed the race, the crash, myself, the world. That's when suddenly I recalled a David Goggins quote I'd read years back—the idea that when you believe you've reached your absolute limit, you've only tapped into about 40 percent of what you're truly capable of. The barrier isn't the body. It's the mind.

Then I found myself thinking about what Julie had said to me, just before the race started that morning: "Remember, it's already done. All you have to do now is show up. Stay present. And show us who you really are."

Show us who you really are.

Nearing the end of that interminable run, as I made the final descent off the Queen K Highway toward the Old Airport landing strip for the last stretch to the finish line, I was swept off the ground by Julie, my crew, Tyler, and Trapper—all cheering wildly for me. And once again, those all-too-familiar tears returned.

I was proud of myself. I'd showed up. I'd played hard when I was hurt. And I'd gotten it done. I'd crossed the finish line not just intact, but alive. *Truly alive.* That third day I'd covered 52.4 miles in seven hours and fifty-one minutes. It was a full seventy minutes faster than my 2008 effort—good enough for sixth place overall in a total time of twenty-four hours and thirty minutes. I was the top American finisher with a time that would have actually won the race outright in both 2005 and 2006. Remarkably, I'd actually gone *faster* than David Goggins had in 2006—the man whose stunning athleticism first inspired this harebrained adventure to begin with.

Is this it? I wondered. *Will I ever top this feeling, ever top this performance?* I couldn't know then that an even more arduous test was waiting in my future.

During the 2009 holiday season, Jason Lester, my Ultraman training partner who had talked fancifully about trying to complete five consecutive iron-distance triathlons on five different Hawaiian islands—a feat he called the EPIC5—visited my family at our house in Los Angeles. On New Year's Eve, Julie organized a "visioning" project for the family and a few close friends, Jason included. We took the better part of the afternoon of December 31 to itemize the things that no longer served us, qualities we wanted to overcome, ideas we needed let go of, and dreams we wished to see materialize in 2010. Gathering everyone together at dusk around our outdoor fire pit, Julie kicked things off with a brief but powerful blessing. Then we went around in a circle, each of us mustering the courage to share a few of our private items aloud. Then we cast our notes in the fire. It sounds simple but it was a potent gesture, bringing us all closer. I remember glancing across the fire at Jason, watching as a small smile played at his lips.

The next morning, he joined me as I sipped on a green smoothie in our backyard and kicked absently at the ashes in the fire pit from the night before. He cleared his throat and began.

"Big Bro. I've been doing a lot of thinking. I think you're supposed to do EPIC5 with me. And there is nobody else I'd rather have with me than you. What do you think? Are you in?!"

My immediate reaction was a surge of adrenaline. Because despite my prior dismissive eye rolling, I'd been secretly hoping that he'd ask this very question. *Am I in?!? Are you kidding me?* But now that the possibility was actually on the table, my closeted aspirations were quickly replaced with terror. *Holy crap! Five iron-distance triathlons in five days. Can it be done?*

What he proposed was more than daunting. It was almost unimaginable—indeed, it was verging on impossible. EPIC5, as Jason had conceived it, was far more than a race. Rather, it was an unprecedented crazy-ass, down-the-rabbit-hole, into-thin-air adventure.

In our modern world, there are few remaining untried challenges. Endurance junkies have raced their bikes across America without sleep, swum the Amazon, pedaled from Alaska to Chile, and paddled the Pacific. Three guys have even run across the Sahara, from Senegal all the way to the Red Sea! And of course, men have walked on the moon. The days of great adventurers such as Lewis and Clark, Sir Edmund Hillary, Amelia Earhart, and Ernest Shackleton are long over. It seems as though everything has been done.

Yet here it was—a challenge not yet attempted that just sat there, almost begging for a go. The proposition fascinated me precisely because it was so lunatic.

As tempted as I was, I ruminated on the decision for a few days, letting the reality of it all properly sink in. I wanted to ensure that I had the support of my family and could follow through on the commitment required.

"I'm in," I finally announced to a bemused Jason. Sealing the deal with a hug, I was immediately struck by a foreboding thought: *What have I gotten myself into?*

Jason promptly returned to Hawaii to face the full-time task of hammering out the logistical challenges of pulling off EPIC5. Alone, he traveled to each of the five islands, meeting with local community leaders, firming up the travel itinerary, securing lodging, and recruiting locals to provide the critical volunteer crew services we'd need just to get from point A to point B each day intact.

As for me, it was time to roll up my sleeves and get back to work. After having taken a month off from training following the 2009 Ultraman, I'd gotten soft—gaining weight and indulging the feeling of being a "normal person." But now, with a firm EPIC5 start date of May 5, I had an urgent need to get back on the horse with a solid training plan. There was no time to waste.

My first move was calling up my coach to let him know I was ready to resume a training program.

"Great!" said Chris. "What are we training for?"

I took a deep breath. "You're going to laugh" was all I could muster.

Although I'd raced two Ultramans, I was still very much an endurance neophyte in Chris's eyes—inexperienced and easily excitable. But my coach didn't laugh—as I'd thought he might. Instead he responded with tempered enthusiasm. It wouldn't be easy, he said, but it was doable. And he was excited by the challenge of devising a training regimen for something never before attempted. I remember at that moment feeling relief. I knew that if Chris thought I could do it, then it could be done.

How do you prepare for five iron-distance triathlons in five days on five different islands? The question had never been asked, so there existed no proven protocol. With only four short months to prepare, my inclination was to cram as many miles and hours as possible into each day. But that wasn't the answer. Instead, Chris devised a program built around a single premise: *slow down.* To be sure, plenty of miles. But the intensity of all my sessions was capped far below what I'd grown accustomed to. Whether swimming, biking, or running, the idea was to acclimate the body to be *always moving.* To adapt to the progressive fatigue I'd face, I even experimented with sleep deprivation, pulling very late nights at work followed by full days of training on little more than two or three hours of sleep.

But the main thing I had to remember was that this wasn't a "race." EPIC5 had nothing to do with going fast, let alone winning. Rather, it was better to frame it as an adventure, the goal being nothing more than finishing each day hand in hand with Jason. All for one and one for all.

Julie and the kids wanted to join me in Hawaii to support the challenge, but we quickly realized that the daily inter-island travel would prove too daunting for our little ones. So we decided I'd have to take this one on without the crew that had supported me so well at the 2009 Ultraman.

Thus it was that on April 30, 2010, I flew alone out to the lush garden isle of Kauai several days before our start date to get acclimated to the tropical heat and humidity, as well as to aid Jason with the last-minute details. When I arrived, it was immediately apparent just how much work Jason, along with his friend and Kauai local Rebecca Morgan, had put into the preparations. Rebecca's condo in Princeville, on the north shore, had been transformed into EPIC5 headquarters, every inch of floor space covered with gear contributed by sponsors. Courtesy of bicycle manufacturer Specialized: helmets and cleats to go with high-end S-Works Transition time-trial bikes. From Zoot Sports: dozens of new running shorts, shoes, socks, visors, and compression gear. And from Vega, CarboPro, and Hammer: countless oversized jugs of performance nutrition.

I didn't know it at the time, but Rebecca would become our sherpa, event producer, and overall lifesaver. She was the only person who traveled with Jason and me to every island. She never left our side and never lost sight of the goal of getting us home in one piece. It's not an exaggeration to say that we could never have done this without her help. Never. Completely devoted to the cause, she was the true embodiment of the *ohana* spirit that defines the best of not just Hawaii, but humanity. She was our angel.

We spent the last few days running errands, doing some light training, nailing down final support-crew arrangements, and pinpointing the final iron-distance route on each island. An event like this is won or lost on these types of preparations. With such enormous distances to cover, tiny issues can become huge problems if not handled properly. For example, forgetting the Vaseline to put between one's toes can result in a blister that could easily derail the entire adventure. So lists were made, bins packed and meticulously labeled. And Rebecca, bless her soul, took care of all of it.

Meanwhile, I was eating like a fiend. I told Jason that my goal was to gain as much weight as possible the week before. Generally, I try to be as lean as possible for a race without jeopardizing power output. But again, we weren't racing, and I felt it was more important to "store the chestnuts." No matter how much we ate during the event, a gigantic caloric deficit was almost inevitable as the days wore on, so like a bear heading into hibernation, I was gorging myself on as much nutrient-dense, high-octane plant-based food as I could get my hands on—heaps of vegan lasagna, mounds of lentils and beans over steamed brown rice, quinoa doused in coconut oil, and my precious superfood Vitamix blends. All told, I probably put on eight pounds that week alone. And Chris advised me that despite the race's immense caloric toll, my body would likely continue to *gain* weight over the course of the five days—only to drop it like a rock in the seven to ten days following. Apparently, when the body senses that it is in caloric jeopardy, it works overtime to retain fluids and store fats to simply survive. I had a hard time believing that Chris was correct on this point. But of course, that's exactly what happened.

DAY ONE: KAUAI

LET THE INSANITY BEGIN

The last flight off Kauai to Oahu on May 5—the first day of EPIC5—was at 7:52 P.M. This was cutting things very close; it meant we had to begin our first day hours before daybreak.

For safety reasons, we didn't want to bike or swim in total darkness, so we decided to kick Day One off with the marathon, starting promptly at 3:00 A.M., then swim the 2.4 miles in Hanalei Bay, and finish with a 112-mile ride across the entire island and back to finish at the airport in time to make our flight to Oahu. Otherwise, we'd be screwed.

With such an early start, we hit the hay the night before at 7:00 P.M. I'm not sure I'd slept a wink when the alarm sounded at 2:30 A.M.

We didn't waste any time. Rebecca had already packed the van, so all Jason and I had to do was throw our running clothes on, grab some quick breakfast—a green smoothie and some quinoa with berries for me—head out the condo door, and start running. Just another early-morning training run, right? Donning headlamps to light our path, we simply began—no press, no fanfare, no cheering, no start gun—just Rebecca with a smile on her face and a quick snapshot taken in her driveway to mark the seemingly uneventful occasion.

"This is it, Roll-Dawg. You ready?"

"Bring it," I said, coasting on the adrenaline of the moment. "Easy is as easy does," I added, channeling my inner Forrest Gump.

Only a couple of miles in, we were calmly running along the dark main highway toward the sleepy north shore town of Hanalei when a car slowed next to us. I figured it must be someone wondering why on earth two people would be running along the highway in the middle of the night with headlamps on! To my surprise, it was a woman who'd heard about what we were doing and just wanted to give us a cheer of support—at 3:30 A.M.! The window rolled down and a face peeked out. "Hi, boys! I knew I'd find you!" the woman exclaimed, grinning broadly. I had no idea who this person was. But it was immediately apparent she knew exactly who we were. "I just had to come see for myself! Make us proud!" And with that she rolled up the window and pulled away, the taillights of her car disappearing down the dark highway. "That was wild," Jason said. "Pretty cool" I responded. This was my first inkling that what we were attempting might mean something to people other than ourselves.

Only moments later, we ran up on a police car, blue and red lights swirling. *Was there an accident? Is someone being arrested? Are we somehow breaking the law?*

As we tentatively approached, the officer leaned out his window. "Aloha! Looking good, boys! Keep going!" Turns out it was Detective Kekoa Ledesma, husband of one of our key Kauai logistics volunteers, Lisa Kaili Ledesma. An avid surfer and water man himself, Kekoa would soon reappear back at Hanaeli Bay to guide my swim on his paddleboard. I was floored by this living example of *ohana*. And we'd barely begun.

The sun started to rise as Jason and I approached the far reaches of Kauai's north shore at Haena—a place resembling the end of the Earth, where the highway suddenly stops at the water's edge, leaving the Napali Coast Trail as the only means of traveling to the island's other side. Green mountains rise straight up above terrain so lush it's like a scene out of *King Kong* or *Jurassic Park*. The end of this road marked the half-marathon mark. So far, so good. *Feeling strong.* But the casual chatter between us was starting to fade as the realization of the work ahead began to settle in. I forced myself to relax and focus, not push our pace. Even so, heading back toward

Hanalei my thighs began to grow heavy and my calves began to tighten. Because no matter how relaxed you try to be, there's no escaping the fact that 26.2 miles is still 26.2 miles.

To complete the run we circled through the town of Hanalei before wending our way down to the bay to finish. We ran through an alcove of beach houses, even passing the set for *The Descendants,* a George Clooney movie being filmed in a Hanalei beach house. I'd traveled three thousand miles from Los Angeles to do this event, yet I still couldn't get away from Hollywood!

As we rounded the final corner to the Hanalei Bay public beach picnic area, we were met by cheers from locals who'd turned up to join us for the upcoming swim. After high-fives all around, I determined that we'd completed the first stage in our long journey in just over four hours—certainly not fast by the usual marathon standards, but in strict accordance with a strategy I affectionately coined "persistent conservation."

To say that the swim part of any race is difficult for Jason is an understatement. I can't imagine swimming more than a few strokes, let alone miles, with only one arm. And doing it *after* a marathon? It's staggering that he'd even attempt it. I reminded myself that Jason and I were doing this together, so there was no sense in being aggressive with the swim. *Just enjoy it.* So I let him get started while I chatted with our new local friends and patiently allowed time for my breakfast of bananas, coconut water, and almond butter to properly digest.

I entered the water with about five locals who'd taken the day off from work to join us. We headed out together along the Hanalei Pier and then turned west to traverse the bay a couple hundred meters offshore, where we encountered considerable adverse currents and chop. I put my head down and followed the path set by Detective Ledesma, who guided me on his stand-up paddleboard while the local group swam right behind. My priority was making sure my stomach and legs didn't cramp, a likely scenario after running a marathon and eating. But all was well; the body held together fine. At 1.2 miles, on the far side of the bay, I turned around to head back and became worried after catching glimpses of Jason struggling against the currents. But Jason is tough and I knew better than to check in on him. With the current at my back, it was smooth sailing home and I was done before I knew it. I felt good as I walked up the beach to greet Rebecca and Molly Kline, who'd flown in to chronicle the event for our sponsor Zoot. While they packed up all the gear in Rebecca's Toyota 4Runner, our support vehicle du jour, I grabbed a bottled water and headed for the beach shower, where I rinsed the salt from my body, donned cycling gear, and reclined, trying to conserve every ounce of energy for the course. But it was hard to relax knowing that Jason was still out there, battling the current. Since heading out on the bike without Jason wasn't an option, there was nothing left to do but wait.

After what seemed like eons, Jason finally dragged his weary body out of the bay. Had we known about that current and the challenge it would pose to Jason, we would have undoubtedly rethought leading off the day with a marathon. Because he only has the use of one arm, Jason is forced to use his legs far more vigorously than the typical swimmer in order to maintain proper body position. In contrast, I can let my legs drag behind during the swim, saving them as much as possible for the bike. The quadriceps are huge muscles and require a lot of energy output without much forward swimming propulsion—it's just not efficient to overwork the legs in the water, because the realized gain is minimal when compared to the energy expended. But Jason simply doesn't have the luxury of "saving" his legs. So having to kick hard to combat the current on legs that had already run a marathon that day almost buried him. It was written all over his face. But his only focus was to keep moving forward—hence his mantra and foundation name-sake: *Never Stop*. Head down, he marched directly to the showers to change. When he emerged, his only words:

"What are you waiting for? Let's go."

And so we did. Heading out on the bike with a large group of local cyclists, we departed Hanalei. My energy was good, and Jason seemed to be slowly recovering. I had to keep telling myself not to ride too hard; a few of the locals were excited, anxious to push a vigorous pace. Tempting, for sure. But they only had this one hard ride—I had the big picture to think about. *Be smart,* I kept telling myself. To adhere to my strategy of persistent conservation, I kept dutiful focus on my Garmin bike computer, fully aware that to complete EPIC5 intact my heart rate and watts must both stay far below my aerobic threshold at all times.

At about forty miles in, I stopped to use a restroom, telling the group to go on without me, certain I'd quickly make up the lost time down the road. Back on the bike, I rode alone for a while before I caught up with a local named Johnny Grout, a strong and excitable guy about my age determined to see what I was made of by forcing a strong pace. I foolishly let him, suddenly riding much harder than advised, my Garmin displaying watts far above my self-imposed cap. But I was caught up in Johnny's enthusiasm. *I should slow down,* I thought. Yet I didn't, knowing full well that I'd pay dearly for this on subsequent days. There were times when I was *too* competitive.

With Jason nowhere in sight, Johnny and I focused on our vig-orous tempo and in the process missed a turn on the south side of the island to a coiled stretch near Poipu. It wasn't until many miles farther that I realized the error, having lost touch with the group entirely. Not sure whether to turn back, Johnny and I settled on continuing onward, realizing that we could regroup on the route back from the southwestern end of the island, where I could tack on additional miles as needed by looping around.

Pushing hard down the long, flat highway that tracks Kauai's western shoreline, my head neatly tucked and my arms outstretched on my Easton carbon aero bars—special time trial–bike handle-bars that allow you to rest your elbows on the bike's cockpit—I was doing my best to cut through the considerable winds that were pushing me all over the road. The pace was solid and I was in the groove, albeit still riding well above my recommended pace. I reached to shift gears, and that's when I heard a loud *snap!* My chain gurgled and sputtered until it locked in on the smallest ring on my rear cassette. I quickly realized that I'd broken not just my rear derailleur cable, but the shifter housing as well, leaving me completely unable to maneuver my chain out of the most difficult gear. *Dammit!*

Johnny and I pulled over to survey the problem. Dripping rivers of sweat on my bike, I felt my anxiety swell in proportion to my sinking heart as I wordlessly surveyed the damage.

Johnny broke the silence, doing his best to stem my obvious agitation. "Dude, no worries. Someone will be here soon to help you fix it. We're cool."

But I was in no mood for this hang-loose Hawaiian approach to my crisis. *How is any of this cool?* I wouldn't be able to repair the problem without a proper bike mechanic and proper spare parts—a tall order on an island with only one bike shop and an ill-equipped crew nowhere to be found. To boot, there was zero cell service, so we couldn't call. And since we'd ventured off-course, Rebecca had no idea where we were. There was absolutely nothing we could do aside from wait until someone showed up. Meanwhile, the clock was ticking, our 7:52 P.M. flight departure time looming heavy in my mind.

"Right. Fantastic." I stared off into the deserted inland. Nothing for miles. *This sucks.*

Close to forty-five minutes later, Rebecca and Molly finally arrived to find me in a semi-manic state and fearing for the collapse of the overall EPIC5 challenge not even 20 percent into its completion. Contacting Kauai Cycles—the island's sole bike shop—for help, the two women did their best to calm my nerves. Unfortunately, the shop was on the other side of the island and nobody seemed able to reach the mechanic. *The only mechanic.* I was losing hope. Realizing I could no longer sit around waiting for someone to solve my problem, I decided to soldier on, grinding it out alongside Johnny in the only gear I had—all the way to the northwestern reaches of the island, where the road turns to a fine sandy dirt at Polihale State Park. In the process, I "buried myself," cycling parlance for overextending my effort. My legs now swelled with rivers of lactate that would seriously undermine my body's ability to rebound for tomorrow's test. I logged another twenty or so difficult miles in my hardest gear and was en route back to the Lihue Airport when Johnny and I met up with Jason and his small crew of local riders near Kekaha. Up ahead a steep ascent loomed, but I allowed myself a whisper of hope as I saw the crew van in the distance. I wasn't sure I could climb that hill in my fixed gear. We labored up the initial portion of the climb to a bluff above the ocean to greet our crew, who informed me that the bike mechanic was now en route. Nothing to do but sit tight, during which time I tried to eat but spent most of the wait anxiously pacing, repeatedly checking my watch against our impending 7:52 p.m. deadline. Half an hour later, the mechanic finally arrived, only to inform me he had no real fix; my shifter was completely stripped and he had no replacement part on hand.

I walked away from the group to brood. If I dug deep, I could probably make it up that hill and through the day, but what about tomorrow? *Damn.*

"Rich, calm down. We'll figure it out. We always do." Jason's words relaxed me; I realized that my competitive nature was getting the best of me, and that I didn't want to derail this for Jason. Knowing he was calm about it went a long way toward easing my nerves.

I returned to check on the progress, happily discovering that the mechanic had successfully jerry-rigged a temporary solution to the problem by installing an ill-fitting gear shifter from another bike model. It wasn't ideal, but provided it held up, it should get me through the day, and hopefully the week.

It was now about 5:30 P.M. That left only a little more than two hours to cover the remaining thirty-five miles on the bike back to the airport, unload the van, pack our bags and bikes, and get checked in at the airport in time for our flight. It was time to put our collective heads down and focus. *Gotta make that flight. Get it done.*

It was dusk when Jason and I pulled into the airport parking lot to greet our two crew vehicles. We were elated that we'd just completed the first day of EPIC5. But there was absolutely no time to celebrate. *Fifteen minutes to takeoff.* We were faced with the task of unloading the gigantic load of belongings that had accumulated over the course of the day in the crew vehicles, packing it all up, breaking down our bikes into travel boxes, and getting everything through security in time to board. Meanwhile, Rebecca—the one person who had a grip on where everything was and where it should go—had already departed for Oahu hours earlier to secure our crew van there and get us checked into our hotel. But with the help of Molly and our local volunteers, we worked like a Red Bull–fueled Indy 500 pit crew, frantically jamming items into bags without regard to what should go where. Though we had 140.6 miles under our belts, Jason and I were denied the luxury of even sitting down. We furiously disassembled our bikes and anchored the various parts in hard-case travel boxes before making a mad dash across the parking lot toward the terminal with as much gear as we could possibly haul.

Ten minutes to takeoff.

Luckily, this was Kauai and not JFK, so there were no real lines to contend with. But with inter-island travel, you must carry even your checked bags through security and out onto the tarmac, a challenge almost as daunting as the day itself. Loaded down with hundreds of pounds of gear, including bike boxes, Jason and I bumbled through the terminal to security. We dared to breathe a sigh of relief. It looked like we were going to make it after all.

However, in our exhaustion, we overlooked one crucial fact. As we passed our gear through the metal detectors, the TSA officials took notice of the copious amounts of liquids we were attempting to "smuggle" on board the flight. All of our performance nutrition for the upcoming days. *Damn! No liquids on the plane! How could we forget?*

Five minutes to takeoff.

Security pulled us aside to interrogate us. *Why are you going to Oahu? What are these strange liquids?* They detained us for what seemed like an eternity as we watched them pour out hundreds of dollars of race nutrition—expensive items like FRS and CarboPro 1200 that we'd be hard-pressed to replace. Bad mistake.

Two minutes to takeoff.

We were finally released by TSA, and Jason and I made a frantic sprint for our flight, our depleted bodies hauling our bikes and bags, straining through this final unofficial Day One challenge. With one minute to spare, we arrived at the gate just as the doors on our flight were closing. Finally seated, we burst out laughing, only then realizing that we were both still wearing our cycling kits, our stenchy spandex fouling the cabin. But we didn't care. Day One was in the books. We'd done it.

"That's why it's called a *challenge,* Roll-Dawg!"

Next up, Oahu.

DAY TWO: OAHU

RETRACING HISTORY

A mere thirty odoriferous minutes later, Jason and I landed safely in Honolulu, fantasizing about the dinner we'd yet to eat, the warm shower that beckoned, and the hotel room bed. But not so fast.

Rebecca greeted us at the arrival terminal with our new crew van and bags of Thai takeout food. Normally, I'd have been pissed. Herself a health nut, Rebecca knew all too well how important good nutrition was to successfully completing this adventure. And this fare was garbage. But one look into her eyes and it was obvious she was overwhelmed, forced to handle the work of four people. And just as fatigued as we were. So I happily let it go, grateful for the calories as we collected our gear from the luggage carousel— with one glaring omission. My bike hadn't arrived. It seemed impossible that Jason's bike would make the flight but not mine, yet that's what happened.

Airline officials informed me that my bike somehow "missed" the flight and would "likely" arrive on a subsequent flight routed through a different island, sometime around midnight. Fearing I'd never see a bed that night, let alone my bike, I asked Rebecca to get us settled in our hotel rooms and return to the airport herself to retrieve my trusty steed.

I was never so happy to get out of my cycling attire and into a hot shower. It was now almost 11:00 P.M., with our 5:00 A.M. alarm looming. So recovery luxuries like organic produce, ice baths, and massages were simply out of the question. I still needed more food, but the kind of food I really wanted—brown rice, steamed vegetables, and hand-pressed juice—was an impossibility under these circumstances and at this late hour. Somewhere in the mountain of luggage there were stores of gluten-free granola, raw almonds, and dried fruit, but I was too depleted to root them out. Forced to make do with what was within arm's reach, foods that under normal circumstances I'd never eat, I inhaled as much of the remaining takeout as my stomach could handle—mostly third-rate noodles and overcooked vegetables soaked in corn oil and white rice. Technically vegan but not exactly healthy. And a far cry from the antioxidant-rich, plant-based-protein superfood Vitamix brews I'd come to rely on for proper recovery.

When I awoke the next morning, my fatigue was deeper than I'd expected or wanted it to be. Maybe I'd run that marathon too hard. Or pushed too aggressively on the bike. *Damn you, Johnny,* I thought. And the gluten-rich takeout from the night before hadn't helped. Then again, even an "easy" iron-distance triathlon is still 140.6 miles. Did I really expect that I'd feel good? But I had to check my brain at the door and focus on what lay ahead. First up, I had to reassemble my bike, which Rebecca had rescued last night, and which now sat unboxed and disassembled at the foot of my bed. Just then, I heard a knock.

"Big bro. We have a problem." Jason looked grave.

Holding his bike frame up, Jason explained how, in the haste of the prior evening's bike disassembly, the lug nut that secured his bike's seat post to the frame had somehow been lost. It was one of those "minor" things that create "major" problems. Without this specific, tiny yet utterly crucial piece of gold-colored, triangular-shaped metal, the seat post wouldn't anchor to the frame, rendering the bike impossible to ride. We had to immediately find a replacement part at a local bike shop, rent a backup bike, or throw in the towel for the day. Obstacle management just became an advanced placement course. Then things got worse.

I returned to my room, lamenting how Jason could allow this to happen—granted, we were in a state of anxiety-fueled delirium when we were breaking down the bikes, but this was a rookie mistake! But as I began to piece my own bike together, I quickly realized that I had the same problem. It seemed that I, too, had managed to lose the same piece of equipment. *Who's the rookie now, smart guy!?*

Jason and I were riding the same bike model—top-of-the-line S-Works Transition time-trial bikes, given to us by Specialized Bicycle Components, one of our key event sponsors. Like high-end race cars, these bikes are composed of a very specific array of modules and components, completely unique to this bike model and no other. That meant that jerry-rigging or swapping parts from another bike was a highly unlikely solution to our problem.

Left with no alternative, we headed across the street from the hotel to the protected lagoon at Ala Moana Beach Park, just west of famous Waikiki Beach, to begin our assault on the Ironman course originally conceived by Navy Commander John Collins back in 1978, before the race was moved to the Big Island in 1981.

It was a beautiful dawn, and despite my fatigue, I welcomed the warm, calm waters as the sun rose. I used the swim to shake off the anxiety of our mechanical setback, losing myself in the metronome of my stroke. I thought of it as an active meditation; I visualized success, balanced my emotional frame of mind, and made firm my resolve that no matter what followed, Jason and I would get through it together.

Meanwhile, our local crew chief for the day, accomplished ultra-runner Rick Vicek, helped Rebecca load up our vehicle with the day's supplies and began the task of locating the precious replacement bike parts needed.

While Jason completed the swim, I used my iPhone to send out a distress call on Twitter and Facebook, hoping that I could recruit some assistance tracking down the parts. I also posted alerts on the EPIC5 website, which displayed progress updates from our crew, periodic video uploads from the course, and a GPS-enabled map that pinpointed our exact location and telemetry (such as average and current speed) in real time from microprocessor chips Jason and I kept attached to our bodies.

To my amazement, the response to my help requests was almost instantaneous. All across the world, people jumped into action, manning their computers, performing the search on our behalf. Before I could even blink, our "outsourced" viral volunteer staff had forwarded more than a few viable leads. I was beginning to understand some important facts. First, social media had the power to marshal the spirit of *ohana* beyond the shores of Hawaii. And second, our crew wasn't limited to feet on the ground. The support evaporated my fatigue and lifted my spirits. We'd yet to solve the problem. Yet right then and there, I knew for a fact that we would.

Luckily, we were on the metropolitan island of Oahu rather than remote Molokai. A nearby shop that retailed Specialized bikes didn't have the scarce parts available for sale, but they did have two Specialized Transition floor models on display. At first, they refused to strip these bikes of their seat-post clamps. But Jason wasn't the type of person who took no for an answer. He pulled the shop manager aside for a private negotiation—a chat that was part pleading, part charm, and part wheedle. And sure enough, minutes later he returned from the recesses of the shop's back office to announce his success: "Done."

The bad news was that this detour had eaten up an unbelievable amount of time. While the mechanics worked on our bikes, Jason and I nervously checked our watches; it was nearing 11:00 A.M. and we'd yet to really even begin the day's journey. At this rate, it was going to be a very, very long day.

But all we could do was accept the situation for what it was.

Let go. We couldn't afford to expend energy on frustration or failed expectations. In truth, we were incredibly lucky to get this mechanical issue resolved at all. Had we been on any other island, we might have been facing 112 miles of cycling on loaned beach cruiser bikes! It was now 11:15, but we were finally suited up and ready to go.

Then it started to rain.

Jason met my growing concern with a smile, repeating his now favorite line. "Like I said, Roll-Dawg, that's why it's called a challenge! The EPIC5 Challenge!"

It took what seemed like forever to ride out of the Honolulu and Waikiki city limits, since we had to stop every half mile or so for a stoplight. But we eventually made it out of town and began heading north around the eastern edge of the island, facing strong headwinds on rolling climbs and a few sharp ascents. Chasing daylight, I once again fought the urge to ride too hard, keeping my energy levels in check. *Persistent conservation.* It was going to be a long day no matter what I did at this point. *Just sit back and enjoy the ride.*

It worked. Taking in the sublime beauty of Oahu's North Shore, I pondered what it must have been like for John Collins and his cohorts back in 1978, attempting this course for the very first time. The reverie was effective in distracting me from my fatigue and soreness that was now quickly creeping into my "undercarriage," polite cycling parlance for the butt region. Anyone who logs a lot of miles on a bike likely knows the unique pain brought about by saddle sores, boil-like infections that creep into the sensitive derma lining the "sit bones." The only real solution is strong disinfectant, a couple days off the bike, and in very serious cases, lancing. Obviously, none of these was an option.

In the weeks leading up to EPIC5, we were well aware that we needed a solid strategy to avoid saddle sores. Responding to the

challenge, Jason had turned up a well-tested "chamois cream" recipe. Conceived by legendary ultra-endurance mountain bike racer
and cycling design pioneer Keith Bontrager, the ointment consisted
of hydrocortisone cream, petroleum jelly, lanolin, and Neosporin.
Before each ride, we liberally applied scoops of this hand-mixed
goopy medicinal mess to our rear ends in hopes of keeping infection at bay. But today I began to realize that our preventive efforts
had fallen short.

In retrospect, it had been unwise to remain in our cycling shorts
during the flight the night before. Every cyclist knows that to avoid
saddle sores you must get out of your bib and shower immediately
after every ride, then apply an antibacterial such as tea-tree oil to
the region to further disinfect. More rookie mistakes. But there was
little I could do about it now.

And no escaping the fact that the sheen of our epic quest was
beginning to loose its luster. Heads down, Jason and I barely spoke
all day, resolved to put this ride and all of its missteps firmly in our
rear view.

After passing through Haleiwa on the island's North Shore, we
turned south en route back to Honolulu and faced a long ascent
made more arduous by blustery trade winds. I love a challenging
climb and felt a sudden resurgence of energy as I dug deep to conquer the pesky grade.

Soon we'd descended back into more populated areas and were
once again tortured by endless stoplights and heavy traffic. The
last twenty miles of the ride should have taken us about an hour.
Instead, it took almost two and a half hours of dodging cars and
constant red-light stops. It was getting dark and we were weary, to
say the least. Along the final stretch of the Nimitz Highway nearing the Honolulu Airport, we stopped at yet again another red
light. Jason and I looked at each other. It wasn't hard to read each
other's mind.

"This is ridiculous," I said, as I munched on an avocado and Vegenaise sandwich that I'd tucked in the back pocket of my jersey, and downed a coconut water handed off to me by Rebecca through the window of the crew van. "How did I let you talk me into this nonsense? Are we really going to run a marathon tonight? We should just call it a night and run the marathon in the morning."

"Don't even think about it," retorted Jason. I shut up.

At Ala Moana Beach Park, Rebecca and Rick greeted us with a change of clothes and a dose of solid nutrition. To my amazement, there were about a dozen local runners and triathletes gathered to join us for the run. The peppy group greeted us warmly. They brimmed with energy reserves, but I could barely muster a smile. With darkness having settled in, I couldn't believe I was about to run a marathon.

I chugged a recovery "Endurance Elixir" that I'd brought—a concoction conceived specifically for me by my friend Compton Rom, a PhD in microbiology and the founder of wellness start-up Ascended Health. An entirely plant-based formula loaded with high-caliber nutrients sourced from the four corners of the globe— fermented greens, adaptogens, probiotics, Cordyceps mushroom extracts, marine phytoplankton, and exotic antioxidants, like nattokinase, resveratrol, and quercetin—it's not particularly flavorful but always revives me like nature's Red Bull (for more information on this and other Ascended Health products, see Appendix III, Resources). During training, I generally only drink a few ounces a day to boost my recovery. But I was a walking dead man desperate for resuscitation, so I downed a full sixteen-ounce bottle and headed for the showers. After rinsing off, I couldn't believe how quickly I began returning to life. *God bless you, Compton* was all I could think. I mustered a smile and introduced myself to the local running crew, grateful for the company to break the monotony and hoping I could absorb their energy. At that moment, I honestly didn't believe that I was physically or mentally able to run a marathon. But the only way out was through.

One foot in front of the other. Turn the brain off. Keep it simple and just begin. And so I did.

We headed out along Kalakaua Avenue, Waikiki's main commercial drag, where I soaked in the warm air and absorbed the electricity of the lively tourist crowds. After spending the last two days traversing the remotely populated and undeveloped corners of Kauai and Oahu's North Shore, it was surreal to now witness flip-flopped teens fiddling with iPods inside a brightly lit Apple Store as we dodged packs of college students pub-crawling their way through spring break, women surveying handbags outside Louis Vuitton, and honeymooning couples dining at the many outdoor cafés. The energy of it all returned needed life to my tattered body. And after about two miles, I felt like a brand-new person. *I actually felt good.*

As we cleared Waikiki and headed up and around Diamond Head to tackle the Honolulu Marathon course, our group slowly dwindled. Twelve became ten; ten became eight. And soon all that remained were Jason, me, and a small core group from the Hawaii Ultra Running Team ("HURT"). Given that it was already nine o'clock on a weeknight, I figured they, too, would drop off soon, so I tried to enjoy the company while we had it. But I underestimated the hard-core nature of this crew. It became evident that these people—endurance junkies with names like Chet "The Jet" Blanton—intended to run the entire marathon with us. No big deal. Apparently, banging out a casual marathon after dinner on a weeknight was just a normal thing to do. And I thought I was nuts.

Beyond Diamond Head, we ran as a group through the night along Kalanianaole Highway, a heavily trafficked, grimy thoroughfare, before turning around at the half-marathon mark. It was here that the rubber began to hit the road. My blinders came down and I stopped chatting. I purposely isolated myself away from Jason and the group to eliminate distractions. I was laying down a decent pace and feeling strong, but I was still facing about nine miles and my thighs were growing heavy. The iPod went on. And even though it was dark, I pulled my visor low on my forehead. At times I even closed my eyes for as long as I thought I safely could, engaging a deep active meditation, enveloped by the dark. I was now deep in the "pain cave," that impossibly dark place where all sensory perception is obliterated and replaced by one overriding and singular sensation—suffering. My peripheral vision narrowed to the oval light cast by my headlamp. Each stride brought shearing pain up my thighs, as if my quadriceps were being julienned by daggers. And the bottoms of my feet were on fire, as if I were running barefoot on hot coals. But that didn't mean I wasn't happy. I was exactly where I wanted to be.

As we entered the marathon's final two-and-a-half-mile stretch in Kapiolani Park, the HURT crew continued to chat, miraculously appearing as fresh as they had during mile 1. In contrast, I struggled. Forget about form and technique—that had dwindled miles ago. Staying upright, moving one leg in front of the other was a victory. *Just get to the next lamppost. . . .* Two laps around the park seemed interminable. But Jason and I made it to the finish and even mustered up enough energy to hug and get out a few celebratory words in the haze of exhaustion. And as we sat on the curb with the HURT crew still cheerfully chatting as the clock ticked past 1:00 A.M., it dawned on me. We'd made it. Two consecutive iron-distance triathlons in the books. Even if we stopped now, we'd accomplished something nobody else had ever done.

But what about tomorrow? Our itinerary called for a 3:50 A.M. wake-up call. If we didn't abide by it, we wouldn't have the time required to get out of bed, pack, check out of the hotel, and make a 6:20 A.M. flight to Molokai to begin Day Three. Jason and I both knew that this wasn't going to happen. I wouldn't say that it was impossible, but it was close. The primary idea was that we'd complete the five iron-distance triathlons. The goal was to do it in five days, but the schedule didn't anticipate the mechanical obstacles that had so severely delayed us. If we adhered to the schedule, we'd face maybe *ninety minutes of sleep* before heading to the airport to do it all over again on another island.

We were too tired. If we stuck to the schedule, the bigger goal—finishing the five—would likely capsize. Better to stick to the challenge than to stick to a schedule that would bury us. So we decided to sleep in the following day and hop an afternoon flight to Molokai. In other words, we'd take a much-needed rest day. It was disappointing to know that we wouldn't be able to complete the challenge within our five-day goal. To be sure, part of me was pissed. But this was something I just had to make peace with—and it turned out to be the right decision.

By the time we got back to the hotel, it was after 2:00 in the morning. And with our nutrition cooler completely depleted until Rebecca could restock at the grocer the following day, we once again found ourselves eating lousy Thai food out of Styrofoam boxes, apparently the only food available at this late hour. All I could think was *Are you kidding me? Again?*

It's easy to criticize Rebecca for failing to ensure an appropriate meal at day's end. In a perfect world, we would have enlisted additional volunteers to avoid such mishaps. But all of us had underestimated the overwhelming logistics of pulling off this adventure, not to mention the sheer volume of food Jason and I ingested each day. Without a doubt, Rebecca had been overworked and underappreciated since the first day. Her hands were more than full. And she was doing the best she could under extremely challenging circumstances. There was simply no point in getting upset. So despite my desperate need for proper nourishment, I happily turned off my morning alarm and instantly lost all consciousness.

DAY THREE: MOLOKAI

THE REAL HAWAII

When I awoke around 10:00 A.M., the fatigue was deep but manageable, especially knowing that we'd have a little recovery time before taking on the Island of Molokai, Hawaii's most remote and mysterious atoll. Rebecca returned our van and arranged for an afternoon flight while I stayed in bed for two more hours, eating and talking to my wife and kids on the phone.

"Hi, Daddy! Are you still riding your bike?" The greeting from Mathis boosted my spirits higher than any double espresso. "Mommy says you're very tired. You should really get some sleep, you know. Sleep is very good."

Truer words had never been spoken. Julie was anxious to hear all the details of our previous day. I did my best to recount the highlights, but in truth I was simply too tired to spin a proper yarn. But that was okay; just knowing I was safe was all Julie needed.

Around one o'clock Jason, Rebecca, and I met in the hotel lobby, where Jason proudly greeted me with a copy of the day's *Honolulu Advertiser,* Oahu's primary newspaper. Right there on the front page was a picture of Jason and me biking along Oahu's eastern shore.

"Cool!" I said, amazed that our adventure had made the news. Reading the piece, my disappointment that we'd blown our tight schedule faded. People were watching, taking notice, reminding us once again that we weren't alone. What was important now was that we finish what we started.

After a brief and stress-free bunny hop of a flight, we landed in the tiny, sparse, and relatively unpopulated island of Molokai. Measuring only thirty-eight miles long and ten miles wide, Molokai is best known for its history as a quarantined leper colony.

Now acknowledged more for its staunch preservation, the arid and tourist-free hamlet was a welcome and stark contrast to the urban landscape of Oahu.

At the airport—more like a landing strip—we were greeted by Jessie Ford, the field administrator for Coffees of Hawaii, a five-hundred-acre premium coffee plantation. The business is family-run by Albert Broyce, a fellow Stanford graduate as well as an accomplished and passionate endurance athlete who'd graciously agreed to sponsor our efforts. And the support was superb, soup to nuts.

Jessie didn't waste time filling the role of our very own Molokai Princess, helping us load our gear and then driving us straight to the plantation. As we pulled away from the airport, we saw a road sign that read: SLOW DOWN, THIS IS MOLOKAI. And as we'd soon discover, Molokai indeed has a velocity all its own.

After a short drive, we arrived at the Coffees of Hawaii plantation, where Jessie gave us the keys to our own guest house—a first-rate home complete with kitchen, laundry, and fully stocked refrigerator. Not to mention our own vegan chef, who later that evening brought us a cornucopia of home-prepared dishes sufficient to feed a dozen people. Talk about *ohana*!

For the first time since we began the journey, I was able to fortify with the foods my body was screaming for. Our host's chef prepared a mind-blowing menu that included organic olive-oil coconut butter; garden-sprouted quinoa; mole with tomatoes, raisins, chopped walnuts, and garlic; vegan fettuccini alfredo made with pureed squash noodles; cashew cheese; beet borscht; mashed potatoes; and a dessert of avocado chocolate mousse with macadamia nut whipped cream. I was in heaven.

After eating as much as we possibly could, we hit the sack early. I slept like a baby and was up before dawn, raring to go for iron-distance triathlon number three. With the sun now rising,

Jessie and Rebecca shuttled us across the island to the western coast, where we met up with Molokai native Phillip Kikukawa and his nine-year-old son, Luke, who'd serve as our morning swim crew. Phillip teaches at the island's only middle school, and he and his wife Sue—a Dartmouth-educated Olympic cross-country skier and yogi from Alaska who continues to train for Alaskan Nordic events by "sand skiing" along local Popohaku Beach—own Molokai Bicycles, the island's sole bike shop. To give you a sense of the pace of life on this sleepy isle, the shop is open only two days a week for three or four hours at a time.

In a battered pickup truck, Phillip and Luke led us down bumpy dirt back roads to Popohaku Beach. The second-largest beach in all of Hawaii, Popohaku is a three-mile stretch of pristine shoreline almost untouched by man. I watched deer dart through kiawe trees alongside us as we made our way to the water, and it was undeniable that we'd found the real Hawaii—a big reason I was even on this adventure in the first place.

Given the strong north-to-south current and considering Jason's swim struggles on Kauai, we settled on a point-to-point swim course beginning at the north end of the beach and exiting 2.4 miles downshore to the south. This would make for an "easy swim" with favorable currents. As we walked down the sand to shore, not one soul could be seen in any direction. "I'm going naked, guys," I said to Phillip and Jason, only half-joking. They laughed, of course, and I chickened out, but in retrospect, I really wish I had.

Feeling like I wanted to make this swim in solitude, I declined any crew aid and hopped in the ocean, leaving Phillip to meet me on the south end while Luke paddled alongside Jason in the family kayak. As I began, it was immediately apparent just how strong the current was, in my favor. I felt as though I could have rolled onto my back and floated to the finish. To put things in perspective, I'm usually able to cover an iron-distance swim in forty-eight to fifty-two minutes, give or take. But this swim required only forty-three minutes, barely raising my heart rate in the process. It was so quick that when I finished, Phillip had yet to arrive. I took solace in the isolation and sat quietly on the beach to meditate for a full fifteen minutes.

Soon, Phillip, Rebecca, and Jessie arrived. As I waited for Jason to complete the swim, I washed down a plate of leftover vegan fettuccini and mashed potatoes with coconut water, changed into my cycling gear, and helped the crew load our van with the day's provisions. Greeting Jason as he emerged from the ocean, I joined him in hauling the kayak almost two hundred yards up the beach to the truck.

"I think this is the only triathlon where the athletes have to haul a boat as part of the swim-to-bike transition," Jason remarked with a wry chuckle.

Because Molokai is only 38 miles long, cycling 112 miles required a creative course that entailed multiple loops crisscrossing the island. Meeting strong headwinds and a sparse terrain, we pointed our bikes eastward and had only tracked a few miles when we were met by local cyclist Will Carlson. A mainlander who'd originally migrated to Molokai to lead mountain biking tours and now worked as a special education teacher, Will was a strong rider who solidified himself as our official bike sherpa and tour guide for the day. He regaled us with stories about the history of Molokai, local political gossip, and points of interest along the way.

Having banked a day of rest, Jason and I were both feeling good on the bike. Back to our normal selves, we took in the landscape of the "most Hawaiian" island of Hawaii (other than the privately owned island of Niihau) and truly enjoyed the ride. Despite the island's population of only 7,400 and almost complete absence of stoplights, there seemed to be an impossible number of churches. "The highest per capita in the state," Will informed us, an artifact of the work of Father Damien, the Belgian priest whose work ministering to the legally quarantined community of people suffering from leprosy came to define Molokai and resulted in his sainthood.

Churches aside, Molokai is also widely known as the "spiritual hub" of Hawaii. People with psychic abilities have widely commented on the power of this particular island, and although I wouldn't consider myself extraordinarily empathic, I did feel—as we cycled through the dilapidated hilltop village of Maunaloa, which had been left essentially deserted in the wake of the anti-development political forces that had compelled closure of the ill-fated Molokai Ranch development many years earlier—the conflict of light and dark energy. For a momentary spell, the effect was so powerful I had difficulty maintaining a straight line on my bike. But as soon as I descended eastward with Maunaloa firmly in my rear view, the aching vanished and my balance returned.

Before I departed for Hawaii, Julie had repeatedly implored me to "respect the power of the islands. No matter what, stay in gratitude. And most important, ask the kahunas for permission to tread their sacred land. Every day. Out loud."

Her urgings had at the time seemed, well, very in keeping with her spiritual outlook on life, but after this disorienting experience in Maunaloa, I was suddenly hyperaware of my tenuous guest status on the island. I'm not sure whether I was drunk on endorphins or truly more conscious of the reality of things, but I actually found myself calling out loud on my bike: "Thank you for letting me experience your home. Please allow my friends and me safe passage; permit us to grace your sacred space. I promise to tread lightly and repay your blessing with gratitude and service."

Did I really just say those words? Out loud?

As we approached the eastern portion of the island, the terrain morphed from parched to lush forest—a welcome break. But that break would be brief. Hugging the rugged coastline, we wended around the craggy shoreline before heading up the climb to Halawa Beach Park, a tough ascent with grades of 14 to 15 percent at times. Though conscious of maintaining our energy reserves, we were nonetheless careful not to slow too much, which would have required grinding gears to climb—something to avoid with a marathon in view. After successfully reaching the top of the ascent at a state park, we took a quick bathroom and nutrition break before heading back down to the western edge of the island without incident. Fatigue was creeping in and the heat was taking its toll, but Jason and I managed a strong and consistent pace through the flats of Kaunakakai town, to complete the ride on the port village's long pier with plenty of daylight to spare.

After a shower at the pier that washed off the salt and grime of the day's ride, we quickly changed into our running gear, anxious to keep moving while we still had plenty of daylight. Jason and I drank some Endurance Elixir and greeted Rodney Nelson, another schoolteacher, training for Ironman Arizona, as well as high school cross-country standout Akona Adolpho, who were both anxious to join us for the entirety of our next leg—the third marathon of EPIC5. Without fanfare, we began with a light jog down the pier, then headed east through town along the main road, where we met up with a large crew made up of more schoolteachers and local schoolkids, pumped to join the fun.

As the sun went down, we welcomed the cool evening air. Jason and I chatted with the excited kids and Jessie, jogging right alongside us. A natural-born runner, Akona told me about his favorite local trail runs and life as a teenager on Molokai. At around the eight-mile mark, in a demonstration of his mettle, he shot ahead, leaving us in the dust.

"See ya in a few miles, youngblood!" I called after him, sharing a knowing laugh with Jason. It wouldn't be too long before he hit that certain wall. We'd all been there. But you can't tell a teenager anything. Soon enough he'd learn for himself.

With the sun now set, we had to make our way along the main road in near-total blackness—there are no streetlamps on Molokai—guided only by our headlamps, dancing beams bouncing off the pavement to the beat of our communal rhythm. At about eleven miles in, I pulled off the road to relieve myself in the bushes. Unfortunately, I made the mistake of doing this right next to an old RV partially obscured in the brush, alarming a group of dogs, supposedly fenced in. Alerted by their furious barking, a man emerged from his house across the street to see the beam of my headlamp darting about in the direction of his dilapidated trailer.

"Hey, you! You're trespassing! If you know what's good for you, you'll get off my property! *Now!*"

I'd chosen what might have been the absolute worst place on the entire island for a bathroom break. The barking escalated in ferocity as the islander marched toward me, intent on rooting out why I was snooping around his property with a headlamp.

"What do you think you're doing!?" the man roared. It wasn't what he thought, but I doubted he'd appreciate my answer. I said nothing.

Worried that he'd release his pack of killer guard dogs, I quickly pulled up my shorts and hightailed it out of there.

"You come back and I'll shoot your ass!"

I must have covered the next mile in under six minutes, not feeling safe until he was well out of sight and earshot. Maybe, I thought, as soon as I could think clearly, something untoward and possibly illegal was going on in that home—something our friendly neighbor didn't want me discovering. I'd just bumped up against some of that dark island energy I'd sensed earlier. Sure, this kind of thing could happen anywhere. But why me? And why now? Then

I remembered my promise to tread lightly, an oath I'd clearly just violated. Karma comes quick on Molokai. *Time to be more careful.* I chided myself, still shaking. "Calm down," I repeated out loud, catching sight of the other runners. *Focus, find your center.*

And just up the road, I found it. As we neared the half-marathon mark, Akona was running out of gas. As predicted, his excitable adolescence was finally getting the best of him.

"Told ya I'd see you soon." It was a good learning experience, well earned.

But I'd soon meet my match in our youngest crew member, Akona's younger brother, CJ, a boy no more than eight or nine years old who joined us about fourteen miles in after convincing his parents to come out and run with us in the dark. He was a shirtless and stubby little island whippet in worn-out sneakers and light blue basketball shorts that draped below his knees; the crown of his head barely reached as high as my waist. But what he lacked in size he more than made up for in focus and concentration. I figured he'd run a mile or so for fun, then head home—maybe get two miles tops. Instead, CJ matched me stride for stride for many a dark mile as his parents and siblings followed us in their nearby minivan. *What's with these Adolpho brothers?* "Hey, buddy, it's a school night. Isn't it past your bedtime?" I asked him with a grin.

But CJ was humorless and silent, intent on getting the job done. I couldn't even get a smile. His only response was an undecipherable grunt before accelerating, his arms pumping furiously as sweat dripped down his tanned back. The only thing more impressive than his technique was his determination and focus.

I took a sip of coconut water from the bottle lodged in my fuel belt. Then I heard him speak for the first time.

"Gimme that coconut water!"

"You got it, CJ." I handed it over to him. Between labored breaths, he took a hit and handed it back to me, his gaze never losing focus on the road ahead, lit by the beam of my headlamp. I couldn't help but grin. Gotta love the passion! Soon up the road, we passed his family, congregated in the minivan.

"Who *is* this kid!?" I called out to his proud parents.

CJ ended up running the entire remaining distance that night, well over ten miles. I'd later learn that when he found out what Jason and I were doing, he'd pestered his parents relentlessly until they agreed to let him come out and run with us that school night. And it didn't just make his day—it made his year. I can honestly say that having him along with us was one of the highlights of the entire EPIC5 experience. Connecting with Hawaii, inspiring people, spreading a message of healthful and positive living—running alongside this kid captured all of it in spades.

Hitting the twenty-mile mark as we reached town, the group began to splinter. I turned around and headed back the way we'd come for a three-mile jaunt up and back to complete the distance, while Jason and a few others opted to head in the other direction for a change of scenery. Now alone, I was back where I'd been in those final miles on Oahu a few days before—iPod on, peripheral vision narrowing, and holding on for dear life. One foot in front of the other. And for the first time I began to feel blisters forming on my feet. I'd been lucky in that I'd never had a problem with blisters. After two Ultraman World Championships and thousands of training miles, not once had I gotten a blister. But now my feet were on fire. Every step sent shooting pains from the bottom of my feet up my legs. *Just keep moving.*

Eventually, I found myself at the finish, the day complete. Jason and his crew of runners soon joined me from the other direction. Gingerly, I removed my shoes and surveyed my feet, certain to find the pads covered in blisters. But to my amazement, there were none. To this day I'm not sure what caused my severe foot pain that night—possibly hotspots, temporary but painful flare-ups on the foot's tender underside, caused by incessant pounding, that make you believe your feet are on fire. But I was grateful I wouldn't be facing Day Four—now a mere eight hours away—with that other, more common but debilitating malady. A small consolation for what would prove—bar none—the most challenging day in my athletic career: *Maui.*

DAY FOUR: MAUI

EMBRACING THE VOID

Without a doubt, Maui would present Jason and me with our most difficult EPIC5 test. But this time, our challenges wouldn't arise in the form of mechanical failures, crew mishaps, or anything else beyond our control. Instead, they'd be struggles of an internal sort, asking us to come to our own private conclusions about how much punishment the body can take.

In my last moments of consciousness before falling asleep the night before in Molokai, I'd felt mired in a welter of emotions— fear, dread, exhaustion. It was as if I were staring down the barrel of a gun. Jason and I were utterly depleted. And every inch of me wanted to quit.

But my *final* thought before I fell asleep in Molokai? *Three down. Two to go. Bring it on.*

Nonetheless, when the predawn alarm bell sounded against the backdrop of crowing Molokai plantation roosters that next morning, I felt as if I'd slept no more than an hour, tops. I could barely lift my body out of bed. Each limb felt like it had been injected with lead. Wobbling to the kitchen, I mumbled a zombie greeting to Rebecca, who'd risen an hour earlier to pack our bags and load the car for the quick jaunt down to the airport for our 7:30 A.M. flight to Maui. She was our Eveready battery, always charged.

We arrived at the Maui airport in a thorazine haze, greeted by the already searing sun and blustery winds—an omen of the challenges we'd meet on the bike later that day. Our apprehension was somewhat tempered by the warm welcome of local Paul Hopwood, an outstanding ultra-runner and member of the HURT crew then diligently training for the legendary Western States 100 trail race, considered one of the most prestigious and difficult trail ultra-marathons in the world. Paul had volunteered to crew for us throughout the day, and so despite vast fatigue, my spirits lifted. I was grateful to have an endurance expert on hand for the ordeal to come as we quickly loaded up and headed down to Kamaole Beach in Kihei.

At the beach parking lot, crowded with tourists looking forward to a lazy day drenched in sun and surf, we donned our swim gear in the public locker rooms. Since our sleep-deprived minds were still clouded in a thick fog and our overworked bodies equally compromised, what should have taken ten minutes, preparing for the swim, took almost thirty. I just couldn't seem to find the where-withal to get moving. I should have been getting warmed up, doing some stretching, applying sunscreen and Vaseline to guard against the painful rash that inevitably develops in my underarms from the rubbing caused by the swim. I should have been reviewing the day's plan with Paul and organizing my nutrition and gear for the swim-to-bike transition. Instead, I sat motionless on the car bumper slowly nibbling a banana, vacantly staring off into the distance, reluctant to even move. Clearly, I was trying to avoid the inevitable, but while I dithered, the sun simply grew hotter.

We'd anticipated a 9:00 A.M. start for the swim; however, it was already inching toward 10:00. No words were exchanged, but at one point Jason and I looked at each other and I saw in his eyes that he felt as I did: Completing an iron-distance triathlon in our current state seemed totally impossible.

I shook my head, then immediately regretted that I'd wasted dwindling reserves on anything negative. *Not helpful,* I thought. *Why are you playing the victim? We're all tired . . .* I strained to affect a positive attitude. But inside, all I could think was *This is beyond ridiculous.* Jason had become a man of very few words—perhaps his means of conserving every ounce of energy for the demands ahead. Or maybe like me, he knew it was just better to keep any fear or negativity to himself, to submerge it below his poker-face exterior. When I looked at him, all I heard in my mind was his mantra, *That's why it's called a challenge.*

As if I could forget. Our eyes locked again, the absurdity of the moment percolating to the surface. We both wanted to complain, but we bit our tongues. And the most unlikely thing occurred. We both burst into uncontrollable, exhaustion-fueled laughter, giggling like teenage girls. Catharsis. The only appropriate response. And a better pain salve than a morphine drip.

Armed with that moment, we ventured down the beach to greet the surf, the sand already burning the soles of my worn feet. Unlike Kauai's Hanalei Bay or the deserted sands of Molokai's Popohaku Beach, Kamaole was a swarming tourist enclave, set against a backdrop of bustling shops and busy restaurants. Everything about the calming atmosphere said, *Relax; take a break; this is a vacation.*

Tempting, to be sure.

As gentle waves soothed my hot feet in a gurgle of white foam, I took comfort in our anonymity, knowing that not a single beachgoer had the slightest clue about our adventure. At the water's edge, a little girl no more than four was busy filling a blue bucket with wet sand. Staring at her and the turquoise beyond, I momentarily lost myself in her vacation moment, recalling carefree days of my childhood spent along the shores of Lake Michigan. I wondered how I'd gotten from there to here.

But the time had come to get to work. With a deep inhale,

I filled my lungs with the warm salty air and gingerly waded in. Submerging my body up to the neck, I closed my eyes and floated spread-eagled, centering myself for a very brief meditation. It was a desperate attempt to release the mind, to put distance between my negative thoughts and my higher purpose, to get in touch with the idea that who I am is not defined by what I "think" or even how I "feel" in a given moment. *You are not your mind, you are not your body* . . .

And for a fleeting moment, I untethered my mind. What followed was a rush of energy, followed by a deep understanding that I could indeed get through this day—without a doubt.

But I knew with a jolt that my own power wouldn't be enough to make it happen. Relying on self-will can take you a certain distance, sure. But not across the ultimate goal line. And definitely not today. I knew that I had to find a way to take myself out of the day's equation—to surrender.

But what does that word "surrender" mean? As I let myself float that morning, my body fully supported by the warm ebb and flow of the sea, the words of writer Daphne Rose Kingma came to mind: "Surrender is a beautiful movement in which you gracefully, willingly, languidly fall, only to find midway that you have been gathered into some unimaginable embrace. Surrender is letting go, whether or not you believe the embrace will occur. It's trust to the hundredth power—not sticking to your idea of the outcome, but letting go in the faith that even the absence of an outcome will be the perfect solution."

Sometimes in life we're lucky enough to receive the precious gift of clarity. I suddenly realized that success wouldn't come if I made today about me. Rather, success would come only to the extent that I could drop my ego and align myself with something higher and more fundamental.

Easier said than done. But it was only by grasping on to this insight that I was able to begin. One small swim stroke. Then another. And another.

I prayed the ocean would bring me back to life much as it had in Oahu, but no such luck. As I stroked past the initial breakwaters, I was greeted with unwelcome swells, a washing machine of stern currents and an offshore break that seemed to thrash my body in every direction but forward. Clearly, this wouldn't be the "easy warm-up" type of swim I was blessed with in Oahu, and I certainly wouldn't have the benefit of the unprecedented tail currents that had jet-streamed me down the Molokai coast. I was going to have to put some backbone into this swim. And if it was hard for me, I couldn't imagine the toll these conditions would take on Jason.

Back to letting go. I couldn't fight the current, that was clear. The only way through was to surrender—to allow myself to get jostled and relax into the idea that it would take three to four strokes to progress the distance it normally takes one stroke to accomplish. *So what. Who cares. I'm here in Maui.* In the throes of this incredible adventure. It was a beautiful day. *Let's enjoy.* Doubt, resentment, and frustration evaporated. I took my thoughts off myself and focused on sending Jason positive energy to get him through the day's first true challenge. The swim course involved eight tightly wound and buoy-marked laps around the bay, during which time I lapped Jason twice, underscoring his struggle. On each occasion I could see him fighting mightily against the current, yet never giving up. I wished I could make it easier for him, but I knew the best thing was to leave him alone.

A little more than an hour later, I exited the water, dodging beachcombers and kids on Boogie Boards who didn't give me a second look—which put everything in perspective. On the beach, I tried to catch my breath and take stock. We were just getting started, yet I was already dehydrated, groggy, and yawning. So much for a refreshing morning swim to get my blood flowing.

Squinting across the water, I scanned for Jason and caught a glimpse of his left arm slapping the surf far offshore. He still had a long way to go yet was steadfast as always. He churned it out—one stroke at a time. I should have known better than to be worried about him.

I washed the salt from my body in the nearby showers and immediately tried to rehydrate and replenish with several liters of coconut water, Endurance Elixir, and avocado sandwiches. But with an already ailing stomach, it was tough to get any calories down without gagging. And as the blood rushed to my gut to digest the nourishment I could hold down, my sense of fatigue increased. Then there was the oven-like heat. The sun was now high and stifling, scorching my beaten corpse with a blistering dryness that far exceeded anything we'd endured on previous days. Fixating on a young couple napping on fluffy white beach towels, I felt my blood boil with jealousy. I had to force myself to turn away. Time to focus. Time to get to work.

As Jason came out of the water, I could tell that it had been a battle. Shunning the aid of Rebecca and Rick, he made it clear he needed to be left alone for a moment. And he also didn't want any sympathy, I knew. There was nothing left to say. Yet so much left to do.

Putting the congested and convivial Kamaole Beach oasis in our rear view, we headed off together on our salt-stained bikes, our backs baking as we pedaled straight uphill from the beach before veering left on Piilani Highway. As we made our way toward the airport, I took a quick look at Jason's feet snapped into his pedals, just beside mine—*up down, up down, up down.* My leg muscles burned with each stroke. We were both in real pain, physical and mental—I knew without a word being spoken that he felt as I did. Our bikes were close—only inches apart from each other—and I felt the heat from Jason's body, felt little drops of sweat fly off of his body onto mine. The sun burned, the pavement sizzled with heat, and ahead of us stretched the road—black and glittering. *Pain, pain, pain.* "Hot," Jason croaked out at one point. I grunted in agreement.

Then came the wind.

As we neared the airport, we were met with fierce trade gusts. I was pushing about two hundred watts on my bike, well within my Zone Two range and a sustainable pace that should have registered at least twenty miles an hour on a typical flat road such as this. Instead, my Garmin read only eight miles per hour. It was a fierce struggle just to maintain a straight line, let alone move forward efficiently. Yet this barrier to progress remained almost invisible, the sparse, low-lying vegetation and open terrain lending no clue to the wind's formidable power, save for the occasional swirling blasts of sand that blanketed our sweaty bodies and nearly blinded me despite my protective Oakley Jawbone sunglasses. With only one arm to stabilize his position, Jason was performing some kind of miracle by not getting blown over into the dry brush that lined the shoulder of this arid furnace freeway.

Time to reconsider our route. We'd originally planned two loops, which would involve long stretches battling this headwind. But we knew if we had to face these gusts again that we'd jeopardize not just our ability to finish but our safety. So when we reached the airport, we U-turned and headed back toward Kihei, the strong tailwinds carrying us to a right-hand turn onto Route 30, where we'd track the coast around West Maui up to Lahaina.

Now somewhat protected from the winds, we both met a new challenge in the form of an old friend. Our rear ends were giving out. After a brief but welcome remission on Molokai, the saddle sores that had begun to develop on Oahu had predictably returned. Despite our diligent application of the Bontrager cure, it was now clear that our preventive efforts had failed. Only forty miles into our ride, both Jason and I began to experience torture in the nether region. Five pedal strokes seated before standing on my pedals was the best I could muster—a herky-jerky, inefficient way to ride a bike even when fresh, and in this situation a disastrous energy sap. But we had no choice; to remain seated was to be stabbed with knives from below.

And this was when I started to lose my mind. To say that I was cranky is an understatement. Ultra-endurance veterans always advise, "Never enlist friends or loved ones to crew for you." Why? Because when deep fatigue and lack of sleep take hold, one's inner beast emerges, causing fracture of even the best of relationships. I never gave this much credence, particularly after experiencing such a bonding experience with my wife and kids at Ultraman in 2009. But now, for the first time, I was beginning to understand. I wasn't just cranky. I was becoming intolerable.

About halfway into the ride, I rode up on our crew parked along the shoulder just outside the town of Lahaina, got off my bike, and demanded a new clean cycling bib, a "Hail Mary" attempt to salve my wounds. Of course, my crew had no idea where to look for such an item. *Why can't they read my mind?!* I lost it.

"Gimme my bag!" I demanded.

Rummaging furiously through the van, I pulled out my duffel bag and threw all my clothes into the dirt until I found what I was looking for. Then I ran into the bushes to change. When I returned, Molly Kline, Paul, and Rebecca all looked at me wide-eyed. Like a man possessed by demons, I was in need of an exorcism. Riding off in anger, I covered several miles before I was able to compose myself and reflect objectively on my behavior. Sure, I was more tired than I'd ever been in my life. But that was no excuse to treat our crew—people who were selflessly giving themselves completely to our cause—in such a manner. Not cool. And definitely not me. *What was I becoming?*

Ironically, I was riding along some of the most beautiful coastline in the world, yet, for the first time, I was unable to enjoy the view. Along Honoapiilani Highway, gorgeous palm trees hugged the tranquil coast, arching their fronds low over impossibly white sands. Offshore, surfers crested perfect curls in the turquoise luminescence. Meanwhile, I couldn't focus on anything beyond my failing legs and the searing pain in my seat. I tried to find a way to savor the moment. But with my body atrociously overheated, I couldn't. I glanced momentarily at the world-class sunset that had now painted the sky a fluorescent pink, but I couldn't summon anything beyond indifference. *So what?* . . .

With Jason drafting behind me, it took all of my concentration just to keep pushing through the wind, in a straight albeit slow line forward. I had no bandwidth at all for nature appreciation. Instead, I began staring at the dusty road shoulder, scanning for a place to nap. *Yearning.* I knew without a doubt that if I set my bike down, I could be asleep in a bush in fewer than ninety seconds.

A welcome distraction from my hypnotic state arrived in the form of a car that began to leapfrog us outside Lahaina. Leaning out of the passenger-side window was a person taking pictures of Jason and me. And it wasn't random; these people seemed to know who we were, what we were doing. They were there to help cheer us on and document our progress. It sunk in once again that we weren't alone. Sure, we had our relentlessly devoted crew, but there were also people we didn't even know who were paying attention—even going out of their way to give us a boost. My saddle sore pain temporarily faded and my energy elevated. I turned to Jason. "People are watching us, man. We're not alone. Maybe we're making a difference—having an impact on people's lives?"

Thinking back, it's embarrassing to recall those words. It's not at all like me to engage in such self-congratulatory hyperbole, but that's what happened. I said it because I was desperate. At that particular moment, I needed to hear myself say it. Because to keep moving forward, I needed to believe that this lunacy held some meaning outside myself. And so did Jason. It seems like such a small thing. But by saying those words out loud we were able to take the focus off the fatigue and embrace an idea that had begun to take root that morning during my pre-swim meditation.

Whether this quest *was* about more than Jason or me or not, as a survival mechanism I had to convince myself that it was. Otherwise, what was the point of all this other than to take a massive ego trip? *Please let it be so.* I had to buy it. So I did. I pushed a little bit harder, getting through the next several miles without obsessing about that nap, my aching rear end, the lower back that was seizing, or the power that was quickly fading from my legs.

Per our improvised route, we logged two loops between Lahaina and Maalaea. On our second pass through Lahaina, the sun set and we took a brief break to put fore and aft lights on our bikes. But we underestimated how dark the island would quickly become. Despite our efforts, we still couldn't adequately see the road in front of us. Time to improvise by strapping our elastic-banded running headlamps across our bike helmets.

However, as we resumed the ride, looking very much like coal miners descending into the earth's innards, my elastic lamp strap kept slipping off my helmet, flipping the lamp down across my salt-stained forehead and inverting the beam such that it shone directly into my eyes, completely blinding me. This made for more than a few scary interludes. On one occasion, I was managing some significant crosswinds while descending quite rapidly just behind Jason on a dark stretch of heavily trafficked road that lacked any true shoulder. I could hear the diesel chug of a big rig truck approaching from behind, when my lamp once again flipped down over my eyes. *Total whiteout!* Anyone who's ridden a time-trial bike knows how unsteady they can be when strong winds blow from the side. It can take all your focus just to prevent the bike from getting blown over. In these scenarios, the last thing you want to do is remove a hand from the bars. Yet I was totally blinded from the shaft of light now piercing my pupils. As the truck quickly reared up alongside me, I panicked, lacking any ability to see where I sat on the road. I desperately tried to call out to Jason, but my voice failed me. My mind raced, trying to figure out my position on the road while running doomsday scenarios. *Was I along the narrow shoulder? Or had I veered out in the middle of the highway, potential roadkill for the quickly approaching truck?* Some primitive fight-or-flight response commanded my left arm to quickly flip the lamp off my eyes and maintain my line just as the truck whirred past, my heart rate jumping twenty beats to maximum in a nanosecond blur.

We had forty miles to go as we put West Maui in our rear view and cut south down State Highway 31 for a straight shot toward Wailea, grateful for a much-needed broad shoulder. I was in such a fog, I barely recall these miles, knowing only that I logged most standing up. I was now entering a new event horizon in my life experience with fatigue. The numbers on my power meter plummeted to laughable digits. *Just keep moving forward.*

As we neared Kamaole Beach—where our day had begun and where we planned to transition for the evening's marathon, I was overwhelmed by the fragrant aroma of food emanating from the many bars and restaurants along this touristy drag. But my stomach revolted at the wafting smells, and banana-flavored stomach acid percolated in the back of my throat. Then I began seeing spots. And every little bump in the potholed road thrust lighting bolts of pain through my carbon fiber bike frame into my saddle sores. The only thing that kept me from completely giving up was our impending arrival at the beach parking lot.

I locked in on the mile markers peppering the road, counting down. . . . T-minus three miles . . . two miles . . . one mile . . . half a mile . . . But with the beach within our grasp, Paul leaned out the window of our crew van to let us know that we were still well shy of our 112-mile bike goal—we'd need to overshoot the beach and keep going for another four miles and U-turn back. *Eight more miles?!?!?* It couldn't be true. But a quick check on my bike computer verified it. Normally, I could tack an extra eight miles onto a long ride just as easily as I could brush my teeth. But today was far from normal. I was now officially at my breaking point. Had I been a spy detained in Guantánamo, I would have happily divulged every state secret I held just to get off that bike. I actually began to cry.

Don't let anyone see. Head down. Tears mixed with sweat from my brow stung my half-blind eyes as I strained to keep focus on the white line of the road. *Just make it to the next mile marker.* What followed was interim goals measured in yards . . . then feet. Those last eight miles were an eternity. And forget about the marathon that we were scheduled to do after this! Clearly, that wasn't going to happen. Not in my state of mind, body, and spirit. I knew Jason would agree. We'd somehow complete this ride. But that was it. We'd given it a solid try, but there was no way running shoes would find their way onto my feet tonight. Maybe we could think about it after a decent night's rest, but not tonight. No way, no how.

As we finally—and quite gingerly—coasted into the beach parking lot just past 10:00 P.M., I'd firmly decided on behalf of both Jason and myself that the evening marathon was officially canceled.

As our crew greeted me, I unclipped from my pedals, somehow managed to rear my leg over the bike's top tube, and just let the bike drop to the ground. Fine by me if I never saw that steaming heap of carbon fiber ever again. In a daze, I stumbled right past Jason, Rebecca, Molly, and Paul, making my way directly to the public shower, where I steadied myself by leaning against the tile wall under a stream of hot water, still fully clothed.

For fifteen minutes, I rinsed the grime, salt, tears, and pain from my worn-out body and watched it circle the drain, mesmerized. Enveloped in the much-needed shower stream, I was consumed with one thought only: *I'm done.* I didn't care that I wouldn't finish the day or that we'd fall shy of what had now become, thanks to social media, a relatively public goal. I knew that I'd given it everything I had, left it all out on the island. I could be happy with that, I guess. The truth is, in that moment, I really didn't care. I didn't need this. *After all, I'm forty-three years old. I have a law practice I've been ignoring. What am I trying to prove?* I'd done enough. I needed my wife. I missed my kids terribly. And for now, all I wanted was a pillow, some fresh sheets, and oblivion.

Firming my resolve to get to the hotel as soon as possible, I got out of the shower, grabbed a towel, and inched my creaking bones to join Jason, sitting on the open-hatched rear bumper of the crew van, head slung low, covered in a wet towel. Together we sat at this makeshift altar, saying nothing.

Rebecca approached, breaking the silence with a question that had something to do with socks. But before she could finish, Jason cut her off. "Don't talk to me right now."

Thank you. Of course, it wasn't Rebecca's fault. As always, she was anticipating our needs, anxious to help. But the energy required to even listen to someone, let alone field a question, was overwhelming. Nothing else needed to be said to clarify that we were finished for the night, and I knew Jason felt the same way, without a doubt. Ten more minutes passed. Paul, Rebecca, and Molly hovered nearby. Not a word was uttered. Jason and I both understood what needed to be said, but neither of us wanted to be the one to say it out loud.

Fearful of passing out, I regained some balance by opening my eyes and staring blankly toward the ocean. Obscured in total darkness, the rhythmic sound of the waves hypnotized me, freezing time and thought. But my excursion into intoxicated exhaustion was interrupted by the very real and sudden appearance of a woman, emerging from the black nowhere of the beach beyond. Stumbling and looking haggard beyond her true years, she shuffled barefoot toward us until she stood directly in front of me, fully illuminated below the glow of the halogen streetlamp above. A teal tank top and brightly colored board shorts barely covered her leathery, sun-damaged skin. In a state as incoherent as mine, she looked me directly in the eye and slurred, "Hey, man, you wanna party?"

Great. Just what I needed. A drunk woman. "Maybe some other time," I managed to mutter, avoiding her glance in the hope that she'd keep moving.

"Suit yourself." She groused in that distinctive rasp native to the veteran alcoholic, and wandered off in search of a partner in crime. But it was enough to break the silence. Putting an end to this chapter, Jason reared up off the bumper, turned to look me in the eye, and said, "Okay, big bro."

Thank God, I thought. *That hotel bed just got closer.*

"Go get your shoes," he said. "Time to run."

What?! He can't be serious! Instantly, my mind raced with all the excuses I wanted to make, all the obvious reasons that this was a bad idea. Instead, I was mute. And oddly, my thoughts turned back to the drunk woman. A flood of emotion welled up inside me as I realized that, shy of the grace that had come my way twelve years prior, I could very easily have been her, staggering around lost and alone, impossibly drunk. *We're not so different, that woman and I.* Yet here I was, not just sober, but meeting reality head-on.

Why did she approach me? I wondered. My only conclusion was that she was an angel, sent to remind me just how blessed I'd been—how far I'd come in my recovery.

Injected with this high-octane dose of gratitude, I did the impossible, slowly raising my body up to meet Jason's pensive, thousand-yard stare. And then . . . *blackout*. Five baffling minutes later I regained awareness, finding myself mysteriously adorned in a new pair of shorts and compression socks, lacing up my running shoes and ready to run. Clearly, I hadn't passed out. I just have absolutely no recollection of doing any of this under my own power.

Without a doubt, this was *the defining moment of EPIC5*. And one of the defining moments of my forty-five years. Getting up off that car bumper to stare down a marathon was the hardest thing I've ever done in my entire life.

Yet I didn't *do* anything. All self-will had drained from me. My resolve had evaporated, replaced with delirium. So what did happen? Somehow, a switch was flicked. But not by me, this I know. The energy to get off that bumper could only have come from something beyond the self.

Bliss in depletion. I finally got it. It's that beautiful place of ascetic purity that is permitted to bloom only when the mind is stopped dead in its tracks and everything else is stripped away, leaving your soul—or who you *really* are—to forge a connection with the truth.

As a boy, I was hooked on the 1970s TV show *That's Incredible!* Each week, hosts Fran Tarkenton, Cathy Lee Crosby, and John Davidson would present the audience with some amazing feat of the human spirit. Sure, it was cheesy. But like most kids my age, I loved the show, tuning in every week. One of their guests was the mystical "Yogi Kudu," a six-foot-tall, fantastically limber yoga master. I'll never forget the episode where Kudu slowly contorted himself into a two-foot-square clear Lucite box, which was then hermetically sealed and placed in a swimming pool, where it sat on the bottom of the deep end with weights on top to hold it down. A stopwatch ticked off fifteen minutes before a crane raised the box back to the surface and the yogi unfurled himself, perfectly fine. By slowing his heart rate to something like five beats per minute, the master was able to remain in the box without air, free from claustrophobia, downright comfortable. It blew my mind. I still think of Yogi Kudu often—as well as the Hindi monks who are able to meditate for weeks, months, even years in some documented cases, with nary a morsel of food—as examples of how, when the mind is controlled and spirit aligned with purpose, the body is capable of so much more than we realize.

Jason and I began our marathon with a step, rounding into a walk. As we went, we ate almond butter sandwiches and took in copious amounts of fluids, slowly restoring some life to the legs that would now have to propel us 26.2 miles in darkness.

"We got all night, bro. Who cares how long it takes. If we have to walk the entire thing, then so be it."

Jason's words relieved my anxiety. And recalling my commitment to surrender, I again let go of the pressure I'd placed on myself to perform. I started to come alive again. After an initial half-mile walk, we found ourselves jogging. Not so bad. And before we knew it, Jason and I were actually running, laughing, cracking jokes. Our ultra-running crew captain for the day, Paul Hopwood, and Zoot's Molly Kline joined us, their enthusiasm a welcome improvement on the dour tapes that had been continuously playing in my mind for the last several hours. As we headed up to Highway 31, we made progress back toward the airport, where we were joined by a few local runners who'd been following our journey online and wanted to join.

With a brightened perspective, we began to actually enjoy ourselves, hitting a good stride—running for a spell, walking for a spell, then repeating. Close to midnight, we were chugging along nicely when a car pulled up ahead and stopped. Out jumped top-ranked local triathlete Dylan Rist, who ran alongside us dressed in his tie, khakis, and leather work shoes, fresh off the clock from his waiter job at a local restaurant. It was now officially a party.

For several miles we alternated running (using this term loosely) and walking, taking our time, chatting, and generally enjoying the company and the sound of the warm breeze on the cane fields that lined the road. Before we knew it, we'd hit the ten-mile mark and everything seemed to be clicking. *We might just get this thing finished after all.* Rolling into the quiet town of Kahului in the dead of night, we cut across the airport before heading up Hana Highway toward a long climb up Haleakala Highway. Then things began to get tough.

As we inched our way up the steep grade of Haleakala Highway, hours into our "run," Jason turned to me and quipped, "Almost there, bro. Keep it up and we'll be done before you know it." I looked at my Garmin Forerunner 310XT wrist computer, a heavy chunk of a watch that displays a variety of custom-set data points: heart rate, pace, the incline of the road, time lapsed, and—most important to me then—distance. The device read 12.4 miles. We weren't even halfway yet! Jason was a purist who always declined to wear any type of data monitor, so he had absolutely no idea how far we'd run. But rather than chip away at his optimism, I kept my mouth shut.

Having run steadily uphill for the last three miles with no end in sight to the elevating slant of the dark road ahead, I began to question Paul's chosen route for the night. Once again, the wheels were beginning to fall off my wagon. I was becoming unhinged, returning to that dark and all-too-familiar place where I could no longer handle light conversation—or any interpersonal interaction for that matter. I was officially "no longer fun to be with." And so, wondering why we would continue running uphill for who knows how many more miles, I began to let loose.

"What are we doing?" I yelled, my teeth grinding as the pressure rose behind my eyes. "Let's turn around and head back to the flats. This uphill route is idiotic."

Content to remain in his own world, or more likely just tired of my attitude, Jason kept to himself. And happy to just be running and fresh as morning dew, Paul couldn't see the issue. "It's not that steep," he replied. *Steep enough,* I grumbled under my breath. He may have been an ultra-runner, but Paul wasn't in the throes of his fourth iron-distance triathlon that week. Anyway, I withheld further comment for another mile and a half, treading uphill terrain I knew little about, unable to see beyond the oval circle of light downcast on the pavement by my headlamp. Then around mile 15, I lost it.

"This is ridiculous. I'm heading back to the airport. Anyone else?" Without taking a vote, I pivoted on my heels and headed back down the hill we were still climbing, dividing loyalties by heading away from the group. Ultimately, the pack fell into line with my hijacked route change, but the damage had been done—I'd further eroded morale by violating the one sacred rule: *No matter what, stick together.*

I was initially grateful to descend for a change, but it wasn't long before the downward grade took its toll, searing my quadriceps. Every step sent lactate screams up my legs—knifelike jabs pleading with my mind to stop the madness. My focus narrowed, signaling it was once again time to shut my mouth, pull the shades tight, and isolate.

Soon we hit the flats, again passed the airport, and began a circuit west through the town of Kahului. I dropped back, tracking Jason as he continued to chat with Paul and Molly. I told myself to focus on them. *Calm down. Take it easy.*

It was amazing to watch Paul's run form. A true ultra-running specialist, he was impressively light on his feet, with an effortless stride. He's the kind of runner who excels at distances upward of a hundred miles. To this day I still have difficulty wrapping my brain around the idea of 100 miles. *Someday . . .* I thought. But not today.

It was now nearing 3:00 A.M. Paul had been working his butt off all day taking care of us, and yet, having run every mile alongside us, he looked entirely fresh. In fact, he ran far more than a marathon that night, because he repeatedly jogged back and forth between Jason and me, bringing us fluids, tending to our every need. But again, I was in that dark place where I couldn't handle the interaction. I was gruff, shunning the nutrition and imploring him to leave me alone. But Paul knew better. Experienced in how it feels to be in the "pain cave," he refused to take no for an answer.

I later felt awful about how difficult I was that night. It was beyond uncool to treat so roughly someone who'd volunteered his time. I apologized to Paul and he said he knew it wasn't personal. Like many endurance and ultra-endurance athletes, he understood; he'd been there himself.

Circling Kahului and heading back toward the airport, we hit the twenty-mile mark. Delirium was really setting in now, placed against a very real backdrop of cane fields burning in the near distance. Hundreds of acres blazing in a controlled burn. The predawn sky glowed a fantastic orange, punctuated by an overwhelming acrid aroma. Like a surreal landscape conceived by Salvador Dalí, or a scene straight out of *Apocalypse Now,* our bizarre environs elevated the strangeness this trip already possessed. But the end was now within reach. Both Jason and I had, for the most part, dispensed with walking, now only running.

We settled on a large circular loop around the commercial section of Kahului, which would place our finish line in the airport parking lot. Grateful to have something to fix my gaze on besides the haunting glow of burning cane fields, I focused on the closed but well-lit storefronts—a Chevron here, a twenty-four-hour Rite Aid there—anything to distract me from the pain. And the miles clicked by. But the closer we inched toward our destination, the thicker the smoke from the burning cane became. Despite removing our shirts and wrapping them around our faces to filter the fallout, it was soon close to impossible to breathe. Time, once again, to divert the route.

According to plan, our crew left us to pick up Paul's car in the airport parking lot. We'd reconvene at an improvised finish line beyond the perimeter of the acrid plume. And so for the last two miles it was just Jason and me, slugging it out against the flaming orange sky, racing against ourselves and the impending dawn. A step at a time, we ran together, silent, just as we'd begun on that first morning of our EPIC5 journey in Kauai—days ago. *Almost there. Just get it done.* I looked at my wrist every minute or so, in intervals of one-tenth of a mile. Our self-chosen assignment seemed endless and ridiculous at the same time: run in circles around this neighborhood until my computer would grant us permission to stop. And then—without fanfare, or even a single soul to greet us, let alone pat us on the back—we were finished.

Too tired to hug, the two of us made do with a quick high-five. Our crew was nowhere to be seen. Nothing to do but wait; they should be here any minute.

I gingerly laid my body down on the hard concrete driveway in front of Royal Hawaiian Tire & Auto, a less-than-romantic backdrop to punctuate the unceremonious completion of our day's travels. No more than ninety seconds had elapsed when . . . *oblivion.* I was fast asleep.

I'm not sure how many minutes passed—maybe ten, fifteen tops. But when Paul, Molly, and Rebecca tracked us down, I was still sound asleep. After shaking me awake, Paul had to literally half-carry me into the van, where I rested my head against the window, trying to remain awake for the short ride to the hotel.

When we arrived at a rather groovy little inn up in the funky town of Paia, Jason helped me out of the car and let me lean on him as he guided me into the lobby. *It should be the other way around,* I thought. I was in very bad shape—far worse than Jason. And I needed that bed like I'd never needed anything in my life. I couldn't speak. I couldn't function. The hotel receptionist was doing her best to get us situated at this ridiculously early hour, but it took a spell for her to locate our room keys and sort out our reservation. I was entirely out of rationality and patience, my irritability once again rearing up. I recall very little of what occurred other than that I needed all the help I could get from Jason just to make it up one simple flight of stairs and into that bed. I knew I needed to eat, but I could only muster a few bites of pasta Rebecca had picked up. And as the sun crept up, I shut the shades, pulled the sheets over my head, and was gone.

DAY FIVE: THE BIG ISLAND

A VICTORY LAP

Waking the next morning around 11:00 A.M., I sought out Jason and our crew, and it was quickly agreed to schedule another rest day before our final assault on the Big Island. A few hours later we caught an afternoon island hopper to Kona, and after quickly checking in at the King Kamehameha Hotel—the HQ for the Ironman World Championships and just a skip away from the next day's swim start at the Kailua Pier—we wasted no time hightailing it directly to Island Naturals, Kona's newest natural foods market. Finally, I was able to nourish myself with good, clean-burning organic vegan fuel—nutrition that hadn't crossed my lips since Molokai. And I took every advantage of it—loading up on a giant fresh kale, spirulina, and beet Vitamix blend and gorging on every conceivable whole-food, plant-based delight in sight.

I could actually feel my body return to life, inching toward homeostasis with every green sip and bite of quinoa and lentils.

I stocked up on raw almonds, gluten-free granola, coconut milk, acai, and kombucha to bring back to the hotel for later that evening and the following day's breakfast, then it was right back to the room to call the family before lights out at dusk.

Eleven hours of dead-to-the-world sleep later, I arose around 6:00 A.M. to greet our final day feeling shockingly refreshed—in stark contrast to the emotional meltdown and near organ failure of the previous day. I actually felt "tapered," a term that refers to that feeling of boundless energy that comes with a couple weeks of rest and easy training after a long, arduous season in the lead-up to a big race. It was as if my body were saying, *Okay, I finally understand what is going on now—why didn't you tell me earlier? All I needed was a decent meal and one good night of sleep! An iron-distance triathlon today? No problem.*

Jason and I convened in the hotel lobby and together walked the twenty yards to the Kailua Pier to ready ourselves for the swim. With the hardest work behind us, we approached the day as a victory lap on home turf. Despite the 140.6 miles that lay in front of us—daunting by any objective standard—after what we'd endured, and invigorated by a day of rest, knocking off an iron-distance workout now seemed like nothing more than a walk in the park. We needn't worry about flights to catch, or what hellish trials the next day would inflict on us. Barring unforeseen disaster, when the day was done, we'd have completed the impossible.

At the pier we met up with some local friends. Grant Miller, the owner of the local BikeWorks bike shop, who'd tuned up our bike gear for Ultraman, was there to tweak and tidy our rides while we got the swim under our belts. And also there to cheer us on was local professional triathlete Bree Wee, with her ever-present smile.

Wasting no time, we jumped in and began. I knew this swim course—one of the most beautiful ocean swims in the world—like

I knew every grouted tile of my local pool. Stroking effortlessly through the crystal-clear water teeming with underwater wildlife, I focused on the schools of fish. A casual out-and-back 2.4 miles, and before I knew it, I was done. Only fifty-one minutes—no big deal on a fresh day, but pretty darn good considering what I'd undergone this week. As I was drying off, Grant smiled, remarking, "Wow, you're already done?"

"Just warming up, Grant!"

"So how did it feel to have so many friends out there with you today?"

Having just performed the swim solo, I was confused. "What do you mean?"

"The dolphins! You had a whole school of dolphins out there swimming right alongside you!"

"I did?" I couldn't believe it. Despite the countless number of times I'd swum in this bay, I'd yet to experience the sensation of swimming alongside a dolphin. How could I have missed it?

"Yeah! Look!" Grant motioned to Jason, still chugging out in the bay. With a hand to my forehead to shade the bright morning sun, I spied Jason far offshore, stroking to the musical rhythm of several dorsal fins undulating alongside him. I took it as a blessing on behalf of the Hawaiian kahunas.

Simply beautiful.

As I awaited Jason's arrival, I put on my cycling gear for the final bike segment of the week, ate an almond butter and banana sandwich, and greeted five-time Ironman champion Luke McKenzie, an Aussie who'd been training in Kona over the last few weeks with his fiancée (now wife), Amanda Balding. I'd very briefly met Luke and Amanda by happenstance almost two years prior—before I'd even raced my first Ultraman—during a Starbucks break while out riding in my local Santa Monica Mountains. Remarkably, Luke remembered our meeting, and was nice enough to swing by on his motor scooter this morning to say hello and wish us well for the day. His encouragement provided an amazing morale boost.

"We have a little run planned for later this afternoon if you're interested in joining," I mentioned to Luke. I imagined how his long, sure strides would likely compare to ours and jokingly added, "But be warned, we might be running a little too fast for you."

Luke laughed. "Good times, mate. I've got a big training day ahead, but I'll think about it. Have fun today, boys!" And with that we parted ways. Given his long slog of serious pro triathlete training that day, I doubted we'd see him again, but I was glad to have made the offer.

And we were off, accompanied by our friend and "sherpa du jour" Warren Hollinger, Kona local and multiple Ironman and Ultraman finisher. As we pedaled uphill to the famous Queen K Highway, I was again amazed at just how fresh I felt. Thanks to the remarkable natural properties of tea tree oil, my undercarriage seemed to have miraculously healed overnight—staying seated on my bike was no longer an issue. And what seemed even more miraculous: The power had returned to my legs, the fatigue not much more than a mild annoyance. What can I say? The body's ability to adapt to stress is nothing short of astonishing. With the sun shining, and my friends as my tailwind, my spirits were running high.

Heading up the Queen K, we followed the world-famous Ironman World Championship course on our way to the tiny town of Hawi, happily baking in sun-crusted lava fields. Sure, it was hot. And windy. But today I was unfazed. After Maui, this was easy. The numbers on my power meter reflected my state of mind and body, registering measurements far above anything I'd generated since our first day in Kauai. I wasn't just feeling good. *I was feeling great.*

With the urge to let the tiger out of the cage a bit, I rode off the front of our little group of three. To the purr of my whirring carbon-rimmed Zipp wheels, I embraced some alone time to connect with my gratitude—not just for what we'd accomplished so far this week, but for all the blessings of my life: the sobriety that had returned me to sanity, the faith that had given me the strength to reinvent my life, and the wife who hadn't just supported my dreams but co-created them. I also gave thanks for the children I was blessed to raise, healthy and happy. And my friend Jason Lester, who believed in me enough to make me part of his lunatic fringe. Centered firmly in the *now,* I allowed myself to genuinely feel the sun on my face, lean into the new strength in my legs, and mentally genuflect in this church of lava—this land that had played such a central role in forging my life's new trajectory.

Before I knew it, I'd arrived in the hamlet of Hawi, and I pulled over to wait for Jason and Warren. Marking the fifty-six-mile halfway point of the ride, this village, with its hippie sensibility, was also the finish line for the Ultraman Day Two bike course, as well as the starting line for the Day Three 52.4-mile run. That's a long way of saying that Hawi is a place of great meaning for me.

Soon Jason and Warren arrived, with Rebecca following just behind in our support vehicle, and we took an extended lunch break. Again, today was a celebration, not a race. The feeling was of a leisurely excursion, not a scramble, and Rebecca produced an impromptu picnic. I swiftly shoveled three Vegenaise and avocado sandwiches down the hatch, washing them down with a quart of coconut water, at which point Jason, who was always amused by how much food I could pack away, remarked, "So, Roll-Dawg, how many avo sammies you figure you've inhaled this week?"

After a quick calculation, I answered. "Sixty, easy. Possibly seventy." It's not an exaggeration to say that my EPIC5 experience had been fueled in large part by avocados, grapeseed oil–based Vegenaise, and coconut water.

Spirits still high, we got back on the bikes and descended from

Hawi down toward the Queen K. Together we rode gently back into Kona town, circling the main commercial drag before completing our ride where the day had begun, at the Kailua Pier. I had 2.4 miles of swimming and 112 miles on the bike under my belt, and I was still smiling. The sun still tall in the sky, my energy ran high, and I was excited for the run—our final leg. Maybe it was the adrenaline, but the idea of running a marathon now struck me as nothing more than an afterthought—just a final jaunt before putting this entire event to bed.

I downed a jar of Endurance Elixir, yanked on my compression socks, and laced up my running shoes. Ready to go, I was cheered to once again find us in the presence of Luke McKenzie. The Ironman champ is one of the biggest names in triathlon and also one of the nicest. Despite Luke's already having put in torrid bike and run workouts earlier that day, he was declining his well-earned right to vegetate in front of the television, so he could join us stride for stride for our marathon's first several miles.

Once through town, and with about seven miles under our belt, Luke bid his adieu as we headed up the steep incline known famously in Ironman parlance as "Palani Hill." And before we knew it, we were back on the Queen K, once again donning our salt-streaked headlamps to cut a path across the black lava. The miles clicked by, and the fatigue began to rise once again, reminding us that we weren't yet free of its grasp. But we kept on, maintaining an even keel. The familiarity of the terrain helped. As it became necessary to start digging deep as we pushed past the marina on the outskirts of town, I recalled a run that Jason and I had completed during our training camp leading up to Ultraman 2009. On this same track of highway, we busted out a very hard two-hour run in the pouring rain on a dark night. It was one of those runs where everything just clicks. And by tapping into that very lucid memory, I felt stronger.

I turned to Jason. "This remind you of anything?"

Jason smiled. He knew exactly what I was talking about. "One of the best runs of my life, big bro."

"Until now," I said, continuing to marvel at just how well my body was holding up after the trauma that visited me on Maui. We certainly weren't running fast, *but we were running.* And most important, we were enjoying the experience. Rather than dread the miles to come and focus only on being done, we were savoring these final steps.

With about six miles to go, a car pulled up and out jumped Grant, further raising our spirits as he jogged alongside us in his Teva sandals. When he remarked that this was his first "run" in years, I responded, "Then you might have considered wearing some running shoes, at least!"

He confessed that he didn't even own a pair. But he didn't want to pass up the opportunity to participate. Ably plugging away, Grant was just happy to be there. Talk about a boost!

Counting down. Five miles to go. Then four. And before we knew it, only three more miles to go. I could feel those mental window shades beginning to drop, and I fought the urge to withdraw as I'd done during the final miles of every previous marathon that week. I battled myself to stay present and, most important, to stay connected with Jason. And just when I thought I couldn't sustain my pace or any semblance of sociability one minute longer, out of the dark appeared Luke and Amanda, riding alongside us in their scooter, snapping pictures, shooting video, hooting loudly, and honking their horn in support. Later, we'd learn that they'd been at home and about to call it a night when they were struck by the urge to venture out and cheer us to the finish.

With the town now within reach, and buttressed by Luke and Amanda's cheering motor escort, which felt a bit like a presidential motorcade, we made our downhill right turn off the Queen K en route to the finish. Then came the goose bumps. As the reality of what was happening began to set in, I felt an energy surge that carried me that final mile. My emotions took over. And with the Kailua Pier now within reach, tears began to stream down my cheeks. Two hundred yards to go and I no longer wanted it to be over. I wanted to *keep going*.

Then came the moment. With the gurgling motor of Luke and Amanda's scooter drowning out the steady fall of our footsteps on the Kailua Pier, and to the backdrop of cheers and whoops from Rebecca, Warren, Luke, and Amanda, we took our final steps. *Done deal.*

Dateline, Kailua-Kona, Hawaii. Approximately 11:00 P.M. In fewer than seven days and on five separate islands, Jason Lester and Rich Roll successfully logged 12 miles of swimming, 560 miles of cycling, and 131 miles of running—703 miles in total.

CONCLUSION

Life is a long, complicated walk. Over the years, I've found myself on many paths, some winding, some clear and straight, and many dark and troubling. My story is about a guy who woke up one morning and found himself on the same worn trail he'd been on for too many years. We've all been there. And far too many of us just can't seem to find the exit ramp, let alone a new and more fulfilling trajectory. But I did. By opening my heart, trusting that it wouldn't lead me astray, and having the resolve to follow its direction, I saw my life change in every conceivable way. The difference, in fact, is epic.

At times the pain of confronting seemingly insurmountable obstacles was so intense that comfort came only through living completely in the moment. Yet with obstacles come the opportunity for growth. And if you're not growing, you're not living. So my mantra has become: *Do what you love; love those you care about; give service to others; and know that you're on the right path.*

There's a new path waiting for you, too. All you have to do is look for it—then take that first step. If you show up and stay present, that step will eventually become a gigantic leap forward. *And then you'll show us who you really are.*

THE NUTS AND BOLTS OF THE PLANTPOWER DIET

Before launching into the specifics of what I eat (see Appendix II, A PlantPower Day in the Life), let's take a look at *why* I eat the way I do. Presented below is a basic plant-based nutrition primer that provides the foundation for the PlantPower Diet.

THIS BUSINESS OF PROTEIN

First, let's address the elephant in the room. The pesky protein question. Rarely does a day go by that I'm not asked: *How do you get your protein?*

There's a powerful and hardened belief in our culture that you need animal protein to be healthy. *A lot of animal protein.* The message is everywhere you turn. From commercials, to food labels, to fitness-expert testimonials: protein, protein, protein. Protein powders, protein shakes, protein supplements. Also omnipresent is the assumption that the only foods that contain an adequate amount of protein necessary for proper human functioning, not to mention peak athletic performance, are animal-based. A T-bone steak. Eggs and a tall glass of cold milk. Or a creamy whey protein shake. Without them, you won't succeed as an athlete, train and race at your peak, build muscle, or recover properly between workouts.

But I've come to see that this pervasive notion is utterly false. Have you ever heard of someone hospitalized for a protein deficiency? I haven't. The whole hullabaloo about protein is much ado about nothing: a red-herring debate, in my opinion, fueled by a campaign of disinformation perpetuated by powerful and well-funded meat and dairy lobbies that have convinced society—including medical professionals, educators, and government bureaucrats responsible for the proverbial food pyramid—that we need these products to live. The protein push is not only based on lies, it's killing us. To be sure, protein is a crucial nutrient, critical not just in building and repairing muscle tissue, but in the maintenance of a wide array of bodily functions, including preserving proper bone mass, immune system strength, and the prevention of fatigue. But what exactly is protein? Does it matter if it comes from plants rather than animals? And how much do we actually need?

Proteins consist of twenty different amino acids, eleven of which can be synthesized naturally by our bodies. The remaining nine—what we call *essential amino acids*—must be ingested from the foods we eat. So, technically, our bodies require certain amino acids, not protein per se. But these nine essential amino acids are hardly the exclusive domain of the animal kingdom. In fact, they're originally synthesized by plants and are found in meat and dairy products only because these animals have eaten plants. I was myself surprised to learn they're found in copious amounts in a wide variety of grains, nuts, seeds, vegetables, and legumes. Things like black, kidney, and pinto beans; almonds; lentils; a quirky seed called quinoa; and even spinach and broccoli. Who knew? I certainly didn't. So in the most generalized sense, if your diet contains a well-rounded variety of these plant-based foods—high in the nine essential amino acids in varying degrees and proportions—it is essentially impossible to be deficient in your body's ability to properly synthesize all the proteins it needs for proper tissue maintenance, repair, and functioning.

In truth, only one out of about every ten calories we eat needs to come from protein. And the requirements of the athlete don't far exceed this recommendation.* And yet the typical sedentary American consumes about twice the amount of protein the body actually needs, which according to the recommended daily allowance (RDA) is only 0.8 grams per kilogram of body weight.† In fact, I agree with many experts who contend that the body's true needs are even lower for most people, with the possible exception of pregnant or nursing women. For now, let's set aside the fact that most people obtain the majority of their protein from ingesting animal products, which tend to be high in unhealthy artery-clogging saturated fats. Take into consideration that on the PlantPower Diet one must obtain the nine essential amino acids from a variety of plant-based foods, which are admittedly digested and absorbed differently from animal-based proteins. And let's get really conservative by factoring in the assumption that an endurance athlete like myself would require even more protein. Let's go so far as to say that this level might even be as high as 1.2 grams of protein per kilogram of body weight. That means that at my current weight of 160 pounds (72.5 kilograms), I'd have a recommended daily intake of 72.5 × 1.2, or 87 grams of protein—although in truth I generally ingest much less than this amount, somewhere in the range of 70–75 grams, even during periods of intense training. Sound like a lot? Ready to break out that gigantic canister of whey protein with the steroid-ripped bodybuilder on the label looking like his head is about to explode? Not so fast. Spread out over the course of a day, eating some almond butter toast and quinoa for breakfast, a black bean and brown rice burrito for lunch, and a healthy portion of

---

* "Nutrition and Athletic Performance—Position of the American Dietetic Association, Dietitians of Canada, and the American College of Sports Medicine," *Journal of the American Dietetic Association* 2000,100: 1543–56.
† Food and Nutrition Board (FNB), Institute of Medicine (IOM), "Dietary Reference Intakes for Energy, Carbohydrate, Fiber, Fat, Fatty Acids, Cholesterol, Protein, and Amino Acids (Macronutrients) (2002)," www.nap.edu/books/0309085373/html/.

tempeh, lentils, mung beans, or quinoa with hemp seeds and some spinach or broccoli for dinner puts me right where I need to be.

Provided your diet is made up of different combinations of these grains, legumes, nuts, seeds, and green vegetables throughout the day, you can't help but get all the essential amino acids you need. This type of regimen has fueled me for years without any issues with respect to building lean muscle mass and properly recovering between workouts.

That being said, during periods of heavy training, when I'm feeling unduly fatigued, or on days I know I haven't ingested enough high-protein plant-based foods, I'll include a modest amount of plant-based protein powder in my daily post-workout smoothie as a supplemental safeguard. When I do, I prefer hemp protein, as this is one of the few plant-based foods that contains a complete amino acid profile. However, hemp isn't the most bioavailable plant-based protein, meaning the body cannot fully assimilate all its nutrients. I have found that it is best used when combined with a variety of other more bioavailable plant-based proteins. To meet this need, and in cooperation with Compton Rom of Ascended Health, I formulated my own plant-based protein formula called Jai Repair, comprised of the purest and most bioavailable pea, sprouted brown rice, and hemp proteins, as well as a robust blend of endurance-promoting Cordyceps mushroom extracts, L-glutamine, vitamin B_{12}, and an array of powerful antioxidants such as resveratrol and more. Jai Repair is a proprietary PlantPower blend scientifically devised to expedite maximum recovery induced by exercise stress and has been instrumental in furthering my continual improvement as an athlete (for more information on this product and more, see Appendix III, Resources, or visit jailifestyle.com). And I always include spirulina in my Vitamix blends. With a protein content of 60–65 percent by weight (higher than any other natural food source), this fresh-water algae phytonutrient superfood is an optimal and complete protein source.

Contrary to popular belief, more protein isn't better. Satisfy your requirement and leave it at that. With respect to athletes, to my knowledge no scientific study has ever shown that consumption of protein beyond the advised 10 percent of daily calories has any beneficial effect on muscle growth or repair. In fact, excess protein is physiologically converted to an inefficient energy source or alternatively stored as fat. And concerning everyone, copious studies have established beyond doubt that over the long term, excess protein intake from animal-based sources can be harmful, significantly contributing to the onset of a variety of congenital diseases such as osteoporosis, cancer, impaired kidney function, and heart disease.

Let's wrap up the protein question with one thought to ponder. Some of the strongest and most fierce animals in the world are Plant-Powered. The elephant, rhino, hippo, and gorilla have one thing in common—they all get 100 percent of their protein from plants.

PLANTPOWER DIET

Plant-Based Foods High in Protein*

FOOD	PROTEIN CONTENT (GRAMS)
Spirulina (10 grams)	6.0
Tempeh (1 cup)	31.4
Seitan (4 ounces)	24.0
Lentils, boiled (1 cup)	17.9
Black Beans, boiled (1 cup)	15.2
Chickpeas, boiled (1 cup)	14.5
Mung Beans (1 cup)	13.5
Kidney Beans (1 cup)	13.0
Baked Beans (1 cup)	12.0

* Physician's Committee for Responsible Medicine, "How Can I Get Enough Protein? The Protein Myth," www.pcrm.org/health/diets/vegdiets/how-can-i-get-enough-protein-the-protein-myth, and "Protein in the Vegan Diet," Reed Mangels, PhD, RD, Vegetarian Resource Group, www.vrg.org/nutrition/protein.htm.

Plant-Based Foods High in Protein (continued)

FOOD	PROTEIN CONTENT (GRAMS)
Pinto Beans (1 cup)	12.0
Kamut (1 cup)	11.2
Quinoa, cooked (1 cup)	11.0
Black-Eyed Peas (1 cup)	11.0
Peanut Butter (2 tbsp)	8.0
Almonds (¼ cup)	8.0
Oatmeal (1 cup)	6.0
Bulgar, cooked (1 cup)	5.6
Spinach, boiled (1 cup)	5.4
Brown Rice (1 cup)	5.0
Broccoli (1 cup)	4.6
Baked Potato	4.0
Whole Wheat Bread (1 slice)	2.7

ALKALINITY: BUILDING YOUR PLANTPOWER BASE

Many of the health benefits of the PlantPower Diet are premised on one powerful concept: alkalinity.

The body is constantly striving to strike a systemic balance of acidity and alkalinity, measured as pH, ranging from 1 (the most acidic) to 14 (the most alkaline, or "base"), with neutral being 7.0. Optimum wellness is achieved when the body is in a slightly alkaline state (7.35–7.45).

The foods we eat, the air we breathe, the toxins we absorb through our skin, and the stress we manage all factor into our body's pH. And although there's a consensus among nutritionists and medical experts well versed in these matters that somewhere in the range of 80 percent of the foods we ingest should be alkaline-forming and 20 percent acidic, the typical American diet—combined with our fast-paced, stress-inducing urban lifestyle—is overwhelmingly acid-forming. Processed foods, sodas, meat and dairy proteins, polluted air, and simple life pressures all contribute to what is called "metabolic acidosis," or a chronic state of body acidity.

Why is this important? When the body is in a protracted or chronic state of even low-grade acidosis, which most people's bodies these days are, it must marshal copious resources to maintain blood pH somewhere in the optimal 7.35 orbit. Over time, the body pays a significant tax that manifests in a susceptibility to any array of infirmities: fatigue; impaired sleep and immune system functionality; a decrease in cellular energy output, nutrient absorption, bone density, and growth hormone levels, which over time lead to a reduction in muscle mass; an increase in inflammation and weight gain, leading to obesity; the promotion of kidney disorders, tumor cell growth, mood swings, and osteoporosis. And I haven't included in that list a variety of bacterial and viral maladies that flourish in the acidic environment.

By way of example, we've been taught since birth that "Milk Does a Body Good," primarily because it's high in calcium. And without it, you risk brittle bones and osteoporosis. But the truth begs to differ. Setting aside the fact that milk contains saturated fat, cholesterol, and, typically, certain hormones, the acidic nature of dairy products can actually *promote* calcium deficiency, which over time can lead to osteoporosis. Unless one ingests a substantial amount of counterbalancing alkaline-forming foods, the body must stabilize blood pH caused by acidic dairy protein intake by leeching precious calcium and other mineral stores from the bones and releasing them into the bloodstream in an effort to achieve pH neutrality. Over time, a person can actually become calcium deficient and his or her bones turn brittle. Funny how that works.

By contrast, plant-based whole foods, when combined with a reduction in environmental stressors, are alkaline-forming. For example, a regimen that contains daily doses of dark leafy greens rich in calcium obviates concerns about bone density and osteoporosis.

I'm talking about fruits and vegetables such as coconut, avocado, bell pepper, tomato, and lemon. Nuts and seeds, like pumpkin, sesame, and almonds, are also helpful, as are sprouted beans and grains, Celtic sea salt, coconut oil and milk, olive oil, and quinoa. They're all great alkalyzers.

Maintaining a diet rich in alkaline-forming foods helps regulate and optimize health on the cellular level, assists in promoting sustained vitamin and mineral levels, and maximizes the body's immune system functionality.

In addition, making the switch to a primarily alkaline-forming diet aids in weight loss. As previously described, metabolic acidosis catalyzes a protective response that results in excess acids being removed from the bloodstream. But where do these excess acids go? The body ends up storing them in fat cells. The more acid, the more fat cells required for storage space. In other words, an acidic diet and environment promotes an increase in body fat while working to erode muscle mass. But this process can be reversed by the ingestion of alkaline-forming foods, which serve to "cleanse" the body of excess acid, negating the need for extra fat cell storage space. The result? Weight loss.

TIP: Squeezing fresh lemon juice or adding a few tablespoons of apple cider vinegar to your water is a simple and effective way to immediately alkalize your system. And it's very effective in combating the onset of head colds and the flu.

As an athlete, I've discovered that, other than sleeping, maintaining a primarily alkaline diet is the best recovery tool available. Such a diet works to reduce exercise-induced inflammation that impedes the body's ability to promptly repair itself while at the same time promoting the repair, growth, and maintenance of lean muscle mass.

TIP: Love your coffee but can't accept letting it go despite its acidic nature? Try *cold press brewing*—an alternative brewing method that not only reduces bitterness but also removes 60 to 70 percent of the acidity found in your favorite cup of joe. For more information, see Appendix III, Resources.

Still not sold? All I can tell you is that over the last five years, despite juggling my rigorous training schedule, full-time job, and hectic family life, I continue to improve athletically. And I've suffered little more than a sniffle. I've missed plenty of training sessions due to family or professional obligations, but never because I was sick. That's amazing in light of the fact that previous to my dietary shift I suffered from a myriad of allergies and could count on getting the flu, a head cold, or a sinus infection every couple months without fail.

I can state with full confidence that an alkaline, plant-based, whole-food diet is the most rapid recovery tool available to the athlete, and a crucial component in my success.

NUTRIENTS: GET DENSE AND BLEND

Another key component of the PlantPower Diet is nutrient density. At least twice a day I prepare a primarily green-based smoothie drink in my beloved Vitamix blender—the one kitchen item I simply can't do without. Neither the Vitamix nor its rival, the Blendtec, are your garden-variety blenders. With motors that could power a Jet Ski, these machines can literally make juice out of just about anything. How powerful? Using the top-of-the-line Vitamix, I once blended an avocado pit and drank it.

In the morning, I pack this turbocharged machine with a variety of plant-based foods to kick-start my metabolism and provide lasting energy for the day. The foundation is always a combination of dark leafy greens high in alkalizing chlorophyll to aid in cell regeneration—foods like kale, spinach, spirulina, and marine phytoplankton. Plus, I add endurance boosters like beetroot, chia seeds, and maca powder, a rotation of avocado, coconut, and hemp seeds high in essential fatty acids, and blueberries and acai for antioxidants. Pepita (pumpkin) seeds provide extra iron, and bell pepper and citrus fruit provide vitamin C, which enhances the body's ability to absorb the iron. And if the blend is too bitter, I add a small amount of orange or apple juice for flavor. But I never overdo it on fruit juices; after pasteurization they're essentially zapped of much of their nutritional value, leaving mostly sugar.

Then I blend everything into hyperspace oblivion. I blend until all the ingredients blur into a foamy liquid. Drinking down the deliciousness, I instantly feel my mood improve and body come alive, alkalized, nourished, and energized for whatever the day may bring. It's a lasting, consistent, and stable energy that keeps me (as well as my wife and kids) fortified and evenly sustained for several hours without the heavy feeling of a carbohydrate-dense breakfast, the inevitable sugar crash of a donut, or the hunger pangs that follow on the heels of empty calories low in nutritional value.

TIP: To jolt your metabolism and start the day right, let go of what you think breakfast should be and get used to the idea of drinking a salad for breakfast.

In essence, the Vitamix not only allows me to eat an incredible amount of low-fat, high-fiber, nutrient-dense foods in one sitting (unlike juicing, which discards the majority of the produce), it does so by essentially "pre-digesting" the foods for me, sufficiently breaking them down *before* ingesting. That, in turn, promotes a high degree of easy absorption, rendering the nutrients readily available for my body to use.

When we eat, our bodies must expend significant resources to digest the food in our gastrointestinal (GI) tract. Energy is required to break down what we've ingested before it can be assimilated and utilized by the body for nutrients and fuel. The more difficult the food is to break down, the more energy is required to digest it. For example, if you eat a steak, it requires an incredible amount of physiological oomph for your body to digest. Your system has to divert a copious amount of resources that could be otherwise used for clear thinking or exercising well or simply being attuned to a beautiful day. The more blood diverted, the more drained and unfocused you become. You experience that "food coma" that only passes when the job is done.

Overall, the calories and the nutrients that you gain from eating the steak have to be counterbalanced against the toll you've paid to digest and eliminate the waste of that steak. And when you do the math, the net energy gain is often not worth the high price extracted.

By contrast, my blends require very little energy to digest, because the blender has done most of the job already. Vegetables that would ordinarily be somewhat difficult to break down are now easily assimilated, availing the body ready access to all the nutrients offered by the food product. It's why you feel good immediately after drinking it.

Moreover, the high nutrient density of these smoothie blends, and plant-based whole foods in general, leads to a natural curbing of the appetite, giving you greater control over weight gain and loss. This is because the body is being properly fortified with all the vitamins, minerals, and nutrients it needs to thrive. *It is sated.* By contrast, when we eat "empty" calories—starchy or processed foods, refined wheat and sugars that may be high in calories, carbohydrates, or fat—we feel full, but only temporarily. Soon we're hungry again, craving to eat. This is because despite the often high calorie count of these foods, they're very nutrient poor. The stomach is full, yet the body remains starved for nutrients, which in turns leads to overeating and inevitable weight gain. Such cravings are often the body's way of alerting you that it needs not just to be fed, but fed *properly.*

People often say to me, "You train so much, you must be gorging on food all day long." But the truth couldn't be more opposite. Back when Brian Nicosia and I were slamming back those doughnuts, we'd convinced ourselves that our bodies needed all that sugar and fat—that we couldn't swim like we did without it. Turns out, the opposite is true. To be sure, my appetite is healthy, but if I'm eating clean-burning, nutrient-dense foods, it stays balanced. In fact, there's no question that despite my training load, I eat far less than I did in my sedentary years prior to 2008.

Ultra-marathon legend and vegan Scott Jurek claims that his body has become so adept at absorbing his nutrient-rich foods that he needs to eat less and operates at a higher efficiency. I can honestly say that I know what he's talking about. I've discovered that the more reliant I become on nutrient-dense foods, the less hungry I become, irrespective of training load. My body is satiated.

Typically, I'll make a blenderful in the morning, drink one large glass, and store the rest in a thermos, taking it with me to sip throughout the day when I begin to feel hungry or feel my energy levels beginning to wane. I find this very helpful in a work/business context. Many people have said to me, "I really want to go plant-based. But there's just no way I can do it because of business lunches and dinners. What am I supposed to do when I have to meet a client at a steak house?" Here's my answer. Brew a large Vitamix in the morning. Bring it in a large thermos to work, along with some other plant-friendly and easy-to-carry snacks like almonds and fruit. And just before you have to head out to that steak house for a work-related lunch, drink a healthy portion of the Vitamix blend. You'll find that your energy increases as your appetite wanes. Then you can attend your lunch and order a light salad, baked potato, or whatever meager offering the plant-unfriendly restaurant has to offer, without starving or cheating.

TIP: Prepare ahead of time for those occasions when you find yourself at a meal where choice is limited—always have a generous amount of green smoothie or other PlantPower snack at your disposal.

Post-workout and/or in the evening, it's back to blending. I prepare another Vitamix before or after dinner as an appetizer or a dessert. I tend to mix it up to keep things fresh and interesting, experimenting with different ingredients and striving not to be rigid about exact ingredients or proportions. But subsequent to training, or as night nears, I always bear in mind what my body needs most to recover from the day's training and professional or life stressors, to ensure I maximize the window to rebuild myself overnight. So the focus shifts away from energizing foods to reparative foods—from catabolic (exertion mode) to anabolic (restorative/growth mode). I'll take some antioxidants to combat stress and exercise-induced free radical damage, but I'm not talking about vitamin pills. I'm talking about blueberries, strawberries, acai and goji berries, spinach, kale, carrots, and spirulina. I'll also think about eating some walnuts for protein and drinking coconut water for electrolytes. And when I crave dessert, instead of ice cream or pie I'll try blending banana and berries with coconut milk and cacao—a chocolate-flavored nutritious superfood high in antioxidants. A guilt-free delight.

PLANTPOWER DIET
Favorite Vitamix Ingredients
Kale

Spinach

Dandelion Greens

Beets and Beetroot

Tomato

Blueberry

Strawberry

Spirulina

Chlorophyll

Hemp Seed, Oil, and Milk

Acai Berry

Coconut, Coconut Milk, Keifer, Water, and Oil

Almonds and Almond Milk

Cacao

Aloe Vera

Orange

Grapefruit

Spinach

Celery

Avocado

Chia Seed

Maca

Marine Phytoplankton

Almonds

Walnuts

Pepita Seeds

Blue Green Algae

Apple Cider Vinegar

Green Sprouts

Goji Berries

Bananas

Jai Repair Performance Recovery Formula

MICROBES, THE BRAIN, AND THE EMOTIONAL AND PHYSIOLOGICAL MECHANICS OF CRAVING

The most common and relatable objections to embracing the Plant-Power Diet that I constantly entertain go something like these: "I wish I could be like you, but I just can't enjoy life without my cheese. . . ." "I can't help myself, I just have to eat ice cream. . . ." "I don't care what anybody says, my body needs eggs. . . ." "I'm powerless when it comes to a nice juicy steak."

In my opinion, the *number one*—and sadly all too often insurmountable—factor that condemns people to persistent unhealthy eating habits is *irresistible cravings*.

Anytime you want something, you have to make a bit of a sacrifice. For better or worse, good things in life come at a price. Training for Ultraman is hard. Often painful beyond my limits. But the reward makes it all worthwhile in the end. So my inclination is to respond harshly with something like "Yeah, you might miss your bacon. But you'll also miss your heart attack. Is it really worth destroying your health?"

But fear tactics, browbeating, and bootstrap shock therapy never really work. They didn't with me, that's for sure. If they did, everyone would eat healthy all the time. So why don't we?

To answer this question we have to take a look at the very nature of cravings—the physiological and emotional underpinnings that cause us to behave and eat the way we do.

At Springbrook, I began to truly understand the emotional nature of human craving in the context of addiction and compulsive behavior patterns. I came to see that our attachment to, and often obsession with, certain substances, behaviors, and even people is often rooted in a form of psychological and chemical imbalance. And food is no different—its pull is capable of creating the same addictive response found in drug addicts.* In fact, studies have shown that for some people, the sight of ice cream stimulates the same pleasure centers in the brain as images of crack pipes do for crack addicts. Over time, we begin to heavily associate certain

---

* Robert Langreth and Duance D. Stanford, "Fatty Foods as Addictive as Cocaine in Growing Body of Science," Bloomberg.com, November 1, 2011, www.bloomberg.com/news/2011-11-02/fatty-foods-addictive-as-cocaine-in-growing-body-of-science.html.

situations and emotions with a particular type of food. These associations become cemented pathways in the brain, establishing addictive patterns that can be seemingly impossible to break. The grip is tight, and more often than not, willpower proves futile. The comfort of your favorite food that can be relied on to take you out of a painful moment becomes a go-to drug of choice, and the more you indulge the more ingrained the habit becomes. What ensues is a cycle so entrenched, it quite literally becomes who we are.

In my case, I had to become introspective about why I ate the foods I did and take an honest inventory of the motivations behind my unhealthy food choices. I had to be honest about how I used food to cope with, deal with, or escape from reality. And so I implore you to do the same: get in touch with your inner workings and explore your psyche, your motivations, and your pain. Develop an understanding of the emotions that drive your unhealthy cravings so that they can be confronted, processed, and ultimately overcome.

Not ready for self-therapy? Well, don't lose hope just yet. There's another aspect to craving that is only recently becoming properly understood—*microbes*. What on earth do microbes have to do with anything? I hope you're sitting down. Because it's time to blow your mind.

We harbor the notion that we're sentient beings commanding full authority and power to control our thoughts. But recent studies provide a new perspective, challenging just how much control we truly have when it comes to our cravings.

What we don't consciously realize is that our bodies are not entirely ourselves. To be certain, our cells cluster together to form tissues, and these tissues compose the organs and systems that make us what we are. And yet we overlook the fact that our bodies act as hosts to trillions of microorganisms. I'm talking about bacteria, fungi, and other invisible organisms that symbiotically inhabit our skin, proliferate in our saliva, and thrive in our GI tract.

The typical human body is composed of about ten trillion cells. And yet we harbor microorganisms *ten times* that number in our digestive tract alone, as many as forty thousand different bacterial strains. In other words, it can be argued that head to toe, we're far more microbe than human. But fear not; to a large extent, these microorganisms are not enemies but friends, performing a wide variety of crucial functions imperative to our health, such as breaking down foods we cannot otherwise digest. And although too often overlooked, maintaining a healthy ecology of these microorganisms is absolutely crucial to optimizing health.

An emerging field of study has begun to evaluate the extent to which this *gut flora* impacts food choice, establishing a fascinating link between microorganisms and the foods we pine for. In other words, there's evidence to support a *microbial basis for craving.*

To illustrate, a team of Swiss researchers recently determined that people who crave chocolate actually harbor different types of microbial colonies in their gut than those who are indifferent to chocolate. And there's evidence to suggest that this may indeed be the case for many other types of food as well.[*]

But what does this mean? Certain scientists, including microbiologist Compton Rom, founder of holistic nutrition products company Ascended Health, submit that there is in fact a very direct and causal connection between our intestinal microbial ecology and the way we think. That, in fact, these microbes message our brains, effectively telling us what to eat. Turns out, it's our microbes that hold sway over our cravings.

Sound fantastical? Consider this. If you saw the documentary *Super Size Me,* you recall filmmaker Morgan Spurlock's quest to see what would happen if he ate nothing but McDonald's food

---

[*] Seth Borenstein, "Scientists Explain Chocolate Cravings," WashingtonPost.com, October 12, 2007, www.washingtonpost.com/wp-dyn/content/article/2007/10/12/AR2007101200019.html.

for thirty consecutive days. For the first few days, we watched him cringe, even vomit from his relentless fare of Big Macs, fries, and shakes. He felt sick. He suffered terrible headaches. But then a funny thing happened. That feeling of sickness went away. The headaches disappeared. Suddenly, he began to crave the food that just days prior had him cringing and buckled over. Then he began to wake up each morning with a headache that wouldn't quit *until* he got his McDonald's fix. How can this be explained? According to Compton, Morgan's dietary shift from a primarily plant-based diet to an entirely fast-food regimen effectively and quite rapidly replaced his healthy gut flora with a pathogenic microbial ecology that thrived specifically on the ingredients present in McDonald's food. This new unhealthy, or "bad," ecology of microflora simply required McDonald's to live. Thus, it hijacked Morgan's nervous system, sending messages to his brain and throughout his body that translated into an acute craving for more of these foods.

But this cycle can be broken by replacing the unhealthy foods you crave with healthy alkali-forming, plant-based foods, which will introduce the proliferation of an entirely new and much healthier microbial ecology to your digestive system. It's a process that can be assisted and expedited with (nondairy) probiotic supplementation (such as that offered by Ascended Health—see Appendix III, Resources). And once established, this new ecology will in turn signal your brain to replace those powerful unhealthy urges with an equally powerful craving for the foods that nourish you. And before you know it, that yearning for ice cream or pepperoni pizza just might vanish, replaced with a longing for a kale and pineapple smoothie, a red lentil pilaf, or even, you might be amazed to discover, sprouted mung beans over brown rice. It happened to me. Once a cheeseburger fanatic, I'm now rarely tempted by McDonald's. And if it worked for me, it can work for you.

TIP: Healthy gut bacteria create a craving for healthy foods, while pathogenic bacteria create a craving for unhealthy foods. *Change your microbes and you change your cravings. Change your cravings and you change your life.*

A WORD ABOUT GLUTEN, GRAINS, AND SPROUTING

Once I began to clean up my diet, I noticed that some technically vegan foods, in particular items containing refined flour—such as pasta, white bread, processed snacks, and pizza crust—left me feeling lethargic, congested, and even puffy-eyed. On occasion, my feet would even swell. I did some research and came to understand that my system has a certain intolerance for gluten, a sticky glue-like (hence the Latin derivation of the word "gluten") protein present in a variety of foods processed from wheat and other related grains, such as barley and rye.

For decades, conventional wisdom was that gluten was harmful only to those suffering from celiac disease, an autoimmune disorder afflicting about 1 percent of the population, in which the ingestion of gluten causes damage to the lining of the small intestine, preventing it from properly absorbing certain nutrients. Celiac patients suffer symptoms ranging from migraines, to skin rashes, muscle and joint pain, and sinus infections.

But in recent years, it's been discovered that far more people suffer a spectrum of ill effects, ranging from mild to serious, caused by the ingestion of gluten. This condition manifests symptoms similar to celiac, but it's generally less severe. The malady is now known as gluten sensitivity, or "GS."

Currently, there's no specific blood test for GS. To determine your personal level of sensitivity, the only solution is to experiment. In other words, simply remove food products with gluten from your diet for a week or two and see what happens. But for this experiment to be effective, you must already be eating well. Because if your diet contains copious amounts of processed snacks, for example, you'll feel better deleting these from your routine irrespective of any gluten sensitivity. So begin the process of getting PlantPowered first, settle into a routine, and when your diet is clean, then experiment.

When I removed gluten from my diet, I experienced a rather dramatic improvement not just in the maintenance of my energy levels, but in my athletic performance as well. For example, I noticed my muscles and joints didn't hurt as much the day after a long run, likely the result of a reduction in inflammation, that pesky impediment to exercise recovery. I also discovered an improvement in my training and digestion, as well as some weight loss. Even my face seemed to narrow.

If you determine that you suffer from GS, then it's incumbent upon you to pay close attention to the foods you eat going forward, since you might be surprised at just how omnipresent gluten is, in so many different foods. Because it's indeed the "glue" that makes certain food products stick together, it's found in everything from most breads and pastas to condiments such as ketchup and soy sauce. And, also, almost all vegetarian or vegan processed meat substitutes. But gluten-free options are becoming more readily available at many restaurants and groceries.

And even if you determine that gluten poses no problems for you, it's always best to trade food products made from refined grains (such as white bread) for those made with whole grains. The milling process that refines the grain effectively strips it of all nutritional value, leaving you with those empty calories discussed above. Conversely, the whole grain retains more of the vitamins and minerals inherent in the food. But the best option is always the *sprouted* whole grain—the seed in its germinated state enhances the nutritional value of the food even further, increasing the protein quality as well as the essential fatty acid, healthy enzyme, and vitamin content. For example, Food for Life makes a wonderful line of sprouted grain breads, called Ezekiel 4:9, available at most health food stores.

There's nothing like sprouted mung beans, lentils, or chickpeas. And without much effort, these foods can be sprouted at home. Soak the dry beans in water for eight to ten hours, and then maintain moistness in a colander or "sprouting vessel" at room temperature. Wash daily for a couple days until they sprout. Eat raw or slightly cooked—over brown rice or a tossed salad, for example—to enjoy the enhanced and bioavailable protein, vitamins, and minerals that are the by-product of the sprouting process.

TIP: If gluten's got you down, ditch the wheat pasta for pasta made from brown rice. Opt for breads and tortillas made from spelt or rice flour. And lose the wheat-based processed snacks like chips and crackers—they're gluten time bombs.

IRON, B_{12}, AND ANEMIA

Vegans are anemic. I hear it all the time. Conventional wisdom states that eating a plant-based whole-food diet fails to provide enough iron to prevent the onset of anemia, a potentially serious condition in which the body becomes unable to make enough oxygen-bearing red blood cells. It's simply not true.

By way of background, iron is a component of hemoglobin, a protein found in red blood cells that acts as a transport system to carry oxygen through the blood to our tissues. Anemia is a decrease in the body's red blood cell count or a reduction in blood hemoglobin caused by an iron deficiency, which undermines the body's ability to perform this oxygen transport and delivery function. The most commons symptoms are weakness, fatigue, poor concentration, shortness of breath, and depression.

Dietary iron is available in two forms: heme and non-heme. The heme variety is the most readily absorbable and is found in meat and dairy products. Non-heme, also found in animal products, is the only source of iron in the plant kingdom, but isn't as readily absorbed by the body. Hence the premise that plant-based diets lead to anemia.

However, studies have shown that the incidence of anemia among vegetarians and vegans is no higher than that among the general population.* It's believed that this is due to the fact that so many common plant-based foods happen to be high in iron. So heme or no heme, a person subsisting on a *well-rounded* plant-based diet that contains a mix of the foods listed in the chart below should experience no issues with respect to anemia.

It takes a long time to exhaust the body's iron stores, and requires a concerted effort to replenish them once depleted. Moreover, the symptoms of iron deficiency often fail to manifest until those stores are significantly diminished. So it's important to stay on top of this issue. But with a little awareness, ensuring proper maintenance of your iron stores is hardly burdensome. With just a modicum of thought and planning, ensuring that I ingest the recommended daily allowance of 18 mg of iron has proved a non-issue.

Here are a few tips to keep you on track:

Combine iron intake with vitamin C. Research has established that the absorption of non-heme (plant-based) iron is significantly enhanced when it's ingested in conjunction with foods high in

---

* R. Obeid, J. Geisel, H. Schorr, et al., "The Impact of Vegetarianism on Some Haematological Parameters," *European Journal of Haematology.* 2002,69: 275–79.

vitamin C—up to sixfold, in fact. Accordingly, I combine red pepper or citrus fruits such as oranges or grapefruit (all high in vitamin C) with dark leafy greens or pumpkin seeds (high in iron) in my daily Vitamix blend. And as an extra step, I always keep a bag of pumpkin seeds in my car, along with some fruit to munch while I drive—a tip I picked up on the friendly advice of Brendan Brazier.

Avoid coffee and tea at mealtime. The tannins contained in coffee or tea (irrespective of caffeine content) impede the body's ability to absorb iron, up to 50 to 60 percent. So if you're concerned about your iron stores, it's best to avoid these drinks an hour or so both before and after meals.

Vitamin B_{12} supplementation. Vitamin B_{12} is another compound required to generate red blood cells. So a deficiency in this vitamin can also lead to anemia. And vitamin B_{12} is the one essential nutrient that simply cannot be found in the plant kingdom. But again, there is no need to be alarmed, run out to the grocery, and start gorging on steaks. The fix is easy. You can simply take a B_{12} supplement, available in capsule form at any health food store. Alternatively, many meal supplements, such as my Jai Repair Performance Recovery Formula, or Brendan's Vega Complete Whole Food Health Optimizer, contain the RDA of B_{12}. Furthermore, nutritional yeast, which we use in a variety of our recipes, such as Cashew Cheese (see Appendix III, Resources, *Jai Seed Vegan eCookbook*), is also high in B_{12}. Finally, a wide variety of packaged foods—including certain grains and breakfast cereals, as well as almond and coconut milk—are generally fortified with this vitamin. Two cups of coconut milk and you've met your B_{12} needs for the day.

Five years PlantPowered and I've experienced zero issues with respect to my iron stores, despite the heavy training tax I impose on my body.

PLANTPOWER DIET

Plant-Based Foods High in Iron*
(RDA 18 mg iron/day; 100 g equals about 2 cups)

FOOD	IRON CONTENT (MG)
Pumpkin Seeds (½ cup)	20.7
Sesame Seeds (1 cup)	7.4
Blackstrap Molasses (2 tbsp)	7.2
Sundried Tomatoes (100 g)	9.1
Dried Apricots (100 g—about 20)	6.3
Lentils (1 cup)	6.6
Spinach (1 cup)	6.4
Quinoa (1 cup)	6.3
Tempeh (1 cup)	4.8
Black Beans (1 cup)	3.6
Kidney Beans (1 cup)	3.0
Pinto Beans (1 cup)	3.5
Potato (1)	3.2
Prune Juice (8 ounces)	3.0
Raisins (½ cup)	1.6

OMEGA MAN: TURNING FAT FROM ENEMY TO FRIEND

One of the incredible benefits of the PlantPowered Diet is that you don't have to overly concern yourself with the fat content of your food. I'm not saying you can go hog wild, but the days of obsessing are over.

How can this be true?

The PlantPower Diet is by its very nature low in fat. When you eat the PlantPower way, you've already removed the "bad" cholesterol and most saturated fat—the nasty artery-clogging, heart

---

* USDA Nutrient Database for Standard Reference, www.nal.usda.gov/fnic/foodcomp/search/.

disease–inducing kind that we generally think of when we think of fat. So right off the bat you've taken a massive step toward reducing your chances of suffering a heart attack or getting cancer, all the while working to reduce your (bad) cholesterol and/or high blood pressure.

But PlantPower is not fat-free. Nor, in my opinion, should it be. It's just that we've replaced those disease-inducing saturated fats with clean-burning, healthy unsaturated fats high in essential fatty acids (EFAs), like omega-3, which we hear so much about. Fats critical to an array of proper body functions. The kind of fats that fight disease, actually improve heart health, keep our energy levels high, our skin bright, and our mood sunny.

Fat associated with the typical American diet is your enemy. But PlantPower fat, in modest amounts, is your friend.

In their various books, plant-based nutrition experts T. Colin Campbell, Dr. Caldwell Esselstyn, and Dr. Dean Ornish all argue that a whole-food, plant-based diet extremely low in fat is best. So they throw out the olive oil and get rid of the avocados. And peanut butter or almond butter? Forget it—no more nuts. How do I feel about that? Well, I concede that if you're obese, fighting cancer, have survived a heart attack, suffer significantly clogged arteries, struggle with critically high cholesterol or blood pressure values, or are afflicted by any chronic disease, then this protocol is best. Your life hangs in the balance, and extreme measures are necessary to back yourself off the ledge. I can't dispute that these authors' programs work, and work well.

However, they're also extreme. Many people unthreatened by imminent demise might not be able to sustain such a strict regimen over time. And as I said earlier, *sustainability is the name of the game.*

The fact is, in cutting out all animal products and most processed foods from our diet, we've already extracted the key culprits in the promotion of heart disease, diabetes, high blood pressure, and cancer. Moreover, there's scientific evidence to support that swapping saturated fat with plant-based unsaturated fat is just as effective at reducing blood cholesterol as a diet entirely devoid of fat.

Another observation worth mentioning is that when people overdo it in their attempt to remove all fat from their diet, they tend to compensate by binging on starchy (nutrient-poor) carbohydrates, which in turn leads to weight gain.

Then there's this confusing business of EFAs—the essential fatty acids known as omega-3 (alpha-linolenic) and omega-6 (linoleic acid). We've all seen the labels. But what exactly are these fats, and why are they so important? Much like the essential amino acids discussed above, EFAs must be obtained from food, since the body can't itself manufacture them. And they're crucial to the maintenance of a wide array of bodily functions, including the activity of the brain, muscles, joints, adrenal glands, and sex organs. And yet many people suffer from a deficiency caused by an imbalance of these crucial fats, which leads to unhealthy skin conditions, joint problems, lethargy, memory impairment, and heart disease.

Balance the omegas. The typical American diet tends to be very high—far too high, in fact—in omega-6, which is found in corn (derivations of which can be found in zillions of food products), processed foods, certain vegetable oils, and meat. To be sure, this EFA is important, particularly with respect to maintaining kidney and skin health. But whether you're a vegan or a meat and dairy eater, ensuring adequate intake of omega-6 is rarely problematic. All of us get more than enough, simply because it's present in so many commonly ingested foods. The problem arises when the ratio of omega-6 to omega-3 is too high. When omega-6 isn't counterbalanced by sufficient intake of omega-3, the result can be depression and inflammation, which over time promotes a variety of chronic illnesses, including cancer—not to mention an impediment to timely recovery from exercise-induced stress.

Experts differ on the proper ratio of omega-6 to omega-3, but land somewhere between 5:1 to 1:1 (omega-6 to omega-3), depending on whom you talk to. And yet the typical American consumes vast multiples of the proper amount of omega-6 while being woefully deficient in omega-3—ratios estimated more in the 10:1 to 50:1 range (again, depending on whom you talk to).

I don't think we need to get overly meticulous about these ratios. Nobody needs to break out the beakers and the scale. Sticking to the theme of keeping things simple and sustainable, the point is this: Reduce your omega-6 and increase your omega-3 intake, which plays a significant role in reducing inflammation, blood pressure, cholesterol, and protecting against coronary disease.

But omega-3 isn't overly prevalent in a plant-based diet—fish oil is the most popular and common source. That opens the door to another argument often used to attack the health benefits of a plant-based diet.

In truth, omega-3 can be found in many plant-based foods. Flaxseed oil is one of the richest sources of omega-3, and until recently it was considered a popular and easy solution to this issue. But recent studies and expert opinion from people like Dr. Joseph Mercola of the Optimal Wellness Center have cautioned against the inclusion of this dietary oil, linking it to an increased risk of prostate cancer and even damage to the eyes. Assuming the correctness of this position, which is mired in ongoing debate, you should opt for an algae-based supplement or a well-rounded diet that includes the following foods high in omega-3:

PLANTPOWER DIET
Plant-Based Foods High in Omega-3 EFAs

Nuts	Brazil
	Walnut
	Butternut

Plant-Based Foods High in Omega-3 EFAs (continued)

Seeds	Chia
	Pumpkin
	Kiwi
	Hemp
	Sesame
Oils	Extra Virgin Olive Oil
	Hemp Oil
	Wheat Germ Oil
	Vega EFA Oil
	Udo's 3-6-9 Oil
Grains	Wheat Germ
Fruits	Avocado
Beans	Fermented Soybeans (Tempeh, Natto, and Miso)
	Navy Beans
	Kidney Beans
Vegetables	Dark Leafy Greens (Kale, Spinach, Mustard, Collards)
	Spirulina
	Algae (available in a variety of supplements)
	Winter Squash

TIP: Reduce your omega-6 intake by cutting out processed foods, animal protein, and oils derived from corn, canola, soy, sunflower, and safflower. Increase your omega-3 intake with nuts, seeds, avocados, dark leafy greens, and extra virgin olive oil. To maximize omega-3 content, eating these foods raw is optimal. But if cooking, do not overheat.

I enjoy my plant-based fats. And so should you. But enjoy them in *moderation*. Personally, I like a light amount of organic extra virgin olive oil on a number of my dishes. Sure it's fat, but it's also high in antioxidants. It's been shown to fight heart disease by lowering blood cholesterol. It even helps in the prevention of colon cancer. And I like to put a little Vegenaise, a grapeseed oil–based, dairy-free mayonnaise replacement, on veggie sandwiches made with gluten-free toast. Not only does this oil promote healthy skin and heart health, it's anti-inflammatory, anti-aging, antioxidant, and anti-cancer. I'm also a huge fan of organic coconut oil. Often misunderstood due to the fact that it's one of the only plant-based foods that contain saturated fat, this oil is actually remarkably healthy. The saturated fat component is quickly converted to lauric acid, a bioavailable energy source that leaves me energized and promotes weight loss as well as heart health by lowering cholesterol and blood pressure. The list of benefits goes on—Alzheimer's prevention, memory enhancement, skin health, improved immunity, better digestion, liver health, mineral absorption, enhanced management and prevention of diabetes—even an antibacterial, antiviral, and antifungal effect. And due to organic coconut oil's ability to sustain high heat without the oxidation that leads to free radical damage in our cells, it's the preferred oil when it comes to cooking. How about nuts? I love 'em. We've already seen that they're useful in terms of omega-3 content. At the top of my list are raw organic almonds, which lower cholesterol and improve heart health due to their high content of L-arginine and vitamin E.

Then there's my all-time favorite, the avocado. Rarely does a day go by that I don't eat one or more. Once maligned for their high fat content (the average avocado has about thirty grams of mostly monounsaturated fat), they're now embraced for their high antioxidant, anti-inflammatory, anti-arthritic, and cholesterol-lowering properties. My perfect food. Not only do they promote heart health and aid in the absorption of other important nutrients, like carotenoids, their anti-inflammatory and antioxidant high-glutathione properties help me recover between workouts. They stabilize blood sugar, keeping my energy even. And if that's not enough, they help prevent the development of both skin and prostate cancer.

Again, this isn't a license to go *nuts*—pun intended. Unless you're training like me, I recommend somewhere in the range of twenty to forty grams of fat per sitting, or 10 to 20 percent of daily caloric intake, depending upon the extent to which (1) your lifestyle is active, (2) weight loss is a priority, and (3) you suffer from chronic illnesses. As a general rule, the more unhealthy and sedentary you are, the less fats you should eat.

TIP: When it comes to cooking with oil, opt for organic virgin coconut. It's far more heat-stable than other oils, which tend to oxidize, causing the proliferation of damaging free radicals. Can't do without your olive oil? Just make sure it's organic and extra virgin, and don't overheat. And ditch that canola and corn oil—no, they're not quite the same, but they're both bad.

If you're an experienced athlete, marathoner, or someone who exercises routinely and rigorously, then in my opinion there's no need to get too concerned about these fats if you adhere to the PlantPower plan. Personally, I don't worry about that aspect.

But if you have a hard time just getting off the couch, or can't seem to lose those extra pounds, then cut back. Maybe even get rid of the oils altogether until your weight stabilizes. Be judicious when it comes to avocados and nuts. But remember, if you skimp too much on the healthy fats because you're concerned about weight gain, you're likely to end up binging on nutrient-poor, high-carbohydrate starchy foods and grains—thus undermining your goal.

And one final note: Get your butt to the gym or a yoga class. Put on the running shoes, play tennis, or tune up that bike collecting dust in the garage. The PlantPower Diet will get you to the twenty-yard line, but if you want to score, daily exercise you enjoy is a must.

PLANTPOWER DIET

My Favorite Plant-Based Fats

Avocados

Almonds (raw) and Almond Milk

Walnuts (raw)

Coconut, Coconut Milk, and Coconut Oil

Olive Oil (Extra Virgin)

Hemp Oil

WHAT ABOUT SOY?

We've been led to believe that foods high in soy (a protein-based legume)—such as soy milk, soy protein supplements, tofu, and many processed imitation meat products—are a healthy and nutritious high-protein replacement for many meats and dairy-based foods. Soy has been historically portrayed as a vegan superfood that protects the heart and fights cancer. But not so fast. There's an expanding field of research that places the health claims of soy in much dispute.

Soy and soy-based products are high in phytoestrogens, a plant-based estrogen. And high estrogen intake has been linked to breast cancer, infertility, and low libido, among other things. High in goitrogens, soy can damage the thyroid, which leads to weight gain, fatigue, and loss of concentration. And unless properly fermented, soy is also incredibly high in phytates and trypsin inhibitors, which block the absorption of minerals and protein, respectively.

Think you're doing your baby a favor by feeding him or her soy infant formula? Think again. The high estrogen content can irreversibly harm sexual development and reproductive health. And for women, just two glasses of soy milk a day over a thirty-day period can actually alter the timing of the menstrual cycle.

For all of the above reasons, I strongly advise against including too many unfermented soy and soy-based food products (such as tofu) in your diet. But maybe you just won't be able to resist those sausage patties unless you can eat that soy-based imitation sausage patty as a temporary bridge as you make the switch. I get it. Just be cautious. And ditch that soy milk in your latte, replacing it with almond, hemp, or coconut milk instead. It actually tastes better anyway.

That being said, I do enjoy a modest amount of tofu in certain recipes from time to time. But as a general rule, I opt for organic, fermented, and non-GMO (genetically modified organism) varieties of soy, such as tempeh, natto, and miso.

VITAMIN D: GO OUTSIDE

Vitamin D isn't found in the plant kingdom.* So is that more ammunition to undermine the advisability of a plant-based, whole-food diet? Hardly. The body produces its own vitamin D with modest exposure to sunlight—ten to fifteen minutes in direct light should do the trick. Hate going outside? Well, then you're probably not reading this book. But if so, or you live where the sun just won't shine, plenty of fruit juices and milk substitutes such as almond and coconut milk are fortified with the recommended daily allowance of vitamin D, thus obviating any legitimate concern regarding a deficiency of this important nutrient.

ORGANIC: DOES IT REALLY MATTER?

We all know that organic food is all the rage, exploding in popularity in recent years. Grocery stores expand their offerings as marketing pushes the message. But does it really matter? Yes, it does.

---

* Studies indicate that white button mushrooms when exposed to ultraviolet B radiation demonstrate vitamin D content beyond RDA levels. But this product is not yet commercially available and the bioavailability of the vitamin D in this context is unclear.

So what's the difference?

Central to traditional, large-scale "factory" farming is the utilization of synthetic fertilizers and other toxins, including pesticides, herbicides, genetically modified organisms (GMOs), and even sewage sludge and ionizing radiation, to grow your food. Invariably, these substances leave toxic chemical residue on the foods we eat, many of which have proved dangerous to human health, even carcinogenic in high doses. There's considerable debate concerning the level of harm presented by such foods, but it's indisputable that caution is in order.

Conversely, organic farming shuns the use of such toxins in favor of natural fertilizers and renewable resources that aim to conserve and enhance the environmental quality of farmland soil, all while reaping foods the way nature intended.

The inherent nutritional content of organic versus non-organic foods is a much-debated issue. But some studies have established that foods farmed in the conventional manner tend to lack the nutritional density of organically grown crops, the importance of which I discussed above. We don't need to get bogged down in the empirical data. I know that when I eat a conventionally grown tomato, it's essentially tasteless. It looks great—large, perfectly round, with a beautiful dark red hue—almost begging you to grab it off the shelf and put it in your cart. But often it has the flavor of sand. By contrast, a small runt of an oddly shaped organically grown tomato bursts with flavor. My research is over.

There's no need for long discourse on this subject. Whenever possible, do your best to eat organic. And strive to eat produce that is locally grown. Not only is it fresher, it's more ecologically sustainable. Becoming a locavore is an easy way to reduce your food's carbon footprint, because locally grown produce doesn't have to be shipped cross-country or internationally, which requires an absurd expenditure of fossil fuel.

It's not always the case, but usually organic foods are more expensive. I know this all too well and am sympathetic to the budgetary constraints of the typical family. Plus, depending on where you live, organic isn't always readily available. Not everyone enjoys the luxury of a nearby Whole Foods or local farmer's market. If you search online, however, you'll likely find a local option or two (for a database of farmer's markets and organic food grown closest to you, visit localharvest.org). Still striking out? You can always start your own garden. It's not as daunting as you might think.

But giving up on a plant-based diet because organic is too expensive or hard to source isn't the answer. It's always better to eat non-organic produce than to eat no produce. Just make sure you wash your items well before eating. If budget is an issue, be selective in your organic choices, since some non-organic foods are worse than others when it comes to pesticide residue.

TIP: Want to get organic but budget and/or availability has you down? Get selective. Here's a list of the top non-organic foods to avoid, due to their high content of pesticide residue:*

Apples	Celery
Strawberries	Peaches
Spinach	Nectarines
Grapes	Bell Pepper
Potatoes	Blueberries
Lettuce	Kale
Cucumbers	Cherries
Pears	

---

* Environmental Working Group, 2011 Shopper's Guide, "The Full List: 53 Fruits and Veggies," www.ewg.org/foodnews/list/.

A PLANTPOWER DAY IN THE LIFE

I've shown you the scientific underpinnings of the PlantPower Diet, and now you understand *why* I eat the way I do. But the question remains, *What precisely do I eat, and when?*

The best way to answer this question is to walk you through a typical day in my life with food.

But before I begin, a disclaimer. I spend the majority of my year training for ultra-endurance events, often upward of fifteen to twenty-five hours per week. Depending on the phase of my training cycle, in a typical week I log 10,000 to 30,000 yards in the pool, 100 to 250 miles of cycling, and 25 to 80 miles of running. And throw in some gym work and yoga to boot. So you might be tempted to assume that my portions and caloric intake so far exceed that of the average person that a look at my daily diet is pointless. To some extent that's true. I ask a lot of my body. In turn, it places a considerable nutritional burden on me. My caloric and nutritional needs are indeed higher than the average person's. And many things I eat are consumed for the express purpose of fueling my training and enhancing athletic performance.

But as previously explained, over the last few years my body has become incredibly efficient in bearing this exercise load. An aerobic bike ride of, say, forty to fifty miles, once daunting, now to me feels equivalent to a light jog to the mailbox. And because of the high nutrient density of the foods I eat, my daily caloric intake isn't as high as you might think. The gap from me to you is actually not that vast—the principles remain the same.

And all science aside, I *enjoy* my food. Far from following a bland deprivation regime, I follow a diet that includes a wide variety of delicious dishes developed by my wife and me to fuel my endurance endeavors *and* please even the finicky palates of our children.

You can find the specific recipes for many of the dishes described below—and more—in our *Jai Seed Vegan eCookbook* (see Appendix III, Resources).

MORNING / PRE-WORKOUT
KICK-START THE METABOLISM

ALKALIZE. Upon waking, I immediately drink a tall glass of water with two tablespoons of apple cider vinegar. This alkalizes my body pH.

ENDURANCE ELIXIR. Prior to a morning training session, I typically drink one-half cup of Ascended Health Endurance Elixir, a thick, dark green concoction I've developed in partnership with microbiologist Compton Rom over the last four years. Containing dozens of live and fermented plant-based ingredients, it's a critical component of my nutrition program and deserves ample credit for keeping me strong, healthy, and fresh while enabling me to bear a rigorous training load. Composed of probiotics, organic greens, marine phytoplankton, the purest form of endurance-boosting maca, fermented seeds and beans, Cordyceps mushroom extracts, enzymes, adaptogens, and some of the purest and most potent antioxidants sourced from all over the world, like resveratrol extracted from the finest Bordeaux grape skins, this get-up-and-go concoction provides me with an immediate source of energy more than sufficient to get me through a morning workout of ninety minutes or less. If you're interesting in learning more about this and other Ascended Health products, see Appendix III, Resources.

PRE-WORKOUT VITAMIX. I also blend a light drink that typically contains dark leafy greens (such as kale, spinach, beet greens, and Swiss chard) as well as a modest amount of organic fruit. Pineapple, grapefruit, orange, apple, blueberries, strawberries, and spirulina regularly find their way into my rotation. Also, chia seeds, beets, and maca root to boost endurance. Another thing I'll add is a few almonds or walnuts, as well as a tablespoon or two of oil (coconut, hemp, Udo's 3-6-9, and Vega EFA top my list) for bioavailable fats to fuel my ride, run, or swim. But let me be clear: I have no singular recipe. Each day is different. I don't wed myself to any particular brew or get overly caught up in exact proportions. Variety is important. I like to cycle and experiment, and the mix generally depends on my level of fatigue, the intensity and duration of the looming workout, and, more often than not, what we happen to have in our refrigerator or pantry that day. The take-away is *don't be rigid.* Stock your kitchen with a wide variety of the healthy items described in this book, then experiment. Pay close attention to how different ingredients impact your energy, mood, and appetite. Find what works for you, which items best suit your taste, and expand from there.

PRE-WORKOUT BREAKFAST. In general, the Vitamix more than suffices. But if I'm feeling worn out, have a big day ahead, or am simply still hungry, a slice of gluten-free toast with almond butter does the trick. Alternatively, cold quinoa with coconut milk and berries serves as a great high-protein breakfast cereal. Sometimes I'll mix in a teaspoon of coconut oil or EFA oil (such as that offered by Vega Sport or Udo's). And I'll feel free to sprinkle some chia seeds on top for a superfood kick. When I'm facing a short workout (1 hour or less) as opposed to a long endurance slog on the bike, higher glycemic (simple sugar) foods such as dates work great for a quick energy boost.

THE FAT-BURNING SESSION. There's evidence to suggest that you can enhance the body's ability to efficiently burn fat as fuel—critical for excelling in endurance sports—by occasionally doing what's called a "calorie deprivation" workout. This is a session—typically a run or a bike ride of varying length—in which you dispense with breakfast altogether and just get out for a morning training session on nothing but water and electrolyte tablets. But this is hardly a daily practice. I recommend only doing it once a week, tops. It's something to integrate very slowly and incrementally into your routine, and a regimen I advise against until you're in solid physical condition. Once the exercise session is complete, it's important to immediately replenish the body's electrolytes and glycogen stores to properly recover in time for the next workout.

DURING WORKOUT
HYDRATE—AND TAKE IN ENERGY

ELECTROLYTES AND HYDRATION. No matter how short the workout, I always make sure I hydrate and replenish my electrolytes every twenty to thirty minutes throughout the session. I prefer coconut water for electrolytes, primarily because it's natural. Vega makes a powdered product called Electrolyte Hydrator, which is also a great source of electrolytes and other natural plant-based nutrients that help sustain energy levels. Alternatively, I'll use an electrolyte supplement such as SaltStick or Endurolytes capsules, readily available at most bike shops and running shoe retailers. But my general rule of thumb is to drink a minimum of twelve ounces of electrolyte-laced water every thirty minutes, depending on heat, humidity, and workout duration.

CARBOHYDRATES. My rule of thumb is to take in about two hundred calories per hour while performing workouts that exceed two hours in length (with the exception of the occasional calorie-deprivation workout). Often this is a challenge for me, since I don't like to eat or drink too much when I'm training. But it's important to do so, not so much to fuel that workout but to avoid feeling depleted or lethargic for the remainder of the day, or the day following. I always prefer to eat "real" foods for this. A lightly baked yam, bananas, almond butter rice balls, and avocado or almond butter sandwiches all work well for cycling. As previously discussed at length, I shun popular sugary drinks and gels. But there are a few bars out there I like—organic and natural varieties such as those offered by WildBar, Vega Sport, ProBar, and Clif (not all Clif Bars are vegan, so check the label). And many people create their own homemade vegan energy bars. If you're so inclined, check NoMeatAthlete.com for some good recipes or do a simple Google search. For running and high-intensity interval-oriented cycling workouts, I find liquid nutrition is most easily digested and assimilated. Amazingly, I can pack up to nine hundred calories of non-GMO maltodextrin-based complex carbohydrate powder, such as Perpetuem by Hammer Nutrition, into one sixteen-ounce bottle. Maltodextrin can also be bought in bulk online. It tastes like pancake batter, so I like to lace it with some fruit juice or coconut water for flavor. On hot days, prepare and freeze the bottled concoction overnight so it slowly thaws throughout your workout, staying cold for several hours.

THINGS TO AVOID. Again, I generally refrain from eating any of the artificially colored sugary products popular among most endurance athletes—like those gooey gels and Gatorade-type drinks such as Cytomax or Powerade. Or "energy" bars (other than those listed above), most of which contain a ton of artificial additives as well as whey protein, a dairy extract derived from cheese production. Chemical additives aside, the high glycemic "simple sugar" content of these products causes a rapid spike in blood sugar. To the extent that a short workout or race induces low blood sugar, this spike can be a good thing, giving the body access to a quick-burning fuel source. But be advised: Once you've boosted your blood sugar in this manner, you must then continuously put into the bloodstream high-glycemic-content foods for the duration of your training session. Fail to do so and the concomitant spike in insulin levels—the body's natural response to a sudden increase in blood sugar—will rapidly pull these sugars out of the blood, causing you to "crash" or run out of steam. Because the duration of my training sessions often exceeds several hours, I prefer to get my energy from a lower glycemic (complex carbohydrate) source (like yams or maltodextrin), which is more effective in maintaining an even and stable level of blood sugar over extended periods of time.

All that being said, I do carry one or two of those gels with me just in case I feel myself starting to "bonk," a common energy crash that occurs if I miscalculate my caloric needs and under-fuel. And to be fair, there's some scientific evidence to suggest that the mere taste of sugar alone sends signals to the brain that fuel is on the way. The brain in turn messages the body that despite fatigue, there's no need for metabolic panic—or shutting down the body. Thus, in certain situations—again, in the context of a race or the onset of deep fatigue in the latter phases of an extended or particularly challenging workout—simple sugar products in the form of gels or drinks have their place. But as a general rule, I do my best to avoid them.

POST-WORKOUT
REPLENISH, REFUEL, REBUILD

Studies have established that the optimal period to begin the post-workout recovery process is within thirty minutes of ending a workout—a time when the body is most capable of directing the appropriate nutrients toward repairing the damage induced by exercise stress. It's thus critical to replenish the body's electrolyte, glycogen, and protein stores within this window.

Because they're most easy to digest, begin with liquids, then add whole foods slowly over the following hour. Immediately after returning from a workout, I drink a tall glass of cold coconut water for electrolytes, plus a quart or two of water, the amount varying depending on heat and duration of workout.

Consensus opinion states that post-exercise one should consume about .75 grams of carbohydrate per pound of body weight—and about 1 gram of protein for every 3 to 5 grams of carbohydrate ingested. But again, I never give these numbers too much thought. Using them more as a thumbnail, I simply pull out the Vitamix. I mix up dark leafy greens, like kale, spinach, and spirulina, with some lemon or apple cider vinegar to quickly alkalize my system. I add foods high in antioxidants, like strawberries, blueberries, acai, and goji berries, to fight the exercise-induced free radical damage. Also: pumpkin seeds for iron, plus fruits high in vitamin C to aid the iron absorption. I'll also maybe add some avocado and chia and hemp seeds for omega-3s. Plus a scoop of Jai Repair Performance Recovery Supplement to ensure a full array of essential amino acids to expedite the rebuilding of weary muscles. There's no need to drink an entire blender's worth in one sitting. Sometimes I'll do that, but not generally. As I said earlier, have a glass or two and thermos the rest.

LUNCH
KEEP IT LIGHT

Once I stabilize my system, it becomes important to replenish glycogen stores with some whole-food (as opposed to liquid) complex carbohydrates. But I don't overdo it (particularly with respect to starchy, nutrient-poor foods), preferring to keep things relatively light so my energy remains high and consistent for the afternoon. So a typical lunch might be lentils, mung beans, quinoa, or steamed vegetables over a modicum of brown rice. Other options might be a salad with mixed veggies and an olive oil–based dressing—and maybe a sweet potato sprinkled with Celtic or Hawaiian sea salt. Why sea salt? In contrast to typical table salt, sea salt is unrefined and high in trace minerals that help balance electrolytes and promote optimal biological functioning.

What else do I eat? Sometimes a veggie burrito—steamed brown rice with black beans, guacamole, fresh salsa, and some veggies such as spinach and peppers lightly sautéed and wrapped in a gluten-free tortilla (Udi's makes a fine version) or mixed in a bowl. And to drink? Water and maybe a detoxifying kombucha tea—I love that stuff.

SNACKS
STOKING THE METABOLIC MACHINE

To avoid lethargy, fatigue, and a loss of mental focus between meals, it's important to continue to feed yourself light snacks to keep your metabolism churning at its peak. Develop a habit of *light grazing*—eating small snacks throughout the day. Nuts are brain food, so a handful of almonds, almond butter on gluten-free or sprouted grain toast, or a healthy trail mix is great, provided you don't overdo it on these fats. And try sipping on that thermos smoothie blend we talked about earlier—always the best snack food option in my opinion, and a solid insurance policy against the onset of cravings that can lead to a sudden unhealthy choice. If you have time to pack a snack, some cold lentils or black beans with hot sauce is a personal favorite. Trader Joe's—a continuously expanding low-cost national grocery store chain—sells (among many other great PlantPower-friendly items) precooked lentils that I often simply eat cold right out of the package, thereby requiring *zero* prep time.

Nonetheless, at least once a week I cook a large amount of brown or basmati rice, black beans, and lentils and store them in the refrigerator. Then I pack a Tupperware bowl with some combination of these items and bring it with me for the day. It's a cheap and easy regimen that keeps me on track should I find myself unable to locate healthy food options during my workday.

And, of course, fruits are a favorite snack. Nothing beats an apple, a banana, or some berries to keep your blood sugar up. Whole foods are always best, but in a pinch, a WildBar, ProBar, Vega Sport, or Clif Bar (again, vegan) are all fine options.

DINNER
MIX IT UP

I tend to eat a large dinner, going heavy on the vegetables. For example, a large arugula salad with avocado, leeks, fennel, cucumber, sprouts, and sesame seeds or pepitas sprinkled with chia seeds and a light olive oil– or apple cider vinegar–based dressing. Also, broccoli, Brussels sprouts, leeks, spinach, artichoke, and asparagus routinely make the list. Maybe I'll have a beet soup with kale chips or a nice warm vegetable broth to warm me up in the winter months, with walnut pâté spread over a baked yam—but I'm careful not to overcook, since excessive heat can destroy much of the nutritional value. And I eat plenty of legumes, such as black beans, sprouted mung beans, lentils, chickpea hummus, and black or kidney bean chili with homemade guacamole and salsa.

What else? Well, I'll eat a sparing amount of starches and grains—brown or basmati rice and quinoa (technically a seed) top my list. Other favorites include vegan mashed potatoes with Julie's tasty mushroom gravy—or her homemade tamales, tempeh-based veggie burgers, or squash-based vegan lasagna. And I allow myself the pleasure of brown-rice (gluten-free) pasta, best with Julie's homemade tomato or vegan pesto sauce—an almond-based recipe that tastes so much like regular pesto I don't even miss the Parmesan. And if you've read the previous chapters in this book, you know I'm a big fan of Vegenaise, a grapeseed oil–based mayonnaise replacement that goes great on avocado sandwiches or in Julie's mashed potatoes and potato salad made with Bubbies brand sugar-free dill relish.

DESSERT
DAIRY-FREE DELICIOUSNESS!

Contrary to popular belief, great-tasting desserts don't require milk, butter, and eggs. How about Julie's Mayan Black Thunder Shake? A fantastic blend of coconut meat and oil, banana, cacao, and kale that rivals the best chocolate milk shake you ever had. If I've trained vigorously on a given day or am feeling overly fatigued, I might add a scoop of Jai Repair Performance Recovery Supplement to the shake to help rebuild my muscles overnight. And the kids' favorite is chia seed pudding. Despite the fact that it contains avocado, you'd be amazed at how much this superfood delight tastes just like the chocolate pudding you're used to. Other favorites: raw cookies, coconut milk–based ice cream, vegan pumpkin pie. These days you can even buy vegan marshmallows, which are surprisingly good. The list goes on and on.

I'm not advocating anyone go crazy on desserts. I'm simply saying that just because you're PlantPowered doesn't mean you should be deprived of the pleasure of a mouthwatering dessert from time to time. There are a wider variety of delicious options available than you might realize. The dessert recipes described above—and more—can be found in our *Jai Seed Vegan eCookbook*. And for information on an array of store-bought dessert options, see Appendix III, Resources.

Just before bed, I often eat a few Brazil nuts. As mentioned previously, this food is high in the trace mineral selenium, a powerful antioxidant activator that has been shown to naturally boost testosterone levels in men, thus aiding in the maintenance of muscle mass and the promotion of general vitality. That's particularly important given that testosterone production in men naturally diminishes with age.

A WORD ABOUT RESTAURANTS

I'm lucky. Living in Los Angeles, I'm surrounded by countless vegan- and vegetarian-oriented restaurants that offer a wide variety of PlantPower-friendly selections and exude a certain "left coast" openness to preparing "off menu" dishes to suit my taste. I realize, though, that not everyone lives in such an environment. Although plant-based and gluten-free menu options are a popular and expanding restaurant trend nationwide, they're hardly pervasive. Therefore, chances are you'll find yourself in an eatery with absolutely no acceptable or appealing entrée possibilities. What then? I'm not immune from this scenario, particularly in a business situation, where I don't always hold sway over what restaurant I'm at. And personally, I hate to make a stink. The last thing I want to do in a restaurant is draw attention to myself. We all know "that guy." The pain in the butt who just can't eat anything and drives the waiter and those he's dining with crazy with annoying requests.

So if you're imagining yourself in just this predicament, I'm sympathetic.

With a little artful and delicate handling, however, these treacherous waters *can* be navigated. First and foremost, if you're polite—and maybe even a bit self-deprecating as opposed to self-righteous—you'll find (as I have) *that people just don't care.* It's the preachy sanctimoniousness that turns people off. So I always try to handle these social situations with a bit of humor and aplomb. What often follows is a reaction of curiosity rather than defensive annoyance. My special requests or exclusions sometimes create an intrigue that spawns a surprisingly dynamic and interesting dinner-table conversation. In the best circumstances, I leave my friends or business acquaintances rethinking their own assumptions about food. The key is to be gracious. If you stand in judgment—or try to rescue or convert—people will run for the hills.

Don't want to cause a fuss? Me neither. So pull the waiter aside when it's time to order and speak quietly with him or her so as not to be "that guy." Or simply excuse yourself from the table and approach your waiter out of table sight. Have a friendly discussion about what you might be able to order off the menu. You may be surprised by the willingness to help.

Even in the most challenging culinary environment, I'm generally able to order something palatable: veggie sushi and vegetables such as spinach, sautéed mushrooms, and seaweed salad at Japanese restaurants; rice and veggies when eating at Chinese or Indian establishments; a veggie burrito or burrito bowl at a Mexican restaurant; a salad, baked potato, and side of steamed vegetables at a steak house; pasta and tomato sauce when dining Italian (although be careful; some homemade restaurant pastas contain eggs, so be sure to ask); and large salads with vinaigrette virtually anywhere.

Veggie burgers also seem to be everywhere these days. The worst-case eating scenario for a vegan? French fries. Obviously, some of these foods are far from ideal. The point is to do the best you can, then move on.

As previously discussed, my best strategy is to be prepared for these scenarios by always having nearby a thermos of home-brewed smoothie, maybe a bowl of rice and lentils, or various healthy snack items. That way I can nourish myself just prior to entering a restaurant that is unlikely to offer proper fare, eat light from the best option available, and leave content.

RESOURCES

JAI LIFESTYLE PRODUCTS AND SERVICES

Roll, Rich, and Julie Piatt. *Jai Seed Vegan eCookbook,*
www.jai-lifestyle.com/cookbook
A digital coffee table–style e-book download for the iPad generation, *Jai Seed*
contains seventy-seven pages of PlantPower nutritional information and easy-to-
prepare recipes that Julie and I have developed and refined over the last five years,
many of which are referenced throughout this book. Containing a delicious array
of Vitamix blends, appetizers, meals, sauces, and desserts, *Jai Seed* is a cookbook
for athletes and families alike.

Jai Repair Performance Recovery Formula, www.jailifestyle.com
A plant-based athletic recovery supplement I formulated in cooperation with microbiologist Compton Rom of Ascended Health, Jai Repair contains a complete
amino acid profile comprised of the purest and most bioavailable pea, brown rice,
and hemp proteins required for proper muscle maintenance and development.
Enhanced with a robust and entirely unique blend of endurance-promoting
Cordyceps mushroom extracts and further augmented with L-glutamine, vitamin B_{12}, and an array of powerful antioxidants such as resveratrol and more,
Jai Repair is a proprietary PlantPower blend scientifically devised to expedite
maximum physiological repair induced by exercise stress and promote optimum
wellness.

Jai Renew Detox and Cleansing Program, www.jailifestyle.com
A comprehensive plant-based detoxifying protocol specifically conceived and
formulated to assist the body in making the transition to a PlantPower lifestyle.
Nourishing and 100 percent natural, Jai Renew is intended as a gentle bridge to
kick-start the changing role of food in your life on the road to long-term optimum wellness.

Jai Release Meditation Programs, www.jailifestyle.com
Thirty-minute instructional guided meditation practice audio programs with musical accompaniment and mantras, produced, arranged, and recorded by Julie Piatt. Beginner and advanced versions available for download.

Jai Lifestyle website, www.jailifestyle.com
Founded by Julie and me in 2009, Jai Lifestyle is a wellness company focused on promoting optimum sustainable wellness through PlantPower nutrition, exercise, yoga, and meditation. The website features PlantPower nutritional information and newsletters, instructional cooking videos, recipe updates, and related products and services, including PlantPower workshops and retreats.

SriMati, www.srimatimusic.com
The debut album of Julie (aka SriMati). All songs written by SriMati; performed by SriMati and our sons, Tyler Piatt and Trapper Piatt.

ADDITIONAL PLANT-BASED NUTRITION PRIMERS AND COOKBOOKS

Barnard, Dr. Neal D. *Neal Barnard's Program for Reversing Diabetes: The Scientifically Proven System for Reversing Diabetes Without Drugs.* (Emmaus, PA: Rodale Books, 2008).

Brazier, Brendan. *Thrive: The Vegan Nutrition Guide to Optimal Performance in Sports and Life.* (Cambridge, MA: Da Capo Press, 2008).

Brazier, Brendan. *Thrive Foods: 200 Plant-Based Recipes for Peak Health.* (Cambridge, MA: Da Capo Press, 2011).

Brotman, Juliano. *Raw: The Uncookbook: New Vegetarian Food for Life.* (New York: ReganBooks, 1999).

Campbell, T. Colin, and Thomas M. Campbell II. *The China Study: The Most Comprehensive Study of Nutrition Ever Conducted and the Startling Implications for Diet, Weight Loss and Long-Term Health.* (Jackson, TN: BenBella Books, 2006).

Esselstyn, Dr. Caldwell, Jr. *Prevent and Reverse Heart Disease: The Revolutionary, Scientifically Proven, Nutrition-Based Cure.* (New York: Avery Trade, 2008).

Esselstyn, Rip. *Engine 2 Diet: The Texas Firefighter's 28-Day Save-Your-Life Plan That Lowers Cholesterol and Burns Away the Pounds.* (New York: Grand Central, 2009).

Freston, Kathy. *Veganist: Lose Weight, Get Healthy, Change the World.* (New York: Weinstein Books, 2011).

Friedman, Rory, and Kim Barnouin. *Skinny Bitch.* (Running Press, 2007).

Friedman, Rory, and Kim Barnouin. *Skinny Bitch in the Kitch: Kick Ass Recipes for Hungry Girls Who Want to Stop Cooking Crap (and Start Looking Hot!).* (Philadelphia, PA: Running Press, 2007).

Fuhrman, Joel. *Eat to Live: The Amazing Nutrient-Rich Program for Fast and Sustained Weight Loss.* (New York: Little Brown, 2011).

Gentry, Ann, and Anthony Head. *The Real Food Daily Cookbook.* (New York: Ten Speed Press, 2005).

Joseph, John, and Dr. Fred Bisci, PhD. *Meat Is for Pussies (A How-to Guide for Dudes Who Want to Get Fit, Kick Ass and Take Names).* (Crush Books, 2010).

Phyo, Ani. *Ani's Raw Food Essentials: Recipes and Techniques for Mastering the Art of Live Food.* (Cambridge, MA: Da Capo Press, 2010).

Ronnen, Tal. *The Conscious Cook: Delicious Meatless Recipes That Will Change the Way You Eat.* (New York: William Morrow Cookbooks, 2009).

PLANTPOWER-FRIENDLY WEBSITE RESOURCES

Rich Roll, www.richroll.com
Jai Lifestyle, www.jailifestyle.com
Physicians Committee for Responsible Medicine, www.pcrm.org
Mind Body Green, www.mindbodygreen.com
One Green Planet, www.onegreenplanet.com
Ecorazzi, www.ecorazzi.com
NoMeatAthlete, www.nomeatathlete.com
OrganicAthlete, www.organicathlete.com
Vegan Body Building, www.veganbodybuilding.com
VegNews Magazine, www.vegnews.com
Vegan Fitness, www.veganfitness.net
Forks Over Knives, www.forksoverknives.com
Local Harvest, www.localharvest.org
Elizabeth Kucinich, www.elizabethkucinich.com
Meatless Monday, www.meatlessmonday.com
Choosing Raw, www.choosingraw.com
Colleen Patrick-Goudreau, www.compassionatecook.com
Engine 2 Diet, www.engine2diet.com
T. Colin Campbell, www.tcolincampbell.org
Dr. Dean Ornish, www.pmri.org
Dr. Caldwell Esselstyn, www.heartattackproof.com
Dr. John McDougall, www.drmcdougall.com
Dr. Joel Fuhrman, www.drfuhrman.com

KITCHEN ESSENTIALS

Vitamix Blenders, www.jai-lifestyle.com/vita-mix-affiliate

Filtron Cold Brew Coffee Systems, www.biogro.us/filtron_cold_brew_coffee
.html

Sprout People Sprouting Devices, www.sproutpeople.org

FOOD STAPLES, CONDIMENTS, AND MEAT AND DAIRY SUBSTITUTES

KAL Nutritional Yeast Flakes, www.iherb.com

Vegenaise (non-dairy mayonnaise), www.followyourheart.com

Earth Balance (non-dairy butter), www.earthbalance.com

So Delicious Coconut Milk and Keifer, www.turtlemountain.com

Living Harvest Hemp Milk, www.livingharvest.com

Amy & Brian Naturals Coconut Juice, www.amyandbriannaturals.com

GT's Kombucha, www.synergydrinks.com

Bragg Apple Cider Vinegar, www.bragg.com

Lily of the Desert Aloe Vera Gel, www.lilyofthedesert.com

Selina Naturally Celtic Sea Salt, www.selinanaturally.com

Bubbies Dill Relish, www.bubbies.com

French Meadow Bakery Organic Breads, www.frenchmeadow.com

Udi's Gluten-Free Bread, www.udisglutenfree.com

Bionaturae Gluten-Free Pasta and Olive Oil, www.bionaturae.com

Nut-rients Nut Butters, www.nut-rients.com

Daiya Non-Dairy Cheese Alternatives, www.daiyafoods.com

Follow Your Heart Vegan Gourmet Cheese, www.followyourheart.com

Follow Your Heart Vegan Salad Dressings and Sauces, www.followyourheart.com

Gardein Meat Substitutes, www.gardein.com

Tofurky Meat Substitutes, www.tofurky.com

Whole Foods 365 (affordable organic food product line),
www.wholefoodsmarket.com

PROBIOTICS AND SUPERFOODS

Ascended Health, www.ascendedhealth.com.

This is a holistic wellness company offering a wide variety of the finest plant-based probiotics and superfood elixirs, including the Endurance Elixir referenced throughout this book. Among other top-shelf products, the company also offers a heart health elixir with high quantities of resveratrol, sourced from the finest Bordeaux grape skins.

iHerb.com, www.iherb.com.
An easy one-stop online shop for many hard-to-find superfood items, with a vast product line that includes most of the items referenced in this book, including chlorophyll, chia seeds, maca powder, marine phytoplankton, acai, resveratrol, and many more.

PROTEIN POWDERS AND NUTRACEUTICAL SUPPLEMENTS

Jai Repair Performance Recovery Formula, www.jailifestyle.com
Living Harvest Hemp Protein, www.livingharvest.com
Vega Whole Food Optimizer, www.sequelnaturals.com
Vega Sport Performance Protein and Protein Bars, www.vegasport.com
Sunwarrior Raw Protein, Activated Barley, and Ormus Greens,
    www.sunwarrior.com
PlantFusion Protein, www.plantfusion.us
BaseAmino, ww.baseperformance.com
ASEA Redox Signaling Supplement, www.richroll.teamasea.com
BioAstin Natural Astaxanthin (antioxidant), www.nutrex-hawaii.com
Sun Chlorella, www.sunchlorellausa.com

DESSERTS

Living Harvest Tempt Hemp Milk Ice Cream, www.livingharvest.com
So Delicious Coconut Milk Ice Cream, www.turtlemountain.com
Uncle Eddie's Vegan Cookies, www.uncleeddiesvegancookies.com
Sweet and Sara Vegan Marshmallows, www.sweetandsara.com

EFA AND OMEGA-3 OILS

Udo's Oil 3-6-9 Blend, www.oilthemachine.com
Vega Antioxidant EFA Oil Blend, www.sequelnaturals.com
Spectrum Organics Coconut Oil, www.spectrumorganics.com
Living Harvest Organic Hemp Oil, www.livingharvest.com

ATHLETIC PERFORMANCE NUTRITION

Hammer Nutrition Perpetuem and Endurolytes, www.hammernutrition.com
Grain Processing Corporation (bulk maltodextrin), www.grainprocessing.com

Vega Sport Performance Optimizer, www.sequelnaturals.com

Vega Sport Pre-Workout Energizer, www.vegasport.com

Vega Sport Electrolyte Hydrator, Endurance Gels, and Bars,
www.vegasport.com

Vega Recovery Accelerator, www.vegasport.com

Vega Energy Bars and Vibrancy Bars, www.sequelnaturals.com

CarboPro and CarboPro1200, www.carbopro.com

SaltStick Electrolyte Capsules, www.saltstick.com

WildBar, www.wildbar.info

ProBar High Performance Energy Bars, www.theprobar.com

Clif Bar Nutritional Products, www.clifbar.com

PLANT-BASED FOOD DELIVERY SERVICES

Thrive Foods Direct, www.thrivefoodsdirect.com

ATHLETIC TRAINING AND RECOVERY PRODUCTS

CEP Compression Gear, www.cepsocks.com

Trigger Point Performance Therapy (foam rollers), www.tptherapy.com

The Stick, www.thestick.com

TRX Suspension Training Products, www.trxtraining.com

Garmin GPS Training Computers and Heart Rate Monitors, www.garmin.com

Polar Training Computers and Heart Rate Monitors, www.polarusa.com

Suunto Training Computers and Heart Rate Monitors, www.suunto.com

CycleOps PowerTap Cycling Power Meters, www.cycle-ops.com

Quarq Cycling Power Meters, www.quarq.com

DZ Nuts Chamois Cream, www.dz-nuts.com

ATHLETIC TRAINING AND WORKOUT TRACKING SOFTWARE

WorkoutLog Training Software, www.workoutlog.com

TrainingPeaks Training and Nutrition Software, www.trainingpeaks.com

Golden Cheetah Cycling Performance Software, www.goldencheetah.org

Garmin Connect, www.connect.garmin.com

Movescount, www.movescount.com

Strava, www.strava.com

Nike Plus, www.nikeplus.com

Daily Mile, www.dailymile.com

Fleetly, www.fleetly.com

ACKNOWLEDGMENTS

"When are you going to write a book?" is a question I've often fielded over the years. Finally having an answer is a reality I wouldn't have thought possible. In truth, this book would have remained simply an aspiration if not for the love, support, and encouragement of almost too many to people to name.

About two years ago I was catching up on the phone with Carter Cast, an old Stanford swimming colleague, when he suggested I meet his friend, literary agent Carole Bidnick. It was an introduction that changed everything. Carter, thank you for the spark that lit the pilot light. And Carole, thanks for taking me on when I knew nothing. Your tireless commitment to championing me can never be repaid. Thank you for always having my back and consistently trudging the extra mile. So much more than an agent, you've changed my life. For that, I'll always be in your debt.

I can't imagine even the most experienced writer having a better editor than Rick Horgan. Thank you, Rick, for taking a flier on a complete unknown. From the very first time we spoke, your belief in my story and my ability to bring this project to fruition has been unwavering. I'm grateful for your friendship, your master class in writing, and your ever-patient mentoring. Thanks also for the late nights, the long hours logged, and your dogged attention to detail—and for pushing me further and harder than any swim coach or boss.

Thank you to my dream team at Crown—which offers no better home for an author. Tina Constable, Mauro DiPreta, Tammy Blake, Caroline Sill, Christina Foxley, Nupoor Gordon, Nathan Roberson, Mark McCauslin, Elizabeth Rendfleisch, Norman Watkins, and everyone else behind the Crown curtain, your tireless parenting of this book from idea to market has exceeded every expectation a writer could have from a publisher.

To my publicity team—Anne Sullivan, Danielle Nuzzo, and Jeremiah Tittle—thank you for undertaking the task of promoting my story to the world.

To my friend Anne Espuelas, my right arm on this journey from the outset, thank you for helping me find the book within the story, mining structure from the chaos of my often muddled mind, and for always keeping me motivated through my many dark lapses of faith. Without your consistently deft editorial eye, ever-honest feedback, and sometimes ruthless proposed revisions, this book would have fallen far short of what it eventually became.

To all the amazing writing mentors I'm lucky to call friends—those who've persistently encouraged me to take this leap, both directly and by living example—I thank you: from Jeff Gordon at Writers Boot Camp, who first took me to task on structure and story, to Belinda Casas-Wells for igniting a fire in my belly and pushing me to believe. Thanks to John Moffet and Mel Stewart for showing me that great athleticism and creative artistry need not be mutually exclusive. Thanks to Tim Ferriss for always finding time to respond to my relentless queries. Thanks to Sacha Gervasi for your unwavering support, devoted friendship, and incessant levity, which lit a path for me to pursue this "war of art" with a semblance of grace. Thanks to Kurt Sutter, for your integrity and indefatigable authenticity as both an artist and a family man. Thanks to Gordy Hoffman, for being the first to help me understand what it means to be a sober man, and your relentless example of veracity in the expression of your art. Thanks to Billy Ray, whose early encouragement strengthened my resolve. And thanks to Mark Gantt, for your loyalty and the way you embody the power of persistence.

Also, my gratitude to Dan Halsted for your constant friendship, honesty, and objective feedback—you've made me a better writer, father, husband, and man. Thanks, too, to Andrew Wheeler, Jeff Newman, Chris Uettwiller, Jesse Albert, Stevie Long, and L.W. Walman for your spiritual counsel. And to Alan Blackburn, Nicole Duran, Brett Blankner, Morgan Christian, Paul Morris, Dave Schraven, Drew Hayden, Gavin Holles, Mike Moffo, Peter Slutsky, Greg Anzalone, Dr. Shay Shani, and Stu Bone. You know why I love you.

To Dr. Garrett O'Connor, as well as the staff and my fellow inmates at Springbrook Northwest, thank you for saving my life and and providing the foundation for a new way of living. Without you, it's safe to say I wouldn't have a story worth telling.

To the two Skips in my life—Kenney and Miller—thank you both for being tough but fair mentors, urging me to push beyond my self-imposed limits and guiding me to a greater understanding of who I am and what it means to be a man.

Chris Hauth, you didn't just believe in my athletic abilities before I did; you showed me what it meant to pursue *true endurance*. I could never have achieved my athletic accomplishments without your steady and firm mentorship, and I can't thank you enough.

To my training buddies Dave Meyer, Darren Wald, Bob Steinberg, Tony Pritzker, Gary Bub, and Jamie Halper, thank you for always brightening those early and long Saturday-morning rides. I'm grateful to Sheri Zeibell for providing me with a quiet writing sanctuary away from the cacophony of home. And to Steve Kaplan, the most supportive law partner I could imagine, thank you for your friendship and the latitude to pursue this dream.

To Danielle Dellorto and Dr. Sanjay Gupta at CNN, I'm in your debt for so generously casting such a bright spotlight on my story, which created the broad audience that made this book a plausible reality.

To Julian Franco, Hector Rodriguez, Stormin' Norman Houck, and Ryan Correia of Franco Bicycles, thank you for your loyal support and for always promoting my efforts and keeping me fully geared while undertaking the herculean task of trying to write this book while simultaneously training for Ultraman.

Thanks as well to all my inspiring PlantPower mentors who've fearlessly blazed this path before me—Brendan Brazier, Dr. Caldwell Esselstyn, T. Colin Campbell, Kathy Freston, Brian Wendel, Lisa Lange, and Dr. Neal Barnard. And especially to Rip Esselstyn, who enthusiastically encouraged me to write this book as far back as 2009. Your friendship and living example have given me more faith than you'll ever know.

So many extraordinary athletes have graciously bestowed on me their camaraderie and wisdom throughout this journey of discovery. Pablo Morales, John Moffet, Craig Beardsley, Mel Stewart, Garrett Weber-Gale, Byron Davis, Mac Danzig, James Wilks, Ryan Hall, Chris Lieto, Luke McKenzie, Terenzo Bozzone, Jordan Rapp, Chris McCormack, Paul Ambrose, Vinnie Tortorich, Dr. Andy Baldwin, Alexandre Ribeiro, Jonas Colting, John Hirsch, James Bowsted, Dave Zabriskie, Levi Leipheimer, Ben and Eric Bostrom, and Ivan Dominguez—you inspire me with your remarkable talent, devotion to excellence, and example. I'm honored to know all of you.

Ultraman is a beautiful and curious world to which I was most graciously and quite miraculously permitted entry. I'm forever indebted to Jane Bockus for taking a chance on me back in 2008 and permanently altering the trajectory of my life. And I'd be remiss if I didn't thank the entire Ultraman *ohana*—most notably Sheryl and Dave Cobb, Cory Foulk, Gary Wang, John Callos, Jamie Patrick, Suzy Degazon, Marty Raymond, Nino Cokan, Miro Kregar, Erik Seedhouse, Mike Rouse, Jochen Dembeck, Vito Biala, Peter McIntosh, Kathy Winkler, Timothy Carlson, Rick Kent, Warren Hollinger, Rebecca Morgan, Verne Sekafetz, and Grant Miller, among many others. To every athlete and crew member who has taken the leap into this lunatic fringe, you're all heroes.

To Mike Field and Todd Clark—my Big Island brothers from another mother—thank you for your boundless generosity and friendship and for always going the extra mile to ensure that my family and I feel at home in Hawaii. I can only aspire to your selfless example of *aloha, kokua,* and *ohana.*

Thanks to photographer extraordinaire John Segesta, for never failing to take remarkable images of me and for always making me appear far better in print than I actually do in person. And thanks to James Gilbert and Reis Paluso at Sandbox Studios for your graphic genius and for giving me a web presence that is the envy of my peers.

To my Ultraman comrade Jason Lester—you're a rare warrior and your spirit transcends athleticism. Thank you for ushering me into the realm of the unknown, for your incredible fortitude, and for being a beacon of inspiration to so many. But most of all, thank you for being my friend.

To Larry and Vylna Mathis, I'm grateful for your steadfast and loving support of my family and me, particularly during the more challenging periods we've faced this past year.

To my beloved parents, Dave and Nancy Roll, thank you for never giving up on me, always believing in me, and selflessly having my back in countless times of need. Thank you for your sacrifice and for instilling in me a tireless work ethic, keen sense of responsibility, and drive to succeed. Dad, you're my writing compatriot, my unceasing ally, my model of what it means to be a gentleman, and my hero. Mom, thank you for giving me a love of the water and a passion for learning, and for always ensuring the best for me. And to my beloved sister, Molly, thank you for being my number one fan. I love you.

To my namesake and the grandfather I never knew, thank you Richard Spindle for being a shining beacon from the beyond—my anchor. My life—and this book—is a living homage to your powerful and persistent legacy.

And of course, I must not leave out my beautiful children: Mathis Indigo, Jaya Blue, Tyler, and Trapper—the absolute joys of my life. Thank you for fortifying my days with meaning and keeping me firmly grounded in what is truly important. In your own unique way, each of you teaches, inspires, and amazes me daily, and I cherish every moment of watching you grow into the rare and amazing people you're quickly becoming. I can never repay you enough for tolerating me and for meeting the herculean challenges that come with having a father who does the things I do. I honor and love you all dearly.

Most of all, I'm forever indebted to my greatest love. Thank you, Julie, for always seeing the better man lying dormant within me and for always pushing me out of my comfort zone, ever expanding my awareness and urging me to deepen my faith in the pursuit of our collective dreams. You've never wavered in your loyalty, love, and constant support, despite the myriad arduous and stressful challenges that have come your way as a result of my endurance dreams and my attempts to bring this book to life. A true spiritual warrior, you are my constant. Thank you for giving me the courage to show you who I really am. Without you, I am nowhere.

In closing, I wish to thank each and every one of the countless unnamed who've found a spark of hope in my story and have taken the time to reach out and confide in me your private struggles and pain. You can't know how much you've touched me. To all those out there who feel stuck, lost, in a rut, or just unable to reach escape velocity, know that I'm with you. And I honor your journey. This book is for you.